LOW CHOLESTEROL CUISINE
Mabel Cavaiani

Contemporary Books, Inc.
Chicago

Library of Congress Cataloging in Publication Data

Cavaiani, Mabel.
 Low cholesterol cuisine.

 Includes index.
 1. Low-cholesterol diet—Recipes.   2. Salt-free
diet—Recipes.   3. Cookery, International.
I. Title.
RM237.75.C39   641.5′63   81-65190
ISBN 0-8092-5945-1   AACR2

Copyright © 1981 by Mabel Cavaiani
All rights reserved
Published by Contemporary Books, Inc.
180 North Michigan Avenue, Chicago, Illinois 60601
Manufactured in the United States of America
Library of Congress Catalog Card Number: 81-65190
International Standard Book Number: 0-8092-5945-1

Published simultaneously in Canada by
Beaverbooks, Ltd.
150 Lesmill Road
Don Mills, Ontario M3B 2T5
Canada

FOR MY MOTHER, Ida Sniffin, whose zest for living and whose fortitude in the face of death inspired all of us who were lucky enough to have known her.

Contents

Acknowledgments

Many recipes in this book have been provided by friends of mine and I have indicated on these recipes, the sources of the recipes and something about them whenever pertinent.

I would also like to give special thanks to Frances Nielsen, Oak Lawn, Illinois, who taught me so much about cooking and who tested so many of these recipes as well as providing many of them; and to my husband Chuck Cavaiani who tested and commented on recipes and who put up with me when I was working so hard to put all of the information together for publication.

Some of the friends who were especially helpful include: Della Andreassen, R.D., Dietary Consultant, Lafayette, Louisiana; Harriette Bepler, Product Counselor, Best Foods, Englewood Cliffs, New Jersey; Mabel Frances Gunsallus, R.D., M.S., Miami, Florida; Mary Agnes Jones, R.D., Chief Therapeutic Dietitian, Holy Cross Hospital, Chicago, Illinois; Anita Kane, Shorewood, Wisconsin; Frances Lee, R.D., M.S., Dietary Consultant, Kerens, Texas; Edith Robinson, R.D., M.S., Atlanta, Georgia; and Muriel Urbashich, R.D., Chief, Dietary Department, South Chicago Community Hospital, Chicago Illinois.

I would like to thank the following organizations for background information and resource material used in this book:
The American Heart Association
The American Dietetic Association

Foreword

I am happy to know that Mabel Cavaiani has written another excellent cookbook. Actually, this volume is a companion to two of her earlier publications, *The Low Cholesterol Cookbook* and *The High-Fiber Cookbook*; the three books complement each other. In *Low Cholesterol Cuisine*, the author responds to the interests of people long accustomed to their own unique ethnic dishes who are highly resistant to new programs of restricted dietary intake. Mrs. Cavaiani is convinced, as I am, that if a diet is to succeed it must include foods people are accustomed to eating. Otherwise, they will soon abandon what seems like a tasteless, overly restrictive, alien regime—however important the diet may be to their health. The difficulty is compounded when everyone else at the table is eating all of the tempting dishes the dieter enjoys most. Mrs. Cavaiani cleverly solves both of these problems in the material she presents. She shares with us the particular technique she employs in substituting low cholesterol ingredients for those high in saturated fats. It thus becomes possible for the reader to apply similar guidelines in order to convert other favorite dishes to meet particular diet requirements.

The potential for developing atherosclerosis—a condition that precedes arteriosclerosis, or hardening of the arteries—is known to be increased by high blood pressure, smoking, elevated blood serum lipid levels (particularly serum cholesterol), sedentary habits along with lack of exercise, obesity, and inherited tendencies. It is a well-established fact that the average American's daily food intake includes too much saturated fat. Then, too, those who have a high cholesterol condition often have associated hypertension and need to lower their sodium intake; Mrs. Cavaiani gives information on adapting each recipe to a low sodium diet. Recent research also indicates that increased fiber in the diet helps to reduce serum cholesterol levels; the author provides many high fiber recipes that are suitable on all counts.

As genetic studies reflect, children whose families have a history of circulatory problems and heart disease should be encouraged at an early age to develop the proper living habits and diet to maintain normal serum cholesterol levels. It is with this last point in mind that Mrs. Cavaiani suggests recipes for the entire family that favor the maintenance of reduced cholesterol levels. This answers the problems of familial potential for circulatory difficulties, and it will indeed be a welcome relief for those frustrated people who used to feel their households were turning into diet kitchens when cooking meant preparing two separate menus—food for the dieter and a meal for the rest of the family.

Joseph T. Crockett, M.D., F.A.P.A.
Marina del Rey, California

Introduction

In 1953, when the doctor first told us that my husband Chuck had a high cholesterol count, I couldn't find any recipes, books, or other information about the low cholesterol diet. I can still remember how bewildered we were about what he could and couldn't eat. Those first few weeks we lived on very lean beef, fruits, vegetables, and margarine accompanied by Italian bread. I don't think he missed giving up fat meat and he never did care for bacon, but he hated to give up those rich Italian foods we both liked so well and the cheese omelets that we served frequently.

After that first period of stunned bewilderment, when it seemed like he couldn't have much to eat, I learned the basis of the low cholesterol diet and started to collect and develop recipes we could use for the whole family. I have never thought it wise to give a dieter a special plate unless it is absolutely necessary. It is much better if the special diet can be worked into the framework of the regular menu served to the rest of the family. I think this is particularly true in the case of the low cholesterol diet, because it is such a good and wholesome diet for the whole family. Chuck always insisted I should prepare anything I wanted for myself and not worry that he couldn't eat it, but this seemed like a waste of time. I saw no need to prepare two separate meals when his food was so good for me—and I certainly didn't need any saturated fats in my diet either!

I feel that it is particularly important for everyone in the family to follow a low cholesterol diet if there are children whose parent or parents have a high cholesterol condition. Research has indicated that many children also develop a high cholesterol condition; therefore, they should be started on the proper foods when they are young if the family has shown a tendency to develop a high cholesterol condition. Remember also that most people tend to prefer foods they ate as children for the rest of their lives; and therefore children should be started in the right direction while they are still young.

Chuck followed his diet faithfully and I was very proud of his willpower. Eventually we brought his cholesterol count back to normal, but we have continued to adhere to the diet to keep his count low. I didn't find out until much later that my mother and sister had a great deal to do with Chuck's strict adherence to his diet. It seems that they both took him aside and suggested he take some time off work to relax and do what he wanted to do. He told us later that he decided that if both my mother and my sister wanted him to quit work and live off my earnings he must be sicker than he thought he was and he'd better stick very closely to his diet.

I've often had people ask me why I'm so dedicated to spreading the word about the low cholesterol diet. The reason is simple. My uncle, my father-in-law, and my brother-in-law, who was best man at our wedding, all died while they were still quite young because we didn't know about the low cholesterol diet at the time. We caught my husband's condition in time to save his life, but we are continually reminded that if we had known about it earlier we could have saved their lives as well. I have met a few people who say they don't agree with the principles of the diet. I tell them that thanks to the low cholesterol diet my husband is still alive and that, as for me and mine, we will follow it to the letter.

They can take any chances they like with their own lives and the lives of their families, but I'm not taking any chances with my husband's life. −

I finally decided that since I have a degree in foods and nutrition from Iowa State University, with a major in experimental cookery (I got the credits to qualify as a registered dietitian later, in Chicago), I should be able to develop recipes we would enjoy using the foods allowed on Chuck's diet. I eventually learned that I could often substitute egg whites for whole eggs, margarine and oil for lard and butter, and instant nonfat dry and skimmed milk for whole milk. I now know that some recipes just cannot be converted, and I've never been able to develop a cream puff without egg yolks, but generally I've been very successful in my efforts to develop new recipes.

Since other dietitians were also looking for recipes, I had many requests from my friends for my recipes. I finally decided to put them into book form, and *The Low Cholesterol Cookbook* published in 1972 was the result. It also eventually led me to write this book.

It wasn't too complicated to alter most of the recipes for *The Low Cholesterol Cookbook.* The low cholesterol diet is based on the substitution of polyunsaturated fats for saturated fats in the diet. The American Heart Association explains the principles further:

Too much *cholesterol* in the circulation encourages the development of heart and blood vessel diseases.

We get cholesterol in two ways: it is manufactured by the body from all foods and we get it directly from foods of animal origin.

Egg yolks and organ meats are very high in cholesterol and shellfish are moderately high in this substance. There is no cholesterol in foods of plant origin such as fruits, vegetables, grains, cereals, and nuts; thus, these foods are recommended.

Saturated fats tend to raise the level of cholesterol in the blood. These are fats that harden at room temperature, and they are found in most animal products and some hydrogenated vegetable products.

Saturated animal fats are found in beef, lamb, pork, and ham; in butter, cream, and whole milk; and in cheeses made from cream and whole milk.

Saturated vegetable fats are found in many solid and hydrogenated shortenings and in coconut oil, cocoa butter, and palm oil (used in commercially prepared cookies, pie fillings, and nondairy milk and cream substitutes).

Polyunsaturated fats are usually liquid oils of vegetable origin. Oils such as corn, cottonseed, safflower, sesame seed, soybean, and sunflower seed are high in polyunsaturated fat. Olive oil and peanut oil are also vegetable products, but they are low in polyunsaturated fats. Your daily intake of salad dressings, cooking fats, and margarines should emphasize the polyunsaturated vegetable oils.

Total fat is low in chicken, turkey, fish, and lean veal, and they are recommended.

Hydrogenation changes liquid fats to solid fats. Completely hydrogenated (hardened) oils resemble saturated fats and should be avoided or used in moderation. Most margarines and solid shortenings containing partially hydrogenated oils also contain acceptable amounts of polyunsaturates.

There are four goals to keep in mind in following the heart-saver eating style:

1. To meet your daily need for protein, vitamins, minerals and other nutrients.

2. To control calories and maintain a desirable weight.

3. To avoid eating excessive amounts of foods containing saturated fat and cholesterol by lowering your total intake of such foods.

4. To make sure that more of the fat you eat is polyunsaturated and less of it is saturated.

You may have to change some of your long-standing eating habits, but you won't have to give up all of your favorite dishes. This is what will be involved:

To control your intake of cholesterol-rich foods:

1. Eat no more than three egg yolks a week, including eggs used in cooking.

2. Limit your use of organ meats.

To control the amount and type of fat you eat:

1. Use fish, chicken, turkey, and veal in most of your meat meals for the week; use moderate-sized portions of beef, lamb, pork, and ham less frequently.

2. Choose lean cuts of meat, trim visible fat, and discard the fat that is rendered when you cook meat.

3. Avoid deep-fat frying; use cooking methods that help to remove fat—baking, broiling, boiling, roasting, and stewing.

4. Restrict your use of fatty "luncheon meats" and "variety" meats like sausages and salami.

5. Instead of butter and other cooking fats that are solid or completely hydrogenated, use liquid vegetable oils and margarines that are high in polyunsaturated fats.

6. Instead of whole milk and cheese made from whole milk and cream, use skimmed milk and skimmed-milk cheeses.

In 1976 I started working with Muriel Urbashich and Frances Nielsen on two new large-quantity cookbooks—*Simplified Quantity Regional Recipes* and *Simplified Quantity Ethnic Recipes*. We enjoyed testing the recipes very much and I was fascinated to discover how many of the recipes followed the preceding guidelines and were suitable for use in my own kitchen. Some of them could be used as written, and many of them needed only very minor changes. We enjoyed using them and I found myself reaching more and more for those books when I wanted to prepare something special for my own family. As I began to collect home-size recipes for more and more of the regional and ethnic recipes, I began to think about writing a new cookbook so that I could share them with everyone who is interested in keeping a low cholesterol kitchen. I contacted the firm who had published the first book of low cholesterol recipes. They thought it was a good idea and thus this new book was born.

I would like to think that you would use this book along with my first book, but since that will not always be possible, I have repeated some of the basic information included in the first book in order to explain how and why I altered recipes and how you can change your own family recipes to conform to the low cholesterol diet.

I would like to suggest that you get rid of the bacon, lard, cream, butter, and hydrogenated fats in your cupboards and substitute margarine, skim milk, and vegetable oil. I think that it is easier to conform to the diet if the unacceptable foods aren't available. If they simply aren't within reach, you won't be tempted to use them "just this time." The low cholesterol diet is a long-term diet. It is a way of life and the sooner you get on with it, the better results you will have.

I think you should also be aware that research seems to indicate that a high fiber diet will help lower a high cholesterol count. I am a firm believer in a high fiber diet and have included in this book quite a few recipes that are high in fiber. Readers who are interested in finding additional high fiber recipes should consult an earlier book I wrote, *The High-Fiber Cookbook*, published in 1977 by Contemporary Books, Inc.

It has been my experience that many people who have a high cholesterol condition also need to lower their sodium intake. Therefore, I have included information at the end of each recipe regarding the suitability of that recipe for a low sodium diet. Several people have told me they wished I had included that information in the first book so, for them and for you, if you need it, the low sodium diet information is included.

All the ingredients in this book conform to the guidelines established by the American Heart Association for planning nutritious meals that are low in saturated fat and cholesterol to reduce the risk of heart attack, and many of them are low in calories for weight control. If you have recipes of your own that you want to use, you can check them out using the following guidelines from the American Heart Association.

Meat, Poultry, Fish, Dried Beans and Peas, Nuts, and Eggs

Recommended:

Chicken, turkey, veal, or fish in most of your meat meals for the week.

Beef, lamb, pork, and ham less frequently.

Choose lean ground meat and lean cuts of meat. Trim all visible fat before cooking. Bake, broil, roast, or stew meat so you can discard the fat that is rendered from the cooked meat.

Nuts and dried beans and peas.

Egg whites as desired.

Avoid or use sparingly:

Duck, goose.

Heavily marbled and fatty meats, spareribs, mutton, frankfurters, sausages, fatty hamburgers, bacon, luncheon meats.

Organ meats—liver, kidney, heart, sweetbreads—are high in cholesterol.

Egg yolks; limit three per week, including eggs used in cooking.

Cakes, batters, sauces, and other foods containing egg yolks.

Vegetables and Fruit

Recommended:

One serving each day should be a source of vitamin C. This could be broccoli, cabbage (raw), tomatoes, berries, cantaloupe, grapefruit or grapefruit juice, melon, orange or orange juice, strawberries, or tangerines.

One serving each day should be a source of vitamin A—dark green leafy or yellow vegetables or yellow fruits. This could include broccoli, carrots, chard, escarole, greens, peas, rutabagas, spinach, string beans, sweet potatoes and yams, winter squash and yellow corn, apricots, or cantaloupe.

Other fruits and vegetables are also nutritious.

Avoid or use sparingly:

If you must limit your calories, use vegetables such as potatoes, corn, or lima beans sparingly. To add variety to the diet, a half cup serving of any one of these may be substituted for one serving of bread or cereals.

Breads and Cereals

Recommended:

Breads made with a minimum of saturated fat—white enriched, enriched raisin, whole wheat, French, Italian, oatmeal, pumpernickel, and rye breads; English muffins.

Biscuits, muffins, and griddle cakes made at home using allowed liquid oil as shortening.

Hot and cold cereals, rice, melba toast, matzo, and pretzels.

Pasta, macaroni, noodles (except egg noodles), and spaghetti.

Avoid or use sparingly:

Butter rolls, commercial biscuits, muffins, doughnuts, sweet rolls, cakes, crackers, egg bread, cheese bread, commercial mixes containing dried eggs and whole milk.

Milk Products

Recommended:

Milk products that are low in dairy fats—fortified skimmed (nonfat) milk and fortified milk powder, low-fat milk.

Buttermilk made from skimmed milk, yogurt made from skimmed milk, canned evaporated skimmed milk, cocoa made with low-fat milk.

Cheeses made from skimmed or partially skimmed milk such as creamed or uncreamed cottage cheese (preferably uncreamed), farmer's, baker's, mozzarella, and sapsago cheeses.

Not recommended:

Whole milk or whole-milk products—chocolate milk, canned whole milk, ice cream, whole-milk yogurt; all creams, including sour, half-and-half, and whipped.

Nondairy cream substitutes that usually contain coconut oil, which is very high in saturated fat.

Cheeses made from cream or whole milk.
Butter.

Fats and Oils

Recommended:

Margarines, liquid oil shortenings, dressings, and mayonnaise containing any of these polyunsaturated vegetable oils—corn oil, cottonseed oil, safflower oil, sesame seed oil, soybean oil, sunflower seed oil.

Margarines and other products high in polyunsaturates can usually be identified by the label, which lists a recommended liquid vegetable oil as the first ingredient and one or more partially hydrogenated vegetable oils as additional ingredients.

Not recommended:

Solid fats and shortenings—butter, lard, salt pork fat, meat fat, completely hydrogenated margarines and vegetable shortenings, products containing coconut oil.

Peanut oil and olive oil may be used occasionally for flavor, but they are low in polyunsaturates and do not take the place of recommended oils.

Desserts, Beverages, Snacks, and Condiments

If you have eaten your daily allowance from the first five lists, these foods will be in excess of your nutritional needs and may exceed your calorie limit for maintaining a desirable weight.

Recommended:

Low in calories or no calories—fresh fruit and fruit canned without sugar, tea, black coffee, cocoa powder, water ices, gelatin, fruit whip, puddings made with nonfat milk, low calorie drinks, vinegar, mustard, catsup, herbs and spices.

Not recommended:

Coconut and coconut oil; commercial cakes, pies, cookies, and mixes; frozen cream pies; commercially fried foods such as potato chips and other deep-fried snacks; whole-milk puddings; chocolate pudding, which is high in chocolate and therefore high in cocoa butter and therefore high in saturated fat; and ice cream.

Moderation should be observed, especially in the use of alcoholic drinks, ice milk, sherbet, sweets, and bottled drinks.

Acceptable, though not recommended, are these foods, which may be used if you are on a low cholesterol diet but do not need to lose weight—frozen or canned fruit with added sugar; jelly, jam, marmalade, and honey; pure sugar candy such as gum drops, hard candy, and mint patties (not chocolate); cakes, pies, cookies, puddings, and ice creams made with approved ingredients; angel food cake; nuts; nonhydrogenated peanut butter; bottled drinks and fruit drinks; ice milk and sherbet; wine, beer, and whiskey.

LOW CHOLESTEROL CUISINE

1

Ingredients and Equipment

Ingredients

I believe that following a low cholesterol diet should be a family project. Doctors tell us that everyone should cut down on intake of saturated fats, so, do everyone in the family a favor and change to a diet that is healthier for all of you.

Since the most important purpose of the low cholesterol diet is to cut down on saturated fats, there are certain items you should be purchasing and others that are taboo. I don't really believe in tables, but occasionally they are helpful. The following one may help you reorganize your shopping.

* *Items to Keep on Hand*
Instant nonfat dry milk
Low fat buttermilk
Low fat yogurt
Low fat cottage cheese
Skimmed milk, plain or
   evaporated
Low fat cheeses

Vegetable oil
Margarine, Butter Buds
Liquid egg substitute
Dehydrated egg whites (optional)
Fresh, frozen, or canned plain
   vegetables
Lean meats, poultry, fish, imitation
   bacon bits
All-purpose and cake flour
Yeast, baking powder, soda
Cocoa
Plain candies made without butter,
   chocolate, or cream
Ice milk, fruit ices, sherbets
Fresh, frozen, and canned fruits

Items You Should No Longer Use
Whole milk, sour cream, and
   whipping cream
Whole milk buttermilk
Whole milk yogurt
Creamed cottage cheese or cream
   cheese
Evaporated or condensed
   sweetened whole milk
Whole milk cheeses
Lard, shortening, any
   hydrogenated fat
Coconut oil
Butter
Egg yolks (you can keep whole
   eggs on hand to use the egg
   whites and discard the yolks)
Vegetables canned or frozen in
   cream sauces or sour cream
   sauces
Bacon, fat meats, or commercially
   prepared meats, poultry, or fish
   in a fatty sauce or without the
   fat removed
Commercially prepared cakes,
   cookies, sweet rolls, doughnuts,
   etc.
Chocolate

Chocolates, candies made with
  cream, butter, or coconut
Ice cream or ice cream drinks or
  items containing ice cream

I use instant nonfat dry milk frequently in this book. My friends tell me they think I must have stock in a milk processing plant because I am so enthusiastic about it. I don't, unfortunately, have any stock in a plant, though we do live a few miles from one of the world's largest milk processing plants. I've never even been inside it and probably never will be. I like to use instant milk because it is easy to store, handy, and less expensive than the fresh milk. Instant whole milk is made, but I have never seen it on the shelves in any store—probably because it doesn't keep as well as the instant nonfat dry milk. Therefore I just use the phrase *instant dry milk* in this book; it is the kind you should use and is the kind that is the most available.

Instant dry milk can be used in several ways: it can be reconstituted and used as regular skimmed milk, it can be added dry to dry ingredients in a recipe, and it can be added to ingredients for dishes such as meat loaf without reconstituting it. When used as a beverage, instant dry milk should be mixed with water and then chilled before it is served. It can also be used to enrich the skimmed milk you buy in the store, which I think is a pretty poor beverage when used as is. I find that adding about 1 cup instant dry milk to 1 quart skimmed milk gives us a beverage that is much better than plain skimmed milk.

If you can't buy low fat buttermilk, you can make your own by adding ½ cup regular buttermilk to 1 quart reconstituted nonfat dry milk. Let it stand at room temperature about 5 to 6 hours or until clabbered (thickened). Stir until smooth. Refrigerate and use as a beverage or as an ingredient for baking. You can often use buttermilk as a substitute for sour cream as well. I use ⅔ cup buttermilk and ⅓ cup melted margarine for 1 cup sour cream in some cakes and cookies and it works very well.

Measures for instant dry milk vary from manufacturer to manufacturer. Therefore, read the directions on the package carefully and use the amounts as directed. I have used 3.2 ounces instant dry milk (or 1⅓ cups) to reconstitute a quart of liquid milk. Most manufacturers use this measure.

Since instant dry milk is whole milk with fat and water removed, it may not act the way whole milk does in some recipes. Certain adjustments are sometimes necessary. The most important thing to remember is that there is a correct way to use it in each recipe. If you have any doubts about how to use it correctly in a particular recipe of your own, look up a similar recipe in this book and prepare your recipe using the same general idea. Generally speaking, you can use the directions on the package when substituting instant dry milk for whole or skimmed milk. However, I like to make the reconstituted milk a little stronger when using it for cream sauces and puddings. Therefore, the exact amounts of instant dry milk and water used in the following recipes may not always agree exactly with the proportions specified on the package.

The following table may be of help to you in deciding how to substitute instant dry milk for whole milk in your recipes.

Instant Dry Milk Conversion Table

Instant Dry Milk	Water	Fluid Skimmed Milk
⅓ cup	1 cup	1 cup
⅔ cup	2 cups	2 cups
1 cup	3 cups	3 cups
1⅓ cups	4 cups	1 quart (4 cups)

Note: This table uses a little more water than the table in *The Low Cholesterol Cookbook.* Either table may be used correctly. The first one was the ratio I generally used in baked or cooked products and this table will give you an equal volume of reconstituted fluid skimmed milk.

If the package of instant dry milk suggests you use butter in your recipe to compensate for the loss of butterfat, ignore it. Getting rid of the butterfat is the most important reason for using the nonfat dry milk.

Since instant dry milk can be added dry to dry ingredients, it is handy for baked goods. It is also wonderful for breads because you no longer have to scald the milk. Just use the dry milk as is because it was treated when it was being dehydrated.

If you like to use sweetened condensed milk in recipes, you can substitute the following milk combination, which Jean Smith, a friend of mine from Clancy, Montana, sent to me. It is handy to have because there are several very good recipes available that use the sweetened condensed milk.

SUBSTITUTE FOR SWEETENED CONDENSED MILK

1 cup instant dry milk
⅔ cup sugar
⅓ cup boiling water
3 tablespoons margarine

Place the dry milk, sugar, boiling water, and margarine in a blender or food processor and mix until smooth. Refrigerate until used.

Yield: equivalent of 1 large can

Please don't underestimate canned evaporated skimmed milk. I always keep it on hand and use it often. I like it for soups, for sauces, and for thinning salad dressing. It can be used in coffee, though some people prefer to use dry milk in their coffee.

Low-fat cottage cheese is available in most stores. If it isn't available, you can always wash off the cream by putting it into a strainer and running cold water over it. Drain it well and put it back into the container dry or with a little skimmed milk.

Most hard cheese is now prohibited, but some cheeses are available that are made with skimmed milk and/or vegetable oil. They are labeled *low fat* or *low cholesterol* and can be purchased in many stores. If you can't find any of the low cholesterol cheeses, you should probably stick to cottage cheese, farmer's cheese, sapsago, mozzarella, hoop cheese, or baker's cheese.

If you want to use a coffee lightener, remember that cream is out and most of the coffee whiteners are also taboo because they contain coconut oil. Be sure to read the label and avoid buying them unless the type of oil is listed. This is important because coconut oil is often included as a vegetable oil. Rich's coffee whitener and whipped topping are made with an acceptable fat, but other than Rich's, I don't know of any acceptable brands.

Sometimes it is a little hard for some women to get used to the idea of cooking with vegetable oil. I know that I had difficulty getting used to the idea of cooking with oil. I knew that many nationalities used it, but I had been brought up in the Midwest, where we used lard, butter, or bacon fat for frying. However, it doesn't take long to shift to oil when you realize how important it is to use an oil without cholesterol instead of other fats, which are high in cholesterol. There really isn't all that much difference when you are frying foods; you simply wait until any of the fats are liquid. But it does make a difference in baking. You can generally substitute margarine for butter on an even basis, but lard is more concentrated than margarine, so I generally use a little more margarine than lard or shortening in any baked recipe when the fat is being creamed with sugar. If the fat is melted before it is added to a recipe that I'm adapting, I use an equal amount of oil for the lard or shortening.

Oil should be kept at room temperature, but it is a good idea to keep it somewhere that isn't too warm or where the sun doesn't hit it to prevent the oil from getting rancid. It should also be kept covered when it isn't being used. I haven't used any recipes for deep-fat fried foods in this book because the American Heart Association doesn't really encourage the use of deep-fat fried foods. But if you insist on deep-fat frying, be sure to use oil and have it at the right cooking temperature. If it is cooked at too low a temperature, the food will pick up too much of the fat and it will be greasy and unappetizing. If the temperature is too high, the food will be too brown and not cooked in the center.

It is always a good idea to read the list of ingredients in any product before you buy it, but it is doubly so when you are buying margarine. You shouldn't buy any item just because it is called margarine. Read the list of ingredients to see what kind of oil is used. The amount of ingredients in a product depends on how they are listed. The ingredients are listed in order of their quantity in the product; you need a margarine that says that there is more liquid vegetable oil in it than any other ingredient. Therefore, it should be listed first. Most margarines contain some hydrogenated vegetable oil, but it should be down the list and not the first item. One margarine we checked turned out to include lard. You can believe I returned that one to the case in a hurry. If you are in doubt about the kind of margarine to use, your local heart association should be able to tell you the most acceptable ones available in your area. In fact, they should have information about the best kinds of many foods to buy in your area.

There is also another new product on the market that is called Butter Buds. The brand we buy is sold by Cumberland Packing Corporation in Racine, Wisconsin, and is very handy since it comes in a dry form that can be reconstituted with hot water. It is very good on baked potatoes and cooked vegetables. I put the powder on the table and we sprinkle it over hot vegetables and potatoes. Or you can add it to sauces if you want them to have a butter flavor.

Liquid egg substitute was not mentioned in my first low cholesterol book because it wasn't on the market at the time, but I have used it often in this book. It is a big help in many recipes, though I've never been able to make a jelly roll or some of the fanciest French cakes or Hungarian tortes with it. Chuck especially likes it with French toast, pancakes, and omelets. I find that when I'm adapting a new recipe, I can generally substitute egg whites for 1 or 2 eggs. For more than that, I probably will have to use liquid egg substitute. There is a dry egg substitute, but it is a substitute for persons who are allergic to eggs and is much more difficult to use than liquid egg substitute.

Many people ask me what to do with leftover egg yolks. I freeze mine in 1-cup portions with 2 teaspoons of sugar or 1 teaspoon of salt per cup. After they are frozen I give them to my friend, Frances Nielsen. Her family is lucky: they don't have to worry about cholesterol, so she uses them to make some wonderful egg noodles or some of those luscious foreign cakes and cookies that are so good and usually prohibited on our diet. However, she always cooks low cholesterol food when she is with us, so we really can't object to the high cholesterol foods she cooks when we aren't around.

If you can't bear to throw away the egg yolks, and you don't have a friend who can use them, you can buy dehydrated egg whites. Your local heart association should be able to give you a source for them. I find it simpler and less expensive to buy the whole eggs and freeze or throw away the yolks, but I do keep some of the dried egg whites on hand for emergencies. Of course, I live in a rural community where eggs are plentiful, not too expensive, and of a very good quality, so you will have to decide for yourself what is best for you. I have used a measure for egg whites in this book because all egg whites are not the same size and sometimes it is very important to use the right amount of them.

Since it is no longer advisable to use commercial cakes, pies, rolls, doughnuts, etc., you will probably need to make sure that you have the ingredients on hand for baking your own items from scratch. You can make your own dry mixes and use them, but it is not a good idea to buy commercial mixes unless you are sure they don't include any saturated fats. Angel food cake mix is always acceptable and some pancake mixes to which you have to add the eggs and fat are acceptable, but most mixes are made with saturated fat, so they shouldn't be used.

Cocoa can be substituted for chocolate in most recipes. Three tablespoons of cocoa and 1 tablespoon of margarine equal 1 ounce of baking chocolate, so substitution is fairly simple. Most hot cocoa mixes don't include any chocolate or whole milk, but you should always read the list of ingredients to be sure that they don't include any of the coffee whiteners to give them added richness.

Ice milk, fruit ices, and sherbets can be used instead of ice cream, though it is a good idea not to use too much of them because they are high in sugar and occasionally ice milk will have some butterfat in it.

Coconut is forbidden because the coconut oil is high in cholesterol. I really don't know of any substitute for coconut, so if you have a favorite coconut recipe, I'm afraid it will have to go by the wayside if you can't substitute nuts in it. Don't substitute chocolate chips for the coconut as one of my friends did when she made some cookies for Chuck. Chocolate chips are high in cocoa butter, as are regular baking chocolate, semisweet chocolate, and milk chocolate.

Fruits and vegetables are high on the list of goodies for a low cholesterol diet and you can enjoy any and all of them as long as you don't add saturated fat when you are preparing them. It's good to have them on hand for use with meals and as snacks to replace some of the foods that are high in saturated fat such as ice cream and other snack foods you may have been used to eating.

Since so many people who are on a low cholesterol diet are also on a low sodium diet, I have included variations suitable for a low sodium diet for most of the recipes in this book. These are planned for a low sodium diet, not a salt-free diet. I discussed what should be included in these recipes with Mary Agnes Jones, R.D., chief therapeutic dietitian at Holy Cross Hospital in Chicago, Illinois, and Muriel Urbashich, R.D., director of the dietary department at South Chicago Community Hospital, also in Chicago. They both agreed that the low sodium diet is more liberal now than it was previously. Therefore, I have included regular milk in the diet rather than specifying low sodium milk. I did include low sodium baking powder and canned goods, which are available at most stores and at all health food stores. I also included salt-free margarine, which is readily available. If your doctor has told you that you should be on a "no added salt diet," you can omit the salt in recipes and not make any other changes. For anyone whose doctor has prescribed a low sodium or low salt diet, it would be best to follow the information listed after each recipe. Some recipes couldn't be adapted because they contain foods that are high in salt for which there is no substitute, such as soy sauce or Worcestershire sauce, and if this is true, it is noted that the recipe is not suitable for a low sodium diet. I am a registered dietitian also and these are the guidelines I follow when planning a menu or prescribing a diet for anyone on a low sodium diet.

Equipment

It is very important that you have and use the correct equipment when you are cooking. I have tried to use the simplest equipment in this book because I prefer to keep things simple and think that you probably prefer that as well. Some recipes can get very complicated, but you can often simplify them if you really work on it. That is what I have tried to do.

I can't stress too strongly the importance of using standard measuring cups and spoons. Recipes just won't come out well unless you use standard measurements. Some recipes such as soups can get by with using a little of this and a little of that, but cakes, cookies, pies, puddings, and many sauces and other recipes can easily fail if they aren't measured correctly. I think it is a good idea to measure everything that goes into a recipe before you start preparing it, if at all possible. I also like to have two or three sets of measuring cups and spoons handy. If I get a certain-sized cup or spoon dirty, I can use another one from another set without having to stop and wash out the first one, which saves time.

The correct knife is also very important. Every kitchen should have a French knife for chopping, a boning knife, and several different kinds of paring knives. These should all be kept sharp. I've often heard that it is the dull knife that causes trouble because people aren't as careful as they should be with a dull knife and therefore are more prone to accidents. Knives should be kept in a knife holder or in individual cardboard or other kinds of cases when they aren't being used.

A good thermometer will save its cost many times. I know that we used to make candy without a candy thermometer when we were children, but I also remember that we sometimes had failures. A meat thermometer will help you produce the kind of roast you want with much less fuss and trouble.

I have a heavy-duty mixer with a dough hook that I like to use for making breads. I have included directions for a dough hook in this book. If you don't have a dough hook on your mixer, you can prepare the dough as much as possible in your mixer and, when it gets too thick for the mixer, transfer it to a bowl and proceed with the same ingredients, mixing by hand. I also use my mixer for many things. I know that some people feel you should mix cornbread and muffins by hand, but I have found that I get better results using a mixer. The mixer is really invaluable when it comes to beating egg whites or mixing many cake and cookie recipes.

Stainless steel cooking ware is my favorite. I have a stainless steel pot my husband gave his mother before I knew her and it looks as though it were still new. I have several saucepans, frying pans, and a dutch oven in stainless steel and I wouldn't trade them for any other kind. I even have a huge 3-gallon stainless steel pot that I use for making soup when I want to freeze it or for making spaghetti sauce. I find the stainless steel easy to keep clean and it cooks evenly and is a good sturdy material that doesn't dent or wear out with long use.

I do have a food processor, and I use it when I need a lot of chopped foods, but I don't use it for a couple of tablespoons or even a ¼ cup of chopped onions. It is marvelous for larger quantities of chopped foods, but I think it is a bother for a small amount of food. I also have a crockpot, an electric egg cooker, a frying pan, a toaster-oven, a knife sharpener, and a grill, but I like to keep my cooking as simple as possible. I'm sure you do also, so I haven't specified using them in this book unless I felt they really added something to the finished recipe. If you want to use them, be my guest. Each person knows best what is best for him or her, but I find that most people prefer to keep life as simple as possible.

2
Soups

It always fascinates me that so many different soups are based on the simple ingredients of meat, poultry, fish, and vegetables. Each country seems to have developed its own favorites throughout the years, and each nationality is convinced that its soup creations are the very best. Some soups occasionally cross national boundaries, such as potato soup, which is popular here and in Great Britain, France, and Germany in slightly different forms. Even in this case, however, you can tell which country originated the recipe just as you can distinguish between the cabbage soup of Russia and the one from Switzerland.

I have always thought soup was the greatest. I like it for lunch and could eat it every day as they do in Europe. I like to make soup in large amounts and then freeze portions of it for later use, especially minestrone. It is sometimes difficult to consume a large pot of soup without getting tired of it, but freezing allows you to serve part of it now and the rest in a couple of weeks. This way, no one gets bored with the soup, and it is great to have on hand for unexpected guests.

Most people enjoy a variety of soups. The local chapter of the Business and Professional Women's Club to which I belong generally serves a soup dinner for the February meeting. I've been in charge of it a couple of times and we discovered that the members really enjoy a variety of foreign soups. We served mulligatawny and fruit soup one year. Many of the women had never tasted either of them, but they decided they were really good and several of them went back for seconds. We served them with crackers, relishes, and dessert so that the soup would be the focal point of the meal—an honor any good soup deserves.

Soups are easy to fit into the low cholesterol diet as long as you avoid animal fats. I like to cook the meat or chicken the day before and let the broth refrigerate overnight. The next day I skim off any fat that has risen to the top and then continue preparing the soup. I refrigerate the meat or poultry separately from the broth so that I can take the meat or poultry off the bones and discard any gristle or fat more easily than if it was still in the liquid. Sometimes, when I have time, I prepare a big container of broth, remove the fat, and freeze it in 2-quart containers so that it is ready when I want to make soup at a later date.

I often use the concentrated beef or chicken soup bases as well; once in a while I have even used the ham base. The only trouble with these bases is that they are high in salt and can't be used on a low sodium diet. I like to use them in the European way, combining two or more soup concentrates for an interesting flavor or adding concentrate of another kind to a broth that isn't rich enough to suit me.

Many of the foreign soups require cream or sour cream. I find that the addition of evaporated skimmed milk generally replaces the regular cream. However, sour cream is another matter, so I try to avoid those soups that need sour cream for flavor. You can also reconstitute instant dry milk at double strength (1 cup instant dry milk to 2 cups warm water) for use in soup when the recipe calls for cream. It won't be as rich but it will be tasty.

All vegetables are cholesterol-free, so feel free to use any variety of vegetables in your soups as long as you skim any fat from the broth and add to the soup no other animal fat such as butter or cream. I like to add leftover roast or chicken to my soups. I seem to feel more secure that all the fat has been removed when I do it that way, though it is just as good to cook the meat or chicken, skim the fat off the broth, cut off any visible fat from the meat, and add it to the soup.

Fruit is also fat-free and the Scandinavians make a great variety of hot and cold fruit soups. I've included only one fruit soup recipe here, but there are many available and they are all good unless you blow it all by serving them with whipped cream or other toppings that are taboo.

Frances Nielsen and I are both great soup makers, but you can always tell our soups apart. Hers are richer and spicier than mine. She likes to use barley to thicken soup and I almost never use it unless the recipe specifically requires it.

Perhaps I should take this chance to introduce Frances Nielsen to you, because I keep mentioning her in the book. She is a good friend of mine with whom, along with Muriel Urbashich, I have done a couple of large-quantity cookbooks. She grew up in Luxembourg and came here to the United States when she was eighteen, so she knows and appreciates the cuisine of most of the European countries. She was married to Denny Nielsen and learned from his mother to cook the Danish way and has always been interested in learning any new ways of preparing foods. She is truly one of the most dedicated cooks I've ever known. If she is tired and tense she goes out into the kitchen and whips up a batch of cookies or some bread to relax when the rest of us would probably collapse on the nearest sofa. She and her husband, who were friends of ours in Chicago before my husband retired and we moved to Iowa, visited us out here often and loved it so much that they moved here about a year after we did. Unfortunately, her husband, Denny, died a year and a half after we moved out here, so she moved back to the Chicago area to be near her children. However, I still talk to her often and see her frequently so that we still feel like we are in touch with each other.

As I will continue to say in this book, I am a firm believer in the importance of fiber in the low cholesterol diet, and vegetables provide a good supply of fiber without any cholesterol, which makes them a nearly perfect food. All vegetables have fiber, but the bean and cabbage families seem to provide a little more than others.

Since we are supposed to eat more fish on a low cholesterol diet, it might be interesting for you to try some of the fish chowders and soups that are popular around the world. Feel free to use any of them except the shrimp variety, which is a no-no. Many of them have a tomato base, which is good, and if a milk or cream base is used you can always use evaporated skimmed milk or instant dry milk. I include only a few of them, but there are many versions of fish chowder. You may already have some of them among the recipes of your own heritage. Of course, if you live inland, fewer fresh fish are available to you than to cooks in some foreign countries and in certain areas of the United States, but you'll be amazed at the many varieties of frozen and/or fresh fish available in your own supermarket. Salmon isn't often thought of as a soup ingredient, but it does make a wonderful chowder that I am sure you will enjoy, and salmon is almost always available.

Before buying a canned soup be sure to check the list of ingredients since they often contain saturated fats. Many of them don't, and there are a large number you can use, but do read the label before you buy them. Dehydrated soups are also available and they are almost always cholesterol-free because eggs and fats, which are high in cholesterol, just don't keep well for soup. Do read the label, anyway.

It isn't a good idea to use many soda crackers because they are generally made with saturated fats, but melba toast, bread sticks, croutons, toast, and some of the specialty crackers are free of saturated fats and may be used freely. I like to serve bread sticks or toast cut into strips with soup and I've even used popcorn on occasion. Rye rounds toasted in the oven are good with soup as are many other specialty breads that you can make at home using approved ingredients.

BAKED BEAN SOUP (New England)

2½ cups beans baked without
  pork or fat meat
1 cup finely chopped onions
½ cup finely chopped celery
5 cups fat-free beef broth
1 29-ounce can crushed
  canned tomatoes
1 teaspoon salt
⅛ teaspoon pepper
2 tablespoons all-purpose
  flour
2 tablespoons melted
  margarine

Crush beans slightly with the back of a spoon. Place beans, onions, celery, broth, tomatoes, salt, and pepper in a pot. Cover and simmer about 1 hour. Taste for seasoning. Add salt, if necessary. (The amount of salt will depend on the saltiness of the broth.)

Mix flour and margarine together until smooth. Stir into the soup. Cook and stir over medium heat about 5 minutes or until soup is slightly thickened. Serve hot.

Low sodium diets: Omit salt. Use low sodium beef broth, beans, and tomatoes or use beans cooked without salt and fresh tomatoes.

Yield: about 2 quarts

CABBAGE AND RICE SOUP (Switzerland)

1 pound (about 5 cups)
  shredded cabbage
1 cup thinly sliced onions
3 tablespoons margarine
5 cups fat-free beef broth
1 quart fat-free chicken broth
⅛ teaspoon pepper
¼ teaspoon grated nutmeg
Salt
½ cup long-grain rice

Fry cabbage and onions in margarine in a heavy saucepan over low heat, stirring frequently, until onions are transparent and cabbage is limp.

Add beef and chicken broths, pepper, and nutmeg to the vegetables. Stir lightly and taste for seasoning. Add more salt, if necessary. (The amount of salt necessary will depend on the saltiness of the broths.) Bring to a boil. Add rice to the soup. Cover and simmer about 20 minutes or until rice is tender. Do not allow the rice to overcook. Serve hot.

Low sodium diets: Omit salt. Use salt-free margarine and low sodium broths.

Yield: about 2 quarts

CATFISH GUMBO (Louisiana)

½ cup chopped celery
½ cup chopped fresh green
  peppers
½ cup chopped onions
1 minced garlic clove or ¼
  teaspoon garlic powder
2 tablespoons vegetable oil
2 cups fat-free chicken broth
2 cups (16 ounces) canned
  crushed tomatoes

1 pound fresh or frozen okra,
  cut into 1-inch pieces
¼ teaspoon pepper
¼ teaspoon ground thyme
1 crushed bay leaf
½ teaspoon tabasco sauce
Salt to taste
1¼ pounds skinned and
  boned catfish
Hot rice

Fry celery, green peppers, onions, and garlic in vegetable oil in heavy pot until vegetables are limp but not browned, stirring occasionally. Add broth, tomatoes, okra, pepper, thyme, bay leaf, and tabasco sauce to fried vegetables. Taste and add salt to taste. Cover and simmer 30 minutes.

Cut catfish into about 1-inch pieces and add to the hot sauce. Simmer, uncovered, 10 to 15 minutes or until the fish flakes easily. Serve gumbo hot over hot rice.

Low sodium diets: Omit salt. Use low sodium broth and tomatoes or fresh tomatoes.

Yield: about 1½ quarts

CREAMY GREEN STRING BEAN SOUP
(Germany)

Frances Nielsen says that, in Germany, this soup is made to use the green string beans in the garden that are a little too old to use as a plain vegetable. Canned green beans do not yield as flavorful a soup as fresh or frozen beans, but they may be used, if necessary. If canned green beans are used, they should be added to the hot broth with the onions and potatoes.

2 cups chopped onions
3 tablespoons vegetable oil
6 cups chopped fresh or
   frozen green beans
1 quart fat-free chicken
   broth
3 cups cubed fresh white
   potatoes

2 tablespoons chopped
   parsley
¼ teaspoon white pepper
1⅔ cups (1 13-ounce can)
   evaporated skimmed milk
Salt

Fry onions in vegetable oil in heavy saucepan over moderate heat, stirring frequently, until soft but not browned. Add beans, cut into about 1-inch pieces, and chicken broth to onions. Cover and simmer 30 minutes.

Add potatoes, parsley, and pepper to soup. Cover and simmer another 20 minutes or until potatoes are tender. Add the evaporated skimmed milk and reheat to serving temperature, but do not let the soup boil after the milk is added. Taste for seasoning and add more salt, if necessary. (The amount of salt needed will depend on the saltiness of the broth.) Serve hot.

Low sodium diets: Omit salt. Use low sodium broth.

Yield: about 2 quarts

CREAMY SALMON CHOWDER
(Northwestern United States)

1-pound can red salmon
1 quart fat-free chicken broth
1 cup diced fresh white potatoes
½ cup chopped onions
¼ cup diced fresh green peppers

¼ cup thinly sliced celery
½ teaspoon salt
⅛ teaspoon white pepper
½ cup instant dry potatoes
2 tablespoons margarine
1⅔ cups (1 13-ounce can) evaporated skimmed milk

Drain salmon and reserve juice for later use. Discard salmon skin and bones and break salmon into small pieces. Refrigerate until needed.

Combine salmon juice with chicken broth, fresh white potatoes, onions, green peppers, celery, salt, and pepper. Cover and simmer 15 to 20 minutes or until potatoes are tender. Add instant potatoes and margarine to chowder. Simmer, stirring frequently, for 5 minutes. Add salmon and evaporated milk. Reheat and serve hot.

Low sodium diets: Omit salt. Use low sodium broth and salt-free margarine. Add ¼ teaspoon ground thyme.

Yield: about 1½ quarts

FISH CHOWDER (New England)

1½ pounds fillet of haddock, halibut, or other white fish
1 cup diced raw white potatoes
2½ cups boiling water
½ cup finely chopped onions
¼ cup diced fresh green peppers

⅓ cup (⅔ stick) margarine
⅓ cup all-purpose flour
2 teaspoons salt
¼ teaspoon white pepper
2½ cups cold water
1⅔ cups (1 13-ounce can) evaporated skimmed milk
Imitation bacon bits (optional)

Remove any skin or bones from the fillets and cut the fish into about 1-inch cubes. Place fish, potatoes, and boiling water in a heavy saucepan. Cover and simmer 20 minutes.

Fry onions and green peppers in margarine over moderate heat, stirring frequently, until onions are golden. Sprinkle the flour, salt, and pepper over the onion mixture and cook and stir over moderate heat until the vegetables are coated. Add the cold water and cook, stirring constantly, over moderate heat until smooth. Add the undrained fish and potato mixture to the sauce. Cover and simmer another 20 minutes, stirring occasionally. Remove from the heat; add evaporated milk and reheat to serving temperature but do not let the chowder boil after the milk is added. Serve hot, garnished with bacon bits.

Low sodium diets: Omit salt. Use salt-free margarine.

Yield: about 1½ quarts

FRUIT SOUP (Scandinavia)

Fruit soup is another one of those dishes that can vary with each and every cook. My mother liked it with pineapple chunks instead of peach slices. You can use light or dark raisins, and there is another version with dried apricots instead of prunes. Some people like to use wine in it, and you can use stick cinnamon instead of ground cinnamon for a slightly lighter color. Tapioca is often used to thicken it, and juice drained from canned fruit may be used instead of the sugar and water. Fruit soup is pretty served in a clear glass bowl for dessert, and I like it used as a sauce over sherbet or plain cake.

2 quarts cold water
¾ cup sugar
8 ounces chopped pitted
   prunes
½ cup raisins
2 tablespoons cornstarch
¼ cup water

2 tablespoons lemon juice
½ cup frozen orange juice
   concentrate
½ teaspoon ground
   cinnamon
1 cup drained, chopped
   canned peaches

Place 2 quarts water and sugar in saucepan. Cook and stir over medium heat until sugar is dissolved. Add prunes and raisins. Cover and simmer 30 minutes.

Stir cornstarch into ¼ cup water to make a smooth paste. Add to soup along with lemon juice, frozen orange juice concentrate, and cinnamon. Cook and stir over medium heat until slightly thickened and the starchy taste is gone. Add peaches to soup and reheat to serving temperature, if necessary. Serve hot as a first course or chilled as a dessert.

Low sodium diets: May be used as written.

Yield: about 2 quarts

GAZPACHO (Spain)

2 cups fat-free beef broth
1 10¾-ounce can condensed
   tomato soup
2 tablespoons lemon juice
3 tablespoons prepared
   Italian-style oil and
   vinegar dressing
⅓ cup finely chopped onions
⅓ cup finely chopped fresh
   green peppers

2 tablespoons finely chopped
   celery
1 cup diced peeled and cored
   fresh tomatoes
¼ teaspoon garlic powder
Salt
¼ to ½ cup finely chopped or
   thinly sliced fresh
   cucumbers

Combine broth, tomato soup, lemon juice, dressing, onions, green peppers, celery, tomatoes, and garlic powder. Taste for seasoning and add salt, if necessary. (The amount of salt necessary will depend on the saltiness of the broth.) Cover and refrigerate overnight or at least several hours.

Served chilled soup in chilled bowls garnished with cucumbers.

Low sodium diets: Omit salt. Use low sodium tomato soup and salad dressing.

Yield: 6 ¾-cup servings

GOLDEN SQUASH SOUP (South America)

¾ cup chopped onions
¼ cup (½ stick) margarine
⅓ cup all-purpose flour
1 cup instant dry milk
2 cups hot water
6 cups hot fat-free chicken broth

2 cups cooked winter squash
⅛ teaspoon pepper
½ teaspoon celery salt
¼ teaspoon curry powder
Salt
Chopped parsley or chives

Fry onions in margarine in heavy saucepan over moderate heat, stirring frequently, until golden. Sprinkle flour over onions and continue to cook and stir until flour is lightly browned. Stir the dry milk into the hot water. Combine with the hot chicken broth and add to the onions. Cook and stir over moderate heat until the sauce is smooth and the starchy taste is gone.

Beat squash until smooth or use frozen precooked squash. Add to soup along with the pepper, celery salt, and curry powder. Taste for seasoning and add salt if necessary. (The amount of salt needed will depend on the saltiness of the broth.) Simmer 5 minutes. Serve hot garnished with chopped parsley or chives.

Low sodium diets: Omit salt. Use low sodium chicken broth and squash. Use salt-free margarine and ¼ teaspoon celery seed instead of the celery salt.

Yield: about 2 quarts

GOULASH SOUP (Hungary)

2 cups chopped onions
Vegetable oil
1 pound beef round, cut into about ¾-inch pieces
2 quarts fat-free beef broth
1 minced clove garlic

2 teaspoons paprika
½ cup crushed, drained canned tomatoes
Salt
1½ cups cubed fresh white potatoes

Brown onions in vegetable oil in heavy frying pan over moderate heat, stirring occasionally. Transfer onions with a slotted spoon to a heavy saucepan. Brown beef in the same frying pan over moderate heat, stirring occasionally. Transfer meat with slotted spoon to saucepan with onions. Pour off as much fat as possible from the frying pan and remove as much as possible of the remaining fat with a paper towel. Add the beef broth to the frying pan and cook and stir over low heat to get all of the brown particles out of the pan. Pour the hot broth into the saucepan with the onion and meat.

Add the garlic, paprika, and tomatoes to the meat mixture. Stir lightly and taste for seasoning. Add salt, if necessary. (The amount of salt needed will depend on the saltiness of the broth.) Cover and simmer over low heat until the meat is tender. Add potatoes. Cover and simmer another 15 to 20 minutes or until the potatoes are tender. Serve hot.

Low sodium diets: Omit salt. Use low sodium broth and tomatoes
   or fresh tomatoes.

Yield: about 2 quarts

OKRA AND TOMATO GUMBO (Louisiana)

1 cup chopped onions	1 teaspoon paprika
¼ cup vegetable oil	¼ teaspoon cayenne pepper
1 pound okra	⅛ teaspoon black pepper
2 tablespoons all-purpose flour	½ teaspoon leaf oregano
2 teaspoons sugar	1 29-ounce can tomatoes
1 teaspoon salt	½ cup boiling water
	Hot cooked rice

Fry onions in as much of the oil as needed in a heavy saucepan over moderate heat, stirring frequently, until golden. Add okra, cut into 1-inch pieces, to the onions. Cook, stirring frequently, over moderate heat 5 minutes using the rest of the oil, if necessary.

Stir flour, sugar, salt, paprika, peppers, and oregano together and add to vegetables. Cook and stir over low heat until the spices are blended into the vegetable mixture. Crush tomatoes and add tomatoes and juice to vegetables along with the water. Cover and simmer about 15 minutes or until the okra is tender. Serve hot over hot rice.

Low sodium diets: Omit salt. Use low sodium canned tomatoes.

Yield: about 1½ quarts

MINESTRONE (Italy)

This thick Italian soup is luscious. There are as many variations of this soup as there are of the American vegetable beef soup, and this is one of my favorites. Many different combinations of vegetables can be used, but most recipes include beans, pasta, and Italian seasonings. This soup freezes beautifully and I always try to keep some of it in the freezer for emergencies.

1 cup chopped onions
¼ cup chopped fresh geeen peppers
½ cup diced carrots
2 tablespoons vegetable oil
3 quarts fat-free beef broth
1 cup diced fresh white potatoes
1 cup crushed canned tomatoes with their juice
½ cup shredded cabbage
2 cups (1-pound can) cooked dried beans

½ teaspoon garlic powder
¼ teaspoon pepper
1½ teaspoons Italian seasoning
1 teaspoon oregano
½ teaspoon basil
1 teaspoon salt
Hot water
½ cup macaroni or other small pasta
2 cups chopped cooked lean beef, cut into about 1-inch cubes (optional)

Fry onions, peppers, and carrots in vegetable oil over moderate heat in a heavy saucepan, stirring occasionally, until the onions are limp but not browned.

Add broth, potatoes, tomatoes, cabbage, beans, garlic, pepper, Italian seasoning, oregano, basil, and salt. Cover and simmer for 30 to 40 minutes or until the vegetables are tender. Taste for seasoning and add more salt, if necessary. (The amount of salt necessary will depend on the saltiness of the broth.) Add enough hot water, if necessary, to bring the volume of the soup up to about 3 quarts. Refrigerate any soup not to be served at the next meal. When the soup is to be served, add the macaroni or other small pasta and the meat, cover and cook about 10 minutes or until the pasta is tender. Serve hot.

Low sodium diets: Omit salt. Use low sodium broth and tomatoes or fresh tomatoes. Cook beef without salt.

Yield: about 3 quarts

MULLIGATAWNY SOUP (India)

This soup is beautiful and tastes so good. I can never understand why it isn't as popular here as it was in India when the British were stationed there.

¼ cup finely chopped onions
¼ cup finely chopped fresh
  green peppers
¼ cup finely diced carrots
2 tablespoons finely diced
  celery
¼ cup (½ stick) margarine
⅓ cup all-purpose flour
2 cups hot fat-free chicken
  broth
¾ cup drained, crushed
  canned tomatoes

1 small cored and diced tart
  apple
¼ to ½ teaspoon curry
  powder
⅛ teaspoon ground
  cloves
Sprinkle of white pepper
Salt
1 cup cooked diced chicken
  with the skin and fat
  removed
1 cup cooked rice

Fry onions, green peppers, carrots, and celery in margarine in a heavy saucepan over moderate heat, stirring frequently, until the onions are limp but not browned. Remove vegetables from the fat with a slotted spoon and set aside for later use. Add flour to the fat in the pan and cook and stir over moderate heat until lightly browned. Add the hot chicken broth and cook and stir, using a wire whip to form a smooth sauce. (The whip is important to make the sauce smooth. If you don't have a whip, it is better to add cold chicken broth and cook and stir until it forms a smooth sauce.)

Add vegetables, tomatoes, apple, curry powder, cloves, and pepper to the sauce. Mix lightly and taste for seasoning. Add more salt, if necessary. (The amount of salt necessary will depend on the saltiness of the broth.) Cover and simmer 45 minutes.

Add the chicken and rice just before serving the soup. Reheat to serving temperature and serve hot.

Low sodium diets: Omit salt. Use salt-free margarine and low sodium broth and tomatoes or fresh tomatoes. Cook the chicken and rice without salt.

Yield: about 1½ quarts

PASTA FAGIOLI (Italy)

1 cup navy or great northern beans
Water
1 quart fat-free beef broth
2 tablespoons vegetable oil
½ cup finely chopped onions
¼ cup finely chopped celery
1 tablespoon chopped parsley
¼ teaspoon powdered rosemary
¼ teaspoon powdered thyme
¼ teaspoon garlic powder
⅛ teaspoon pepper
½ cup tomato sauce
Salt
1 cup elbow macaroni or other small pasta

Wash beans well in cold water, removing any dark or discolored beans. Place beans in heavy saucepan. Cover generously with water and bring to a boil. Boil 2 minutes. Remove from heat, cover, and set aside for 2 hours. Drain beans well.

Place broth and oil in heavy saucepan. Bring broth and oil to a boil. Add drained beans, cover, and simmer 1 hour or until the beans are tender.

Add onions, celery, parsley, rosemary, thyme, garlic powder, pepper, and tomato sauce to the beans. Taste for seasoning and add salt, if necessary. (The amount of salt needed will depend on the saltiness of the broth.) Cover and simmer 30 minutes or until the vegetables are tender.

Before serving, add the macaroni or other small pasta, cover, and cook about 10 minutes or until the macaroni or pasta is tender. Serve hot.

Low sodium diets: Omit salt. Use low sodium broth and tomato sauce or fresh tomatoes.

Yield: about 1½ quarts

POTATO SOUP (Midwestern United States)

This is the basic potato soup that my mother served. Chuck likes it thickened and some people like to put some noodles in it, but this is the way my mother always prepared it and it is still my favorite way to serve it.

3 cups diced fresh white potatoes
1 cup chopped onions
2 cups water
1 teaspoon salt

⅛ teaspoon white pepper
1⅔ cups (1 13-ounce can) evaporated skimmed milk
2 tablespoons margarine
Chopped parsley or chives

Combine potatoes, onions, water, salt, and pepper. Cover and simmer 25 to 30 minutes or until the potatoes are mushy. Remove from heat and add milk and margarine. Reheat, if necessary, to serving temperature, but do not let it boil again after the milk is added. Serve hot, garnished with parsley or chives.

Low sodium diets: Omit salt. Use salt-free margarine.

Yield: 1¼ to 1½ quarts

RED BEAN SOUP (Portugal)

2 cups coarsely chopped onions
¼ cup vegetable oil
2 cups (1-pound can) washed and drained kidney beans
3 cups diced white potatoes
1 minced garlic clove
1 crushed bay leaf
2 cups (1-pound can) tomato sauce
5 cups fat-free chicken broth
¼ teaspoon allspice
⅛ teaspoon black pepper
Salt to taste

Fry the onions in the vegetable oil until soft but not browned. Remove onions from frying pan with a slotted spoon and put them in a heavy soup pot. Add beans, potatoes, garlic, bay leaf, tomato sauce, chicken broth, allspice, pepper, and salt to taste. (The amount of salt necessary will depend on the saltiness of the chicken broth.)

Cover the soup pot and simmer over low heat for 1½ hours. Taste and add more salt if necessary. Serve hot.

Low sodium diets: Omit salt. Use kidney beans that have been cooked without salt and low sodium tomato sauce or fresh tomatoes.

Yield: about 2 quarts

TOMATO BOUILLON (United States)

This is good served hot or cold. In cold weather I like to serve it in the living room with crackers or toast squares before we serve dinner in the dining room.

1 cup chopped celery
1 cup chopped onions
2 cups fat-free chicken broth
3 cups fat-free beef broth
3 cups tomato juice

1 teaspoon Worcestershire
  sauce
⅛ teaspoon pepper
Salt to taste
Croutons

Combine celery, onions, and chicken broth. Cover and simmer 30 minutes. Drain well. Discard vegetables and combine broth with beef broth, tomato juice, Worcestershire sauce, and pepper. Taste for seasoning and add salt to taste. Serve hot or cold with croutons, crackers, or toast squares.

Low sodium diets: Omit salt. Use low sodium broths and unsalted tomato juice. Delete Worcestershire sauce. Add ¼ teaspoon ground thyme, ¼ teaspoon leaf oregano, and ¼ teaspoon basil along with the broths.

Yield: 2 quarts

VEGETABLE BEEF SOUP (United States)

A recipe for vegetable soup is really a pattern rather than a recipe since each person gives it his or her signature with the choice of favored vegetables. This is the way we like it, but if you want to use more tomatoes, tomato juice instead of tomatoes, some barley or corn or cooked dried beans, you can proceed happily according to your own instincts knowing that everyone else who uses the recipe probably changes it a wee bit also.

1½ pounds beef stew meat
2 quarts cold water
1½ teaspoons salt
¼ teaspoon pepper
2 cups diced white potatoes
½ cup diced carrots

1 cup diced onions
½ cup shredded cabbage
1 pound crushed canned
  tomatoes
½ cup green string beans

Trim gristle and fat from the stew meat. Put meat into a heavy saucepan and cover with cold water; add salt and pepper.

Simmer about 1½ hours or until the meat is tender. Drain the stock from the meat; strain and refrigerate the meat and stock separately. Remove and discard the fat from the chilled stock and return the stock to the saucepan. Measure stock after the fat has been discarded and add water, if necessary, to total 7 cups. Add potatoes, carrots, onions, cabbage, tomatoes, and green beans, which have been cut into about ½-inch pieces. Cover and simmer 30 to 45 minutes or until the vegetables are tender. Taste for seasoning and add additional salt and pepper, if necessary. Trim meat and discard any fat or gristle; add meat to soup. Reheat to serving temperature, if necessary, and serve hot.

Low sodium diets: Omit salt. Use low sodium canned tomatoes or fresh tomatoes.

Yield: about 2½ quarts

3

Meats

It is always interesting to discover how the people of any region or country adapted the foods available in their area for their own use. Each group has developed its own kind of stew that uses available ingredients to tenderize and extend the meat supply. The French use wine, the Italians use tomatoes, and the Germans use vinegar to tenderize their meat. The gumbos of Louisiana, the tamale pie of southwestern United States, and the clam chowders of New England are examples of the way the immigrants to this country used available food supplies to create really outstanding foods.

Many of these regional and ethnic recipes are readily adaptable to the low cholesterol diet because they use the leaner portions of meat and turn them into works of art that you can be proud to serve to your family and friends. The whole trick is to make those around your table think this is something you whipped up just for them without going into the fact that it is a low cholesterol recipe that you need to serve.

In my first low cholesterol book I included the basic methods for preparing roasts and steaks that are suitable for the low cholesterol diet. In this book I include some of the stews and other meat extenders that are most popular in this and other countries. Many researchers seem to feel that we are eating too much meat these days. What better way to handle that problem—as well as to fight inflation—than to serve stews, meat pies, and other meat extenders?

Most of the meat you will find in the stores today is choice beef. The prime beef generally goes to the big hotels, so you don't need to worry about getting it without knowing about it. Actually, the good grade of beef is best for you because it is the leanest, but unless you are lucky enough to be able to get it, you will probably have to settle for choice beef, removing all the visible fat with a sharp knife and trying to cook most of the rest of the fat out of the meat. We are lucky enough to live in a rural area where we can buy a whole beef, and the man we buy it from gives us a steer that has not been fed corn at the last for what they call "finishing" the beef. This way we avoid that last push for putting fat on the meat and we find the meat very tender and good. However, we still have to trim the meat after we get it and use all the techniques for cooking as much fat as possible out of the meat.

If you aren't lucky enough to be able to buy good-grade beef or beef that hasn't been processed without that last push for fat, you will need to be especially vigilant about cutting the fat off and cooking the fat out of your meat.

Specific cuts of meat with low fat content that I suggest you buy include the following.

Beef: round, rump roast, sirloin, tenderloin, dried beef, flank steak, and lean ground beef.

Pork: loin, center-cut roasts or chops, tenderloin, lean ham, ham steak, and Canadian bacon.

Veal: round, rump roast, leg roast, sirloin, arm steak, and loin chop.

Lamb: sirloin roast, leg roast, and sirloin chops.

As you can see, roasts are still included in your diet. The most important thing to remember is to select a lean cut and then prepare it to get rid of most of the remaining fat. The roast should be placed on a rack so it doesn't cook in the drippings. If it is dry and needs to be basted, it should be basted with a marinade, vegetable oil, margarine, or bouillon. However, drippings should not be discarded. They should be chilled, the fat should be removed, and then they can be used for gravies or soups.

Fortunately for those of us who like pork, growers are really working on raising pigs that are leaner, and the average pig today is a far cry from what we used to think of as a pig. They are longer and leaner, so to speak, than the pigs of even twenty years ago. If you trim all the visible fat off the pork and then cook it to get rid of the remaining fat, there is no reason why you can't enjoy an occasional meal of pork.

Since many of the leaner cuts are not the most tender cuts, this is a good time to think about using tenderizers. You can use either the commercial tenderizers or the natural ones, such as wine, lemon juice, vinegar, tomatoes, orange juice, and others that add flavor as well as tenderness to meats. These natural tenderizers have been used for ages and are the basis for some of our best recipes.

All cooking temperatures should be followed as closely as possible, though most cooking times are approximate since so much depends on the thickness of the meat and the temperature at which it was put into the oven. A roast-meat thermometer should be used whenever possible.

When you use a recipe that includes ground beef you need to buy very lean ground beef or you must cook all the fat out of the regular ground beef. I like to use ground round for recipes that specify ground beef since it is the leanest ground beef I can buy. Most butchers will cut the fat off the beef round after you have bought it and grind the meat for you. I like to brown the meat well, if it isn't ground round, and then drain off the fat and liquid, which are discarded. After that I pour a little very hot water over the meat to get rid of any remaining fat. This is possible only when you brown the meat first and then go on cooking the meat with other ingredients. You should use only the very leanest ground meat for meat loaves because the crumbs or other starchy basis for the loaf absorb the fat and you can't get rid of it as well as you can when you are cooking ground beef alone.

Canadian bacon may be used on a low cholesterol diet because it is very lean, but the use of ham is rather controversial. If the ham is very lean it is acceptable, and there are many lean hams on the market today. If the ham is fat, however, it is better just to forget it.

Precooked hams generally tend to be rather lean. I don't think they have the flavor of the other hams, but it is almost impossible to get any other kind these days. Ask your butcher to remove any fat from the precooked ham and slice and tie it for you, if you decide to use it. Fully cooked hams should be cooked according to the directions on the container to an interior temperature of 130 to 135° F. This will take about 15 to 20 minutes per pound at 325° F.

It isn't a good idea to order a hamburger when you are out, but if you get into a spot where that is all that is available, take a paper napkin and press it against both side of the hamburger to absorb the fat clinging to it. I'm sure you will be amazed at how much fat you can get from one hamburger. A plain boiled ham sandwich, which is leaner, is preferable to a hamburger. A hot or cold roast beef sandwich without gravy is the best of all.

Many people dearly love the various kinds of sausages available, but they should be avoided, including frankfurters, because they have a high fat content that isn't all cooked out when they are served. Frankfurters, even turkey ones, generally have a fat content of more than 30 percent.

Although many foreign recipes use the fat in the meats to enhance the flavor of the other ingredients, many of these recipes can be adapted to fit into the low cholesterol diet. There is just nothing we can do to adapt some of the regional recipes that call for frying foods in bacon fat or deep-fat frying, but I have included my favorites among the recipes that are suitable for the low cholesterol diet. I hope you and your family and friends will enjoy them as much as my family and friends do.

SAUERBRATEN (Germany)

6 pounds boneless bottom
  round of beef
½ cup brown sugar
1 quart boiling water
2 cups vinegar
1 tablespoon salt
¼ teaspoon black pepper
2 teaspoons ground mustard
1 teaspoon ground cloves
1 minced garlic clove

1 crushed bay leaf
1½ cups finely chopped
  onions
1 cup finely chopped carrots
½ cup finely chopped celery
Vegetable oil
4 ounces crumbled
  gingersnaps
¼ cup sugar

Trim any visible fat from meat and place in a stainless steel or glass container.

Dissolve brown sugar in water. Add vinegar, salt, pepper, mustard, cloves, garlic, bay leaf, onions, carrots, and celery. Mix lightly and pour over beef. Cover tightly and refrigerate for from 24 to 48 hours. Remove meat from marinade. Drain thoroughly. Reserve marinade for later use.

Brown roast thoroughly in oil in heavy frying pan over moderate heat. Transfer browned meat to roaster. Pour marinade over roast. Cover tightly and bake 2½ to 3 hours at 325° F. or until meat is tender. Marinade should not be less than 1 inch deep and should not cover more than half the height of the roast. Remove meat and keep it warm. Strain sauce and return the liquid to the roaster. Bring the liquid to a boil. Add the cookies and sugar and cook and stir until the cookies are dissolved and the juice is thickened. Vegetables that were strained from the sauce may be returned to the sauce, if desired, before the meat and sauce are served. Slice the meat thin and serve warm with the hot sauce over the meat.

Low sodium diets: Omit salt.

Yield: about 12 servings

STEAK RANCHERO
(Southwestern United States)

½ cup all-purpose flour
1 tablespoon salt
1½ teaspoons chili powder
1½ pounds boneless beef
  round steak
¼ cup vegetable oil
½ cup chopped fresh green

peppers
½ cup chopped onions
1 cup fat-free beef broth
1 cup tomato sauce
1 teaspoon chili powder
¼ teaspoon garlic powder
¼ teaspoon ground cumin

Stir flour, salt, and 1½ teaspoons chili powder together to blend well. Trim any gristle and visible fat from the beef and cut it into 6 equal portions. Dredge the steak in the flour mixture and brown it in vegetable oil in a heavy frying pan over moderate heat. Transfer steaks to a casserole and fry the green peppers and onions in the frying pan used for the steak. Remove the vegetables with a slotted spoon and add them to the meat. Pour as much of the oil as possible from the frying pan. Pour the beef broth into the frying pan and cook and stir over low heat to absorb the browned particles in the pan. Add the tomato sauce, 1 teaspoon chili powder, garlic powder, and cumin to the broth and pour over the meat. Cover tightly and bake at 325° F. 1 to 1½ hours or until the meat is tender. Serve the steak hot with some of the sauce.

Low sodium diets: Omit salt. Use low sodium broth and tomato
  sauce or fresh tomatoes.

Yield: 6 servings

BEEF BOURGUIGNON (France)

2 pounds boneless beef round
Vegetable oil
1 4-ounce can mushrooms
½ cup chopped green onions
  with tops

1½ cups chopped onions
½ cup chopped carrots
¼ teaspoon garlic powder
2 tablespoons chopped
  parsley

3 tablespoons all-purpose
  flour
2 tablespoons tomato sauce
¼ teaspoon ground thyme
1 teaspoon salt

⅛ teaspoon pepper
1 cup Beaujolais or
  Burgundy wine
½ cup beef broth
Homemade Noodles or
  Steamed Rice (see recipes)

Trim gristle and visible fat from beef and cut it into about 1-inch cubes. Brown the meat in oil in a heavy frying pan over moderate heat, using as much of the vegetable oil as necessary. Remove the meat from the frying pan with a slotted spoon and put it into a small roaster or casserole. Drain the mushrooms and fry them with the onions, carrots, garlic powder, and parsley in the same frying pan in which the meat was browned until the onions are limp. Add the vegetables to the meat with a slotted spoon. Pour off as much of the oil as possible from the frying pan. Add the flour to the frying pan and cook and stir until the flour is lightly browned. Add the tomato sauce, thyme, salt, pepper, wine, and broth to the frying pan and cook and stir over moderate heat to form a smooth sauce. Add the sauce to the meat and vegetables. Stir lightly to mix. Cover tightly and bake at 325° F. 1 to 1½ hours or until the meat is tender. Serve the hot meat and sauce over Homemade Noodles or Steamed Rice (see Index).

Low sodium diets: Omit salt. Use low sodium broth and tomato sauce or fresh tomatoes and fresh mushrooms instead of canned.

Yield: 6 servings

BEEF STEW (West Africa)

1 pound beef round
¼ cup vegetable oil
2 cups fat-free beef broth
¼ cup smooth or chunky
  peanut butter
1 large tomato, cut into
  wedges

¾ cup thinly sliced onions
½ teaspoon salt
½ teaspoon crushed red pepper
1 tablespoon cornstarch
2 tablespoons cold water
Homemade Noodles or
  Steamed Rice (see recipes)

Remove any fat from meat with a sharp knife and cut into 1-inch cubes. Brown meat in vegetable oil in a large frying pan over medium heat, stirring frequently. Add 1 cup broth, cover and simmer over low heat about 45 minutes or until meat is tender. Add remaining 1 cup broth. Gradually stir peanut butter into the stew. Add tomato, onions, salt, and pepper. Cover and simmer over low heat for 25 minutes. Combine cornstarch and water to form a smooth paste and stir into the stew. Cook and stir 1 minute or until thickened. Serve hot over Homemade Noodles or Steamed Rice (see Index).

Low sodium diets: Omit salt. Use low sodium broth and peanut butter.

Yield: 4 to 6 servings

BEEF AND BEAN STEW (Spain)

2 pounds lean beef stew meat
¼ cup vegetable oil
2 cups coarsely chopped onions
2 cups carrots, cut into 1-inch cubes
1 cup fat-free broth
1 cup chopped drained tomatoes
1 teaspoon salt

¼ teaspoon black pepper
1 minced garlic clove
⅛ teaspoon ground cloves
¼ teaspoon marjoram
½ cup dry white wine
2 cups drained cooked navy or great northern beans
1 tablespoon chopped parsley
Steamed Rice (see recipe)

Trim any visible fat from meat and brown in as much of the oil as necessary in a heavy frying pan. Transfer meat as it is browned to a small roaster or casserole using a slotted spoon. Fry onions until soft but not browned in the frying pan in which the meat was browned. Transfer onions to roaster or casserole with a slotted spoon. Scatter carrots over the meat and onions.

Pour as much of the oil as possible out of the pan in which the meat was browned. Add the broth and cook and stir over moderate heat until the brown bits in the pan have been absorbed by the broth. Add tomatoes, salt, pepper, garlic, cloves, marjoram, and wine to the broth. Mix lightly and pour over the meat and vegetables. Cover tightly and bake at 325° F. for 1½ hours.

Stir beans and parsley into the stew. Cover and cook another 30 minutes or until the meat is tender. Serve the stew hot over Steamed Rice (see Index). The gravy may be thickened if desired but it is not customary.

Low sodium diets: Omit salt. Use low sodium broth, tomatoes, and beans or fresh tomatoes and beans cooked without salt.

Yield: 6 to 8 servings

BEEF GOULASH (Hungary)

This recipe may look simple, but it is simply luscious. My mother loved it after the first time she tasted it and used to ask for it for special occasions. The sauce is thin, but it is not customarily thickened.

2 pounds beef round, cut about ¾-inch thick
Vegetable oil
2 cups coarsely chopped onions
2 cups fat-free beef broth
1 tablespoon paprika
1 teaspoon salt
⅛ teaspoon pepper
Homemade Noodles (see recipe)

Trim any bone and visible fat from the beef and cut it into about ¾-inch cubes. Brown the meat in vegetable oil in a heavy frying pan over moderate heat, stirring occasionally. Remove the meat from the frying pan with a slotted spoon and place it in a small roaster or casserole. Fry onions in the same frying pan until golden. Transfer the onions to the roaster or casserole with a slotted spoon. Pour off any remaining oil from the frying pan. Add the beef broth to the frying pan and cook and stir until the brown particles have been absorbed by the broth. Add the paprika, salt, and pepper to the broth and pour it over the onions and meat.

Cover tightly and bake 1 to 1½ hours at 325° F. or until the meat is tender. Serve hot over Homemade Noodles (see Index).

Beef and Potato Variation: Peel and quarter 4 medium-size potatoes. Cover with boiling water and simmer 5 minutes. Add to the goulash after the meat is tender. Cover and continue to cook about 20 minutes or until the potatoes are tender. Noodles are not customarily served with this variation.

Low sodium diets: Omit salt. Use low sodium broth.

Yield: 6 servings

BEEF STEW WITH RED CABBAGE (Germany)

2 pounds lean beef stew meat	1 teaspoon caraway seed
Vegetable oil	¼ cup vinegar
2 cups coarsely chopped onions	1 coarsely chopped medium-sized head red cabbage
2 cups water	½ cup broken gingersnaps
1 crushed bay leaf	¼ cup water
¼ teaspoon black pepper	Hot cooked noodles
1½ teaspoons salt	

Trim any visible fat from the meat and brown in oil in a heavy frying pan. Transfer meat as it is browned with a slotted spoon to a small roaster or casserole. Sprinkle onions over meat. Pour as much of the fat as possible out of the frying pan in which the meat was browned. Add 2 cups of water and cook and stir over moderate heat until the brown bits have been absorbed by the water. Pour over the meat. Sprinkle the bay leaf, pepper, salt, and caraway seed over the meat. Mix lightly. Cover tightly and bake at 325° F. for 1½ hours.

Pour the vinegar over the meat. Mix lightly. Spread the cabbage evenly over the meat. Cover tightly and continue to bake for another hour or until the meat and cabbage are both tender.

Combine gingersnaps and ¼ cup water. Let stand a few minutes so the gingersnaps will absorb the water.

Using a slotted spoon, transfer the cabbage and meat to a serving dish when they are tender. Add gingersnaps and liquid to liquid in the roaster or casserole. Cook and stir over moderate heat to make a smooth gravy. Mix the gravy lightly into the meat and cabbage. Serve hot over hot noodles.

Low sodium diets: Omit salt.

Yield: 6 to 8 servings

TZIMMES (Jewish)

Anita Kane says this is one of her husband Rudy's favorite recipes and I can certainly see why it would be. It is really a luscious combination.

1 pound fresh yams	4 large white potatoes
2 cups diced carrots	1 small onion
1½ pounds leg of veal or beef round	½ cup liquid egg substitute or whites from 3 large eggs
⅓ cup brown sugar	⅓ cup vegetable oil
½ teaspoon salt	⅓ cup matzo meal or matzo crumbs
¼ teaspoon pepper	
1 cup water	

Peel and dice yams and carrots into about ¾-inch cubes. Trim any fat from the meat and cut into about 2-inch cubes. Place the meat in the bottom of a 4-quart pressure cooker. Place the yams and carrots over the meat. Sprinkle the brown sugar, salt, and pepper over the vegetables. Add the water. Cover and cook at 10 pounds pressure for 30 minutes.

Grate the potatoes coarsely and squeeze as much liquid as possible out of them. Grate the onions and add to the potatoes along with the egg substitute or egg whites, vegetable oil, and matzo meal or crumbs. Mix thoroughly. (I use a food processor for grating the potatoes and onions and mixing the ingredients.) Spread the potato mixture evenly over the vegetables after the 30 minutes of cooking. Reseal the pressure cooker and cook another

30 minutes at 10 pounds of pressure. Serve hot. (When the food is served the potato mixture on top falls apart like dumplings.)

Low sodium diets: Omit salt.

Yield: 6 servings

BEEF PACKAGES (United States)

This was one of my mother's favorite recipes. She loved to fix these beef packages in the oven in the winter and on the outdoor grill in the summer.

2 pounds beef round, cut about ¾-inch thick	12 small onions
	Salt
3 large potatoes	Pepper
6 carrots	1 cup tomato sauce
6 turnips (optional)	

Trim any bone and all visible fat from the beef. Cut into about ¾-inch cubes. Set aside until needed.

Clean and peel vegetables. Cut the potatoes into quarters and halve the carrots and turnips. Arrange equal portions of meat and vegetables on 6 12-inch squares of heavy aluminum foil. Season with salt and pepper and top with 2 to 3 tablespoons tomato sauce. Close foil securely and place on a shallow baking pan. Bake at 350° F. for 1½ hours or place on the grill and cook about 1½ hours or until the meat is tender. Serve in the foil packages.

Low sodium diets: Omit salt. Use low sodium tomato sauce or fresh tomatoes. Sprinkle each packet with a mixture of 1 teaspoon Italian seasoning and a dash of pepper.

Yield: 6 servings

MEAT PIE (England)

1 recipe crust for meat pie
  (see recipe)
12 ounces boneless beef
  round
1 cup diced white potatoes
¾ cup diced carrots
¾ cup chopped onions
½ teaspoon salt
Dash of pepper
⅓ cup canned cream of
  mushroom soup

Prepare pie crust according to recipe (see Index). Remove from refrigerator to let it come to room temperature about 15 minutes before assembling the pie.

Trim all visible fat from the meat with a sharp knife and cut into about ¾-inch cubes. Combine meat, potatoes, carrots, onions, salt, pepper, and soup in a bowl. Mix lightly but thoroughly and let stand at room temperature while you are rolling out the crust. Place bottom crust in a 9-inch pie tin. Spread filling evenly over the crust. Place top crust over the filling and roll the bottom crust at the edge around the top crust so that no liquid will escape around the edges. Cut 3 or 4 slashes in the top crust to let the steam escape. Bake 45 minutes to 1 hour at 400° F. or until the crust is nicely browned. Cut into 4 equal wedges and serve hot.

Low sodium diet: Omit salt. Use low sodium crust for meat pies.

Yield: 4 servings (1 9-inch pie)

MEAT PIE (United States)

This is one of our favorites. I always try to prepare a large enough beef roast so that I will have some left to make meat pie the next day. I know that making the sauce with chicken broth may not be exactly the way everyone else does it, but we think it gives it a better flavor.

FILLING
1½ cups diced white potatoes
½ cup chopped onions
¼ cup diced carrots
2 cups fat-free chicken broth
3 tablespoons all-purpose
  flour
⅓ cup cold water
1 tablespoon margarine
Salt and pepper to taste
2 cups diced cold roast beef

TOPPING
1 cup all-purpose flour
2 tablespoons instant dry
  milk
2 teaspoons baking powder
½ teaspoon salt
2 tablespoons margarine
About ½ cup water

Simmer potatoes, onions, and carrots in chicken broth in a covered pan over low heat for 20 minutes or until the vegetables are tender. Stir 3 tablespoons flour into ⅓ cup cold water to form a smooth paste. Add to the simmering vegetables and cook and stir until thick. Add 1 tablespoon margarine and beef, which has had all fat and gristle removed. Reheat to serving temperature and set aside.

For topping, stir together 1 cup flour, dry milk, baking powder, and ½ teaspoon salt. Cut 2 tablespoons margarine into the flour mixture until it resembles coarse meal. Add as much of the water as necessary to make a soft dough. Use a serving spoon to spread the dough around the inside of the casserole, being careful to seal it to the sides of the casserole. Bake at 375° F. about 25 to 30 minutes or until the topping is browned. Serve hot.

Low sodium diets: Omit salt. Use salt-free margarine and low sodium broth and baking powder.

Yield: 4 servings

ROAST BEEF HASH (New England)

1 cup finely chopped onions   1 minced garlic clove

1 cup chopped fresh green
  peppers
2 tablespoons (¼ stick)
  margarine
3 cups cooked beef with all
  fat removed, cut into ½-
  inch cubes
4 cups cooked, peeled, diced
  white potatoes

1½ cups hot fat-free beef
  broth
⅓ cup catsup
1 teaspoon Worcestershire
  sauce
1 teaspoon salt
¼ teaspoon pepper

Fry onions, green peppers, and garlic in margarine over medium heat, stirring frequently, until onions are golden. Remove vegetables from the margarine with a slotted spoon and add to beef. Add potatoes to beef mixture. Mix lightly and place in a 9-inch-square baking dish that has been well greased with margarine.

Combine stock, catsup, Worcestershire sauce, salt, and pepper. Mix well and pour evenly over meat and potato mixture. Mix lightly.

Cover dish with aluminum foil and bake 30 minutes at 350° F. Remove the foil and continue baking until lightly browned. Serve hot.

Low sodium diets: Omit salt and Worcestershire sauce. Add ¼ teaspoon thyme. Use low sodium catsup and broth and salt-free margarine.

Yield: 6 to 8 servings

CHILI (Chicago)

This is Chuck's recipe; he used it when he had a restaurant in Chicago. If it tastes a bit more Italian than Texan, well, that's how it is when it is made and served in Chicago.

1 cup chopped onions
2 tablespoons vegetable oil
2 pounds lean ground beef
1 29-ounce can crushed
canned tomatoes
2 1-pound cans tomato sauce
1 teaspoon salt
¼ teaspoon pepper
1 teaspoon paprika

1 teaspoon sugar
1 to 2 teaspoons chili powder
¼ teaspoon garlic powder
¼ teaspoon ground oregano
¼ teaspoon ground cumin
1 cup hot fat-free chicken
broth
2 cups drained cooked
kidney or pinto beans

Fry onions in oil in heavy pot over medium heat, stirring frequently, until onions are golden. Add meat and cook and stir over medium heat until meat is broken up and well browned. Pour meat and onions into colander and drain off the fat and liquid. Discard fat and liquid and return meat and onions to the pot.

Add tomatoes, tomato sauce, salt, pepper, paprika, sugar, chili powder, garlic powder, oregano, cumin, and chicken broth to meat. Simmer, uncovered, for 1 hour and 15 minutes, stirring occasionally.

Add beans to chili, simmer another 15 minutes, and serve hot. Or, simmer beans separately for 15 minutes. Then serve hot chili, passing a bowl of beans so that everyone can add to the chili as many beans as he or she likes.

Low sodium diets: Omit salt. Use low sodium broth, tomatoes, and tomato sauce or fresh tomatoes.

Yield: 6 servings

CHILI CON CARNE (Texas)

This recipe came from Frances Lee, who is a dietitian in

Kerens, Texas. She says that there are many different versions of the recipe. Coarsely ground beef is generally simmered until tender and then a special seasoning is added. The mixture is usually thickened with masa (corn flour), cornmeal, flour, oatmeal, or instant potatoes. Tomatoes are not generally added in that part of Texas.

2 pounds coarsely ground
  fat-free beef round
1 tablespoon vegetable oil
½ teaspoon garlic powder
1½ teaspoons salt
1 teaspoon ground cumin
2 tablespoons chili powder

1 quart hot water
¼ cup cornmeal
1 cup cold water
1 29-ounce can pinto beans
½ cup chopped onions
Saltine crackers

Fry meat in oil in heavy pot, stirring frequently, until well browned. Drain well. Discard fat and liquid and return meat to pot. Add garlic powder, salt, cumin, and chili powder to meat. Cook and stir for 2 minutes over moderate heat or until meat is well coated with the seasonings.

Add 1 quart hot water to meat. Simmer, uncovered, for 1 hour, stirring occasionally. Stir cornmeal into 1 cup cold water and add to chili. Simmer, uncovered, for 30 minutes, stirring frequently to prevent burning. Add beans and juice to chili and reheat to simmering.

Serve chili in a bowl topped with chopped onions and accompanied by crackers.

Low sodium diets: Omit salt. Use 3½ to 4 cups pinto beans cooked without salt and serve with low sodium crackers or bread sticks.

Yield: about 8 servings

MEAT SAUCE (Italy)

1½ pounds lean ground beef
2 cups boiling water
1 cup finely chopped onions
2 tablespoons (¼ stick) margarine
3½ cups (1 29-ounce can) solid-pack tomatoes with juice
2 cups (1 16-ounce can) tomato puree
1 6-ounce can tomato paste
½ teaspoon garlic powder
3 chicken bouillon cubes
1 teaspoon salt
2 teaspoons ground oregano
½ teaspoon ground thyme
½ teaspoon crushed basil
¼ teaspoon pepper
1 tablespoon sugar
Tomato juice

Brown beef in its own fat in a heavy frying pan over moderate heat, stirring frequently, until well browned and broken up. Drain well. Pour boiling water over the meat to remove any remaining fat. Place meat in a heavy saucepan. Brown onions in margarine in frying pan, stirring frequently, until onions are golden. Add to meat. Break the tomatoes into smaller pieces and add with their juice, tomato puree, and tomato paste to meat. Cook, uncovered, over very low heat for 2 hours. (The sauce should just barely simmer.) Add garlic powder, bouillon cubes, salt, oregano, thyme, basil, pepper, and sugar to sauce and continue to simmer, uncovered, for another hour. Add tomato juice, ¼ cup at a time, to sauce if it becomes too thick. Put 1 tablespoon of the sauce in a saucer. There should be no free liquid. If there is any free liquid, continue to cook the sauce for another ½ hour or until it is thicker with no free liquid. Serve hot over hot, well-drained spaghetti or use for lasagna or other Italian recipes that specify the use of meat sauce.

This sauce will keep in the refrigerator for several days, but if you want to keep it longer, freeze it in whatever amounts you plan to use later.

Low sodium diets: Omit salt. Use low sodium bouillon cubes, tomatoes, tomato puree, and tomato paste. Fresh tomatoes will not give a satisfactory product in this recipe. Use salt-free margarine.

Yield: about 1½ quarts

PIZZA (Italy)

1 pound lean ground beef
1 cup boiling water
½ teaspoon garlic powder
⅛ teaspoon pepper
1 teaspoon salt
3½ cups all-purpose flour
1 teaspoon salt
2 teaspoons sugar
1 ounce compressed yeast
1½ cups lukewarm
   (85–87° F.) water

2 tablespoons vegetable oil
½ cup all-purpose flour
1 tablespoon cornmeal
2 tablespoons vegetable oil
1½ cups Pizza Sauce (see
   recipe)
8 ounces grated or shredded
   mozzarella cheese
1 tablespoon leaf oregano

Brown meat in its own fat over medium heat in a heavy frying pan, stirring frequently, until well browned and broken up. Place meat in a strainer and drain well. Pour boiling water over meat to remove any remaining fat. Drain well. Place meat in a clean frying pan. Add the garlic powder, pepper, and 1 teaspoon salt. Cook and stir over low heat for 2 minutes. Refrigerate until needed.

Place 3½ cups flour, 1 teaspoon salt, and sugar in a mixer bowl in that order. Add crumbled yeast and water. Let stand 5 to 10 minutes. Mix at low speed, using a dough hook, for 6 minutes. Add 2 tablespoons oil to dough and beat at low speed, using a dough hook, for 2 minutes longer or until oil is blended into the dough. Spread ½ cup flour on working surface. Turn the dough out onto the flour and knead, using as much of the flour as necessary, to form a smooth elastic dough. Round dough into a ball and place in a bowl that has been well greased with margarine. Turn the top of the bowl over to grease the top. Cover and let stand in a warm place until doubled in volume.

Turn the dough out onto a lightly floured working surface. Knead lightly. Round dough into a ball, cover and let rest for 10 minutes. (Make 2 equal-sized balls if you intend to make 2 smaller pizzas.) Roll the dough out to form a rectangle about 14″ × 19″ or 2 circles about 10½″ across. Spread the bottom of the pan with cornmeal. Fit the dough over the cornmeal and brush lightly with the 2 tablespoons of oil.

Spread the Pizza Sauce (see following page) evenly over the dough. Sprinkle the cheese evenly over the sauce and then the meat over the cheese. Sprinkle with oregano and bake at 425° F. for 20 to 30 minutes or until the crust is browned and crisp. Serve hot. (The pizza should be at room temperature when it is baked. It can be prepared and then refrigerated before it is baked, but it should be allowed to come back to room temperature before it is baked.)

Low sodium diets: Omit salt. Use low sodium pizza sauce and cheese. Fresh tomatoes will not give a satisfactory product in this recipe.

Yield: 1 18″ × 12″ pizza or 2 10″ round pizzas

PIZZA SAUCE (Italy)

This sauce may be kept refrigerated for several days, but if you intend to keep it for longer periods, it is a good idea to freeze it in whatever amounts you will need later.

1 cup finely chopped onions
2 minced garlic cloves
2 tablespoons vegetable oil
7 cups (2 29-ounce cans) canned crushed tomatoes and juice
2 6-ounce cans tomato paste

2 tablespoons sugar
2 teaspoons salt
¼ teaspoon pepper
2 teaspoons ground oregano
1 bay leaf
1½ teaspoons crushed basil

Fry onions and garlic in oil in heavy saucepan over moderate heat, stirring frequently, until onions are golden. Add tomatoes, tomato paste, sugar, salt, pepper, oregano, bay leaf, and basil. Simmer, uncovered, stirring occasionally, for 1 hour. Remove bay leaf. Put a tablespoon of the sauce into a saucer. There should not be any free liquid with the sauce. If there is any free liquid, continue to cook the sauce for another ½ hour or until it is thicker with no free liquid. Refrigerate unless used immediately.

Low sodium diets: Omit salt. Use low sodium tomatoes and tomato paste. Fresh tomatoes will not give a satisfactory product in this recipe.

Yield: about 2 quarts

RUNZA (Czechoslovakia)

Deann Figgins of Nodaway, Iowa, sent me the recipe for these meat-filled rolls. She says they are very popular in her area and her family loves them. I'm sure the original recipe didn't have the taco sauce in them, but it is a simple way to add spice and liquid to the filling.

1 cup hot water	1 tablespoon margarine
¼ cup sugar	1 pound lean ground beef
1 package active dry yeast	1 cup boiling water
1 cup flour	1 cup shredded cabbage
1 teaspoon salt	1 cup hot or mild taco sauce
1 tablespoon vegetable oil	Beef gravy (optional)
2 to 2¾ cups all-purpose flour	Taco sauce (optional)
¾ cup chopped onions	

Place 1 cup hot water in mixer bowl. Add sugar. Stir to dissolve sugar and cool to 110° to 115° F. Add yeast and let stand for 5 minutes. Add 1 cup flour and mix at low speed, using dough hook, for 4 minutes. Add salt and oil and mix at low speed only until they are absorbed into the batter. Add as much of the remaining flour as necessary to make a smooth elastic dough. Form the dough into a ball and place in a bowl that has been well greased with margarine. Turn the ball over to grease the top, cover and let rise in a warm place until doubled in volume.

While the dough is rising, fry onions in margarine until onions are lightly browned. Transfer onions with a slotted spoon to a heavy saucepan. Add ground beef to the frying pan in which the onions were cooked. Cook and stir over moderate heat until the meat is well browned and separated. Place the meat in a strainer and drain it well. Pour 1 cup boiling water over the meat and allow it to drain off to take away any remaining fat. Place the meat in the pan with the onions. Add the cabbage and taco sauce and cook and stir over moderate heat until liquid has evaporated. Set aside to cool to room temperature.

After the dough has doubled in volume, transfer it to a lightly floured working surface. Knead it lightly. Form it into a roll and divide the roll into 8 equal portions. Form each portion into a ball, cover and let rest for 10 minutes.

Roll each ball out to form a circle about 5″ to 6″ across. Put ⅛ of the cooled filling in the center of each circle. Pull the dough up around the filling and press together at the top. Place on a cookie sheet that has been well greased with margarine. Cover and let stand at room temperature for 30 minutes. Bake at 350° F. for about 25 to 30 minutes or until browned. Serve hot to be eaten as sandwich or with additional brown gravy or taco sauce. (These are good for picnics but should be treated as a meat item and refrigerated until shortly before they are to be eaten cold or placed in foil and warmed over the fire.)

Low sodium diets: Omit salt. Use salt-free margarine.

Yield: 8 servings

BROWN LAMB CURRY (India)

The spices in curry are always a matter of individual taste. This is the right amount for my family, but you will need to adjust it according to your own taste. This is rather mild, but it will vary according to the kind as well as the amount of curry powder used.

2 tablespoons all-purpose
  flour
1½ teaspoons salt
1 teaspoon paprika
⅛ teaspoon pepper
2 pounds boneless lamb stew
  meat
Vegetable oil
2 cups fat-free chicken broth

¼ cup dry white wine
½ cup chopped onions
½ cup chopped celery
1 minced garlic clove
⅛ teaspoon ground cloves
1½ teaspoons curry powder
2 tablespoons (¼ stick)
  margarine
½ cup seedless raisins

1½ cups cored and sliced tart apples

2 tablespoons (¼ stick) margarine

2 tablespoons all-purpose flour

Hot Steamed Rice (see recipe)

Combine 2 tablespoons flour, salt, paprika, and pepper and blend well. Set aside for later use. Remove all gristle and visible fat from stew meat with a very sharp knife. Sprinkle lamb with reserved flour mixture and brown in vegetable oil in a heavy frying pan over moderate heat, stirring occasionally. Transfer lamb to heavy saucepan with a slotted spoon as it is browned. Pour off as much of the oil as possible, blotting any remaining oil with a paper towel. Pour the chicken broth into the frying pan and cook and stir over low heat to absorb the browned particles in the pan. Add the hot broth with the wine to the lamb.

Fry the onions, celery, garlic, cloves, and curry powder in 2 tablespoons margarine, stirring frequently, until the onions are soft but not browned. Add to the lamb. Mix lightly. Cover and simmer 1 to 1½ hours or until the lamb is tender.

Fry raisins and apples in 2 tablespoons margarine over low heat, stirring occasionally, for 5 minutes. Sprinkle with flour and stir over low heat until the flour is absorbed. Add to the lamb mixture. Mix lightly. Cover and continue to simmer for another 10 minutes. Serve hot over Steamed Rice (see Index).

Low sodium diets: Omit salt. Use salt-free margarine and low sodium broth.

Yield: 6 servings

LAMB STEW WITH EGGPLANT AND RICE (Greece)

Beef may be substituted for the lamb if lamb isn't available. It is good both ways.

2 pounds boneless lamb stew meat

Vegetable oil

1½ cups coarsely chopped onions

1 cup fat-free beef broth

1 cup tomato sauce

¼ teaspoon ground cinnamon

¼ teaspoon garlic powder

1 teaspoon salt

⅛ teaspoon pepper

1½ cups sliced carrots

1 small eggplant

½ cup rice

Salt

Trim all gristle and visible fat from lamb with a sharp knife. Brown lamb in oil in a heavy frying pan over moderate heat, using as much of the oil as necessary. Remove the meat from the frying pan with a slotted spoon and place it in a small roaster or casserole. Fry the onions in the same frying pan in which the meat was browned until limp but not browned. Remove the onions with a slotted spoon and place them over the meat. Pour off as much oil as possible from the frying pan. Add the beef broth to the frying pan and cook and stir until the browned particles in the pan are loosened. Add the tomato sauce, cinnamon, garlic powder, salt, pepper, and carrots. Return to a boil and pour over the meat. Cover and bake at 325° F. for 1 hour.

Wash the eggplant. Remove the stem and ends. Cut the eggplant into 1-inch cubes without removing the skin. Stir into the hot stew. Return to the oven and bake another 30 minutes. Stir the rice into the stew and bake another 30 minutes or until the rice is tender. Taste for seasoning and add salt, if necessary. Serve hot.

Low sodium diets: Omit salt. Use low sodium broth and tomato sauce or fresh tomatoes.

Yield: 6 servings

BAKED LAMB STEW (Ireland)

2 pounds lamb stew meat

Boiling water

2 cups diced white potatoes

2 cups thickly sliced onions

1 teaspoon salt
⅛ teaspoon pepper
¼ teaspoon ground thyme
1 tablespoon chopped parsley
½ cup cooking liquid from
  lamb

2 tablespoons all-purpose
  flour
¼ cup cold cooking liquid
  from lamb
Chopped parsley

Remove any gristle and visible fat from lamb with a sharp knife. Place lamb in saucepan and barely cover with boiling water. Cover and simmer 1 hour. Arrange hot meat and vegetables in a small roaster or casserole as follows: ½ of the potatoes, ½ of the lamb, ½ of the onions, ½ of the potatoes, ½ of the lamb, and ½ of the onions, sprinkling each layer with salt, pepper, thyme, and parsley. Pour ½ of the cooking liquid from the lamb over the meat and vegetables. Cover tightly and bake at 350° F. about 1 hour or until the meat and vegetables are tender. Place the roaster or casserole on top of the range. Stir the flour into the cold liquid and add to the stew. Continue cooking over low heat for 5 minutes, stirring only as much as necessary. Serve hot garnished with chopped parsley.

Low sodium diets: Omit salt.

Yield: 6 servings

WIENER SCHNITZEL (Austria and Germany)

6 4-ounce veal cutlets
All-purpose flour
2 egg whites
¼ cup water
½ teaspoon salt

1 cup dry bread crumbs
¼ cup vegetable oil
¼ cup (½ stick) margarine
12 lemon wedges

Remove any visible fat or gristle from veal cutlets with a very sharp knife. Pound veal to flatten it to about ¼-inch thickness. Dip each cutlet in flour. Beat egg whites with water and salt until blended but not foamy. Dip each veal cutlet in egg white mixture and then in the crumbs. Combine oil and margarine in a heavy frying pan. Heat over low heat to melt margarine. Pour some of the oil mixture into a small container, leaving as much as necessary in the pan. Add the remaining fat mixture as necessary while frying the cutlets. Fry the cutlets in the hot fat mixture over moderate heat until golden on both sides. The fried cutlets can be kept in a warm oven, if necessary, for a few minutes until all of them are fried. Serve hot, garnished with lemon wedges.

Low sodium diets: Omit salt. Use salt-free margarine.

Yield: 6 servings

SAUCES AND GRAVIES

BARBECUE SAUCE (United States)

My friend Jean Smith from Clancy, Montana, sent me this recipe, which she uses whenever she needs barbecue sauce. Jean is a fascinating and beautiful woman who makes bread from wheat she has ground herself and who lives as close to nature as possible. Yet she is perfectly at home at a symphony in Helena or at the art shows she attends with her husband, Tucker Smith, a well-known Western artist.

1 teaspoon chili powder	2 cups water
1 tablespoon celery seed	1½ tablespoons liquid smoke
⅓ cup brown sugar	Few drops tabasco sauce
¼ cup vinegar	¼ cup lemon juice
¼ cup Worcestershire sauce	1 minced onion
1 cup catsup	

Combine all ingredients in a pan. Bring to a boil. Simmer briefly and use as a barbecue sauce.

Low sodium diets: Omit Worcestershire sauce and use low sodium catsup.

Yield: about 3½ cups

BROWN GRAVY (United States)

This recipe provides a way to use those drippings and liquids from cooking meats that you have refrigerated so you could skim the fat off them. Remember that the finished gravy will taste as good as the drippings or stock did, so taste for flavor or strength before you use them. You may want to dilute them or you may want to add another bouillon cube for strength.

2 cups cold fat-free drippings
  or stock
¼ cup all-purpose flour
2 tablespoons margarine
Salt and pepper to taste
¼ teaspoon Kitchen Bouquet
  (optional)

Bring drippings or stock to a simmer in a saucepan. Rub the flour and margarine together until blended. Add to the hot stock and cook and stir over moderate heat, using a whip (it won't work with a spoon), until smooth and thickened and the starchy taste is gone. Add salt and pepper to taste and Kitchen Bouquet. Serve hot.

If you prefer not to use a whip, you can add the flour to the cold drippings or stock, cook and stir until thickened, and then add the margarine, salt and pepper, and Kitchen Bouquet and cook over low heat, stirring frequently, until the starchy taste is gone. It takes longer that way, but it will yield a good gravy.

Low sodium diets: Omit salt and Kitchen Bouquet. Use salt-free drippings or stock and margarine.

Yield: about 2 cups gravy

MILK GRAVY (United States)

2 cups fat-free drippings or
  stock
¼ cup (½ stick) softened
  margarine
¼ cup all-purpose flour
½ cup instant dry milk
⅛ teaspoon Kitchen Bouquet
  (optional)
Salt and pepper to taste

Bring drippings or stock to a simmer in a saucepan. Stir margarine, flour, and dry milk together and add all at once to the hot liquid. Cook and stir over moderate heat, using a whip (it won't work with a spoon), until smooth and thickened. Add the Kitchen Bouquet, salt, and pepper and continue to cook and stir over low heat for a couple of minutes or until the starchy taste is gone. Serve hot.

Low sodium diets: Omit salt and Kitchen Bouquet. Use salt-free drippings or stock and margarine.

Yield: about 2 cups

ONION GRAVY (United States)

½ cup finely chopped onions
¼ cup (½ stick) margarine
¼ cup all-purpose flour
2 cups fat-free drippings or
  stock
Salt and pepper to taste

Fry onions in margarine in a heavy frying pan over moderate heat, stirring frequently, until onions are golden. Sprinkle the flour over the onions and continue to cook and stir until browned. Add the drippings or stock and continue to cook and stir over moderate heat until thickened and the starchy taste is gone. Add salt and pepper to taste and serve hot.

Low sodium diets: Omit salt and use salt-free drippings or stock and margarine.

Yield: about 2 cups

4
Poultry

Until recently, chicken was a luxury item in most other countries; consequently, most of them developed special recipes worthy of such a treat. Some of these special recipes are just too rich to use on a low cholesterol diet, but many of them can be adapted easily for the low cholesterol diet.

I remember trying to decide what to serve Chuck's cousin and her husband from Italy when they visited us for a day while they were on a tour of our country. I checked with a friend of mine who grew up in Italy and she suggested I serve them chicken, which was a treat over there. In fact, she told me that on her last trip to Italy everyone had served her chicken until she finally let it be known that chicken was an everyday affair here and she would much rather have some of the Italian dishes she remembered from her childhood in that area.

We prepare chicken in many ways in the United States, but the favorite above all is fried chicken, which is prepared in many different ways in different parts of the country. You can still enjoy fried chicken the way you like to prepare it best as long as you follow the basic guidelines for chicken preparation. Don't buy chicken that is already prepared because the skin and fat are not removed from the chicken before it is fried (even if it has been cooked in oil).

Pointers for Using Chicken

1. Wash the chicken well in cold running water. Pat it dry with a paper towel or clean cloth and then remove the skin and all visible fat with a very sharp knife.

2. Do not use any animal fat, such as lard, butter, cream, or egg yolks, to prepare the chicken. If your recipe includes milk, use skimmed milk, evaporated skimmed milk, or reconstituted instant dry milk. I have found evaporated skimmed milk to be a very satisfactory substitute for cream in many recipes.

3. There is quite a bit of fat in the skin and flesh of some chickens. Therefore you may need to add some fat to the chicken by brushing it with melted margarine or soaking it in a marinade with vegetable oil to replace the fat you have taken away from the recipe when you took away the skin and any visible fat.

4. Chicken can be dipped in egg white beaten with a little water, skimmed milk, or liquid egg substitute with very good results.

5. It is best not to use a commercial preparation for coating chicken without reading the list of ingredients to be sure it doesn't include anything that shouldn't be used. Prepared coatings frequently contain saturated fats that have a better shelf life than unsaturated fats.

6. Chicken, generally speaking, is better when it is cooked at a lower temperature. Stewing chickens should be simmered, not boiled, and baked chicken, except for Roast Chicken from Greece) should be baked at 325° F.

There are also several points to remember when you are buying poultry.

1. Buy frozen or chilled poultry only from freezer or refrigerated cases.

2. Be sure all wrappers are whole and not torn or pierced.

3. After you buy chicken, wash it well and cover it lightly with wax paper or plastic wrap, store it in the coldest part of the refrigerator and use it within two days.

4. Store frozen poultry at 0° F. or lower. It should be wrapped in moisture-resistant material and left solidly frozen until it is to be used.

5. Defrost poultry in the refrigerator or under running cool water. *Never* let poultry defrost at room temperature.

Several recipes in this chapter include 3 cups of cooked boned chicken with fat and skin removed. One 3-pound chicken will generally yield this amount of chicken. The exact amount of chicken in most casseroles is not critical enough that you would need to add or subtract chicken from the yield of a 3-pound chicken for a casserole that specified 3 cups of chicken. A chicken to be cooked and used for a casserole should be washed and the skin and fat removed. Then it should be simmered in just enough water to cover it until it is tender. It should be drained and refrigerated until it is cold and then the meat removed from the bones. The broth should also be refrigerated and may be used after the fat is removed. Salt and other seasonings may be added while the chicken is being cooked if it is not for a low sodium diet. Chicken prepared this way should be used within a couple of days of cooking. If it is to be kept longer, it should be frozen as soon as it is taken off the bones and kept frozen until needed.

Remember that giblets are a no-no. They can be cooked for the rest of the family or for guests but never for yourself. You should also remember to cook some dressing outside the bird. It absorbs too much fat for you when it is cooked inside the bird.

I also find turkey to be a big help on a low cholesterol diet. I like to keep some frozen turkey on hand. I wrap it in smaller quantities so it will be right for a couple of sandwiches or a casserole or salad. I even like to use some of the scraps of turkey that I freeze together for a quick chicken rice soup and no one is the wiser. Frances Nielsen also cooks the turkey carcass in some water the day after she has served the turkey, and uses the resulting broth for some very good soup.

If you are buying a turkey that weighs less than 12 pounds, allow ¾ to 1 pound raw weight per serving. If you are buying a heavier turkey, ½ to ¾ pound raw weight per serving will be about right. The actual number of servings will depend on the skill of the carver and the temperature at which the turkey was roasted.

Frozen turkeys, with the necks and giblets inside the body or neck cavities, must be thawed before cooking. Remove the giblets as soon as the turkey is thawed, cook them promptly, and refrigerate them for somebody else to eat. The thawing method you use will depend on the amount of time you have before you plan to cook the turkey. It can be thawed in the refrigerator or in cold water. Here is an approximate timetable for both methods of thawing:

Pounds	Refrigerator	Cold or Cool Water
6 to 8	1 to 1½ days	3 to 4 hours
8 to 12	1½ to 2 days	4 to 6 hours
12 to 16	2 to 2½ days	6 to 7 hours
16 to 20	2½ to 3 days	7 to 8 hours
20 to 24	3 to 3½ days	8 to 10 hours

Turkey should be roasted in a shallow open pan to allow the heat to circulate around it. A rack at least ½ inch off the bottom of the pan should be used to keep the turkey out of the juices and fat that gather at the bottom of the pan. For best results follow these simple steps.

1. Roast turkey at 325° F. In poultry cooking, as in meat cooking, low temperatures assure better flavor, appearance, and yield.

2. Rinse the thawed turkey with cold water. Pat it dry. Rub the cavity of the turkey lightly with salt. If you plan to stuff the turkey, remember to bake some dressing outside of the turkey for yourself.

3. Push the drumsticks under a band of skin at the tail or tie them together.

4. Place turkey, breast side up, on a rack. Brush the skin with margarine or vegetable oil. Insert a roast-meat thermometer in

the thickest part of the breast. Be sure the thermometer does not touch any bone.

5. Put the pan and turkey in the preheated oven. Do not cover the pan. Baste occasionally with margarine or vegetable oil. Do not baste with the pan juices, which include fat from the turkey. If the turkey becomes brown before it is thoroughly cooked, cover it with a tent of aluminum foil. When the turkey is two-thirds done, cut the band of skin or cord at the drumsticks.

6. The turkey is done when the meat thermometer reads 185° F. If a meat thermometer is not used, the turkey is done when the drumsticks move easily. The turkey should be allowed to sit for 20 to 25 minutes after it comes out of the oven before it is carved. Plan on baking your turkey about 20 minutes per pound if it was at room temperature when you put it into the oven, a little more if it went from the refrigerator to the oven.

Leftover chicken and turkey, like any leftover meat or poultry, should be frozen unless it is to be used within a couple of days. As soon as possible after serving remove every bit of meat from the bones of the turkey and from the chicken if it has been roasted. Cool the meat and gravy and dressing promptly. Refrigerate separately in the coldest part of the refrigerator. Use the chicken, gravy, and dressing within two days and reheat them thoroughly before they are served if they are not to be frozen. If they are to be frozen, they should be wrapped separately in the appropriate amounts in moisture-resistant packaging and frozen promptly. Never freeze an uncooked stuffed turkey or a roast stuffed turkey, and *never* stuff your turkey the night before you roast it. It just isn't safe. Harmful bacteria just love that moist stuffing and it is difficult to get it cold enough in the refrigerator to inhibit the growth of the harmful bacteria.

The boneless turkey rolls are often more suitable for smaller families. The directions for baking them are included on the package. Remember not to eat any of the skin, just as you wouldn't eat any of the skin on a chicken or turkey.

I have included my favorite chicken recipes in this chapter. I didn't include fried chicken, which should be prepared in whichever way you like it best, using the principles included here for preparing chicken. I do hope you will also try some of these other regional and ethnic recipes. They really are good and will make you and your family and guests forget that they are low cholesterol or that you are on a low cholesterol diet. They are suitable for families and guests alike.

APRICOT BARBECUED CHICKEN (Wisconsin)

Marion Bollman, a dietary consultant from Elkhorn, Wisconsin, who was chief of the Menu Planning Division of the U.S. Army before her retirement, gave me this recipe. She says it is popular in her part of the country, where it is also often used for barbecuing very lean pork.

5 whole chicken breasts
1 envelope onion soup mix
1 cup apricot preserves
1 8-ounce bottle Wishbone
**   Russian dressing**

Wash chicken thoroughly under running water. Pat dry with a paper towel or clean cloth. Remove all skin and visible fat with a very sharp knife and then bone the breasts so that you have 10 boned chicken breast halves.

Mix soup mix, preserves, and dressing together. Spread a thin layer of the sauce on the bottom of a shallow casserole. Place the chicken carefully on the sauce in one layer and cover with the remaining sauce. Cover tightly with aluminum foil and bake at 350° F. for 1 hour. Remove the foil and bake for another 30 minutes or until the chicken is tender and browned. Serve hot with Rice Pilaf (see Index) or Steamed Rice (see Index).

Low sodium diets: This recipe is not suitable.

Yield: 5 servings

BAKED CHICKEN AND NOODLES
(United States)

8 ounces (⅓ recipe)
Homemade Noodles (see recipe)
8 cups boiling water
1 tablespoon salt
1 tablespoon vegetable oil
¼ cup (½ stick) softened margarine
½ cup all-purpose flour

⅛ teaspoon white pepper
4 cups hot fat-free chicken broth
Salt
3 cups cooked diced chicken with skin and fat removed
½ teaspoon paprika
¼ cup dried bread crumbs
2 tablespoons margarine

Prepare Homemade Noodles (see Index) and cook in boiling water with 1 tablespoon salt and oil until tender. Drain well but do not rinse the noodles. Set aside for later use.

Combine ¼ cup margarine and flour and cook and stir in saucepan until smooth. Add pepper and chicken broth. Cook and stir over moderate heat, using a wire whip to form a smooth sauce. Taste for seasoning and add more salt, if necessary. Combine sauce, drained noodles, and chicken. Toss lightly to distribute the chicken. Pour into a casserole or small roaster that has been well greased with margarine. Combine paprika and bread crumbs and sprinkle over the mixture. Dot with 2 tablespoons margarine and bake at 350° F. for 30 minutes. Serve hot.

Low sodium diets: Omit salt. Use salt-free margarine and low sodium broth and noodles and chicken cooked without salt.

Yield: 6 servings

BROILED CHICKEN (United States)

4 1-pound broiler halves
½ cup vegetable oil
½ teaspoon garlic powder
½ teaspoon ground thyme

½ teaspoon ground oregano
1 teaspoon salt
⅛ teaspoon ground pepper
½ teaspoon paprika

Wash chicken well under running water. Pat it dry with a paper towel or clean cloth. Remove all skin and visible fat with a very sharp knife. Combine the oil, garlic powder, thyme, oregano, salt, pepper, and paprika and mix well. Brush the halves with the seasoned oil. Place them on a foil-lined broiler rack 6 to 8 inches from the heat. Turn chicken and brush with the seasoned oil as necessary until the chicken is browned and tender. This should take about 25 to 30 minutes, depending on the amount of heat. Serve hot.

Low sodium diets: Omit salt.

Yield: 4 servings

BRUNSWICK STEW (Southern United States)

¾ cup chopped onions
2 tablespoons (¼ stick)
   margarine
3 cups fat-free chicken broth
1 cup canned crushed
   tomatoes and juice
1½ cups diced raw white
   potatoes
1 teaspoon chopped parsley
½ teaspoon salt
⅛ teaspoon pepper

1 10-ounce package frozen
   lima beans
1 10-ounce package frozen
   whole-kernel corn
1 tablespoon Worcestershire
   sauce
3 cups diced cooked chicken
   with skin and fat removed
½ cup diced very lean ham
Salt
¼ cup all-purpose flour
½ cup cold water

Fry onions in margarine in saucepan over moderate heat, stirring frequently, until onions are limp but not browned. Add broth, tomatoes, potatoes, parsley, salt, pepper, beans, corn, and Worcestershire sauce. Cover and simmer about 20 minutes or until vegetables are tender. Add chicken and ham and reheat to simmering. Stir flour into water to form a smooth paste. Add to stew and cook and stir over moderate heat until smooth. Reduce heat and simmer another 5 minutes, stirring frequently until starchy taste is gone. Serve hot in a shallow soup bowl.

Low sodium diets: This recipe is not suitable.

Yield: 6 servings

CHICKEN WITH APPLE JUICE (California)

Dr. Crockett sent me this recipe from California, where he says it is a favorite of theirs.

2 large chicken breasts or 4
  thighs
2 tablespoons all-purpose
  flour
¼ teaspoon salt
Sprinkle of pepper

1 thinly sliced small onion
2 tablespoons vegetable oil
½ teaspoon ground cumin
1 cup apple juice
½ cup sherry or water
2 teaspoons lemon juice

Remove all skin and visible fat from the chicken with a sharp knife. Separate the breasts into halves if they are used. Dust the chicken with a mixture of the flour, salt, and pepper. Fry the onions in the vegetable oil in a heavy frying pan over moderate heat until golden. Add the chicken pieces to the onions and fry over moderate heat until browned. Add the cumin and any remaining flour. Stir lightly to cook the flour and seasonings a little. Add the apple juice, sherry or water, and lemon juice. Cover tightly and simmer about ½ hour or until the chicken is tender. Serve hot with some of the sauce.

Low sodium diets: Omit salt.

Yield: 2 servings

CHICKEN CACCIATORE (Italy)

1 cup chopped onions
1 minced garlic clove
½ cup chopped fresh green
  peppers

2 tablespoons vegetable oil
3½ cups (1 29-ounce can)
  canned crushed tomatoes
  and juice

1½ cups fat-free chicken
  broth
1 teaspoon ground oregano
¼ teaspoon ground basil
¼ teaspoon ground thyme
1 teaspoon sugar
1 teaspoon salt

¼ teaspoon pepper
4 pounds chicken breasts,
  legs, and thighs
1 cup all-purpose flour
1 teaspoon salt
1 teaspoon paprika
Vegetable oil

Fry onions, garlic, and green peppers in 2 tablespoons vegetable oil in heavy saucepan until onions are limp but not browned. Add tomatoes, broth, oregano, basil, thyme, sugar, 1 teaspoon salt, and pepper. Simmer, uncovered, for 1½ hours, stirring occasionally.

Wash chicken thoroughly under cold running water. Pat dry with a paper towel or clean cloth. Remove any skin and visible fat from chicken with a sharp knife. Combine flour, 1 teaspoon salt, and paprika and blend well. Dredge chicken in flour mixture. Shake off any loose flour and brown in a heavy frying pan in oil over moderate heat. Place chicken as it is browned in a small roaster or oblong casserole. Pour the hot sauce over the chicken. Cover tightly and bake at 325° F. for 1 hour. Uncover and bake 30 minutes longer or until chicken is tender. Serve chicken hot with some of the sauce.

Low sodium diets: Omit salt. Use low sodium broth and tomatoes
  or fresh tomatoes.

Yield: 8 servings

CHICKEN CURRY (India)

You will probably need to adjust the amount of curry in this recipe to fit your own taste. This is a rather mild curry, but the strength of curry powder varies so much that it is always wise to taste a sauce before adding more of the powder.

½ cup chopped onions
¾ cup diced cored tart apples
¼ cup (½ stick) margarine
¼ cup all-purpose flour
1 teaspoon curry powder
½ cup instant dry milk
2 cups hot fat-free chicken
 broth

¼ cup seedless raisins
Salt
3 cups cooked chicken with
 skin and fat removed (see
 note)
Steamed Rice (see recipe)

Fry onions and apples in margarine in heavy pan over medium heat, stirring frequently until onions are soft. Add flour and curry powder and cook and stir over low heat until flour has coated onions and apples. Stir dry milk into hot broth. Mix to dissolve milk and add all at once to onion mixture. Cook and stir over moderate heat until thickened. Add raisins and continue to cook, stirring frequently, over moderate heat for another 5 minutes or until the starchy taste is gone from the sauce. Check for seasoning and add salt if necessary.

Add chicken to sauce, reheat to serving temperature, and serve hot over Steamed Rice (see Index).

Note: Chicken may be removed from the bones for 3 cups or the pieces of chicken may be left whole and served in the sauce. If chicken is to be left whole, 3 pounds of breasts, legs, and thighs would provide adequate servings of chicken for each person.

Low sodium diets: Omit salt. Use salt-free margarine, low sodium broth, and chicken cooked without salt.

Yield: 6 servings

CHICKEN AND DUMPLINGS (United States)

Dr. Crockett, who is an excellent cook, sent me this recipe, which he prepares for two. It is much easier to prepare than the chicken and dumplings I prepare, which takes a long time and leaves me with lots of leftovers.

CHICKEN
2 large chicken breasts or 4
   thighs
2 tablespoons all-purpose
   flour
Salt and pepper to taste
2 tablespoons vegetable oil
1 cup fat-free chicken broth
¾ cup sliced celery
¾ cup sliced carrots
1 sliced onion
1 bay leaf

DUMPLINGS
½ cup flour
1 teaspoon baking powder
⅛ teaspoon salt
Sprinkle of pepper
Sprinkle of ground cloves
⅓ cup milk
1 teaspoon chopped parsley

Remove all skin and visible fat from the chicken with a sharp knife. If breasts are used, they should be cut in half and boned, if desired. Dust the chicken with a mixture of 2 tablespoons flour and salt and pepper to taste and brown in oil in a heavy frying pan. Add chicken broth, celery, carrots, onions, and bay leaf. Cover the pan and simmer over low heat for 15 minutes.

Combine ½ cup flour, baking powder, ⅛ teaspoon salt, pepper, and cloves. Stir to blend. Add milk and parsley and stir only until the flour is moistened. Spoon dumplings on top of the cooking chicken. (There should be about 6 dumplings.) Cover and simmer another 20 minutes. Serve chicken hot with a little sauce and the hot dumplings.

Low sodium diets: Omit salt. Use low sodium broth and baking
   powder.

Yield: 2 servings

CHICKEN FRICASSEE (France)

This luscious chicken in a brown sauce reminds me of coq au vin. It is one of Frances Nielsen's specialties, which she likes to serve with homemade noodles. I've always made chicken fricassee with cream sauce and dumplings, but I'm finally forced to confess publicly that I like hers better than mine.

1 cup all-purpose flour	2 cups carrots, cut diagonally
2 teaspoons salt	about ½ inch thick
¼ teaspoon pepper	1 cup celery, sliced
2 teaspoons paprika	diagonally into about 1-
3 pounds chicken breasts,	inch pieces
legs, and thighs	2 cups water
Skimmed milk	Homemade Noodles (see
Vegetable oil	recipe)
1 cup coarsely chopped	
onions	

Combine flour, salt, pepper, and paprika. Stir to blend well and set aside for later use.

Wash chicken well. Remove all skin and fat with a sharp knife. Dip each piece of chicken into the milk and then into the flour mixture. Shake off any excess flour from the chicken and brown it in a heavy frying pan in vegetable oil over moderate heat. Place the chicken pieces in a casserole or small roaster. Scatter the onions, carrots, and celery over the chicken.

Pour any remaining oil out of the frying pan. Return ¼ cup oil and ⅓ cup of the remaining flour mixture to the frying pan. Cook and stir over moderate heat until smooth. Add the water and cook and stir to form a smooth gravy. Pour the gravy over the chicken, cover, and bake at 350° F. for 1 hour and 25 minutes. Serve hot chicken, vegetables, and sauce over hot Homemade Noodles (see Index).

Low sodium diets: Omit salt. Add ½ teaspoon ground thyme to the flour mixture.

Yield: 6 servings

CHICKEN MOLE (Mexico)

4 pounds chicken breasts, legs, and thighs
Margarine
Vegetable oil
½ cup chopped onions
1 minced garlic clove
½ cup chopped fresh green peppers
2 cups (1-pound can) canned crushed tomatoes with juice

1 cup fat-free chicken broth
1 tablespoon sugar
1 to 2 teaspoons chili powder
¼ teaspoon ground cinnamon
¼ teaspoon ground cloves
¼ teaspoon tabasco sauce
1½ tablespoons cocoa
2 tablespoons cornstarch
¼ cup cold water

Wash chicken thoroughly under cold running water. Remove all skin and visible fat with a sharp knife. Brown chicken in a heavy frying pan over moderate heat in an equal mixture of margarine and oil. Place chicken in a small roaster or oblong casserole as it is browned.

Brown onions, garlic, and green peppers in the frying pan in which the chicken was browned, adding more oil, if necessary. Transfer vegetables with a slotted spoon to a dish. Pour off as much of the fat as possible. Add tomatoes to pan and cook and stir over low heat to scrape up as many of the brown particles in the pan as possible. Combine broth, sugar, chili powder, cinnamon, cloves, tabasco sauce, and cocoa. Stir until smooth and add to broth along with the onion mixture. Cover and simmer, stirring occasionally, for 5 minutes. Pour over the chicken. Cover tightly and bake at 375° F. for 1 to 1½ hours or until the chicken is tender. Transfer chicken pieces to a platter with a fork and keep warm. Stir cornstarch into the cold water to make a smooth paste. Add to the sauce and cook and stir over moderate heat until smooth and thickened. Continue to cook over low heat, stirring occasionally, for 5 minutes or until any starchy taste is gone. Pour hot sauce over chicken and serve.

Low sodium diets: Use salt-free margarine and low sodium broth and tomatoes or fresh tomatoes.

Yield: 8 servings

CHICKEN SPAGHETTI (Texas)

This recipe is based on a large-quantity recipe for chicken spaghetti sent to me by my friend Frances Lee, a dietary consultant from Kerens, Texas. It is used frequently for church dinners and other large groups in her area.

½ cup chopped onions
½ cup chopped celery
½ cup chopped fresh green
  peppers
1 to 2 teaspoons chili powder
4 tablespoons (¼ stick)
  margarine

2 cups (1 16-ounce can)
  tomato sauce
8 ounces spaghetti
1½ cups cooked, boned
  chicken with skin and fat
  removed
1 cup (4 ounces) shredded
  low-fat mozzarella cheese

Fry onions, celery, green peppers, and chili powder in margarine in saucepan over moderate heat, stirring frequently, until onions are limp. Add tomato sauce. Cover and simmer over low heat for 5 minutes.

Cook spaghetti according to directions on the package. Drain well. Add cooked spaghetti and chicken to tomato sauce. Mix lightly and pour into a casserole that has been well greased with margarine. Sprinkle cheese evenly over mixture and bake at 300° F. about 45 minutes or until the cheese is melted. Serve hot.

Low sodium diets: Use low sodium cheese and tomato sauce, salt-free margarine, and chicken cooked without salt.

Yield: 4 servings

CHICKEN SQUARES (Midwestern United States)

3 cups chopped cooked
chicken with skin and fat
removed
3 cups dry white bread
crumbs
½ cup finely chopped onions
¼ cup finely chopped celery
2 cups lukewarm fat-free
chicken broth
¾ cup liquid egg substitute

1 teaspoon salt
Dash of white pepper
¼ teaspoon poultry seasoning
⅛ teaspoon ground sage

SAUCE
1 10¾-ounce can of cream of
chicken soup
½ cup skimmed milk

Combine chicken, bread crumbs, onions, and celery. Toss lightly. Combine chicken broth, egg substitute, salt, pepper, poultry seasoning, and sage. Mix to blend. Pour over chicken mixture and toss lightly to coat the chicken and crumbs with the liquid mixture. Spread evenly in a 9″-square pan that has been well greased with margarine. Bake at 350° F. about 1 hour or until lightly browned and firm. Cut into 6 equal portions and serve hot with sauce.

Sauce: Combine soup and milk and cook and stir over moderate heat until hot and smooth.

Low sodium diets: Omit salt. Use low sodium broth and chicken cooked without salt.

Yield: 6 servings

CHICKEN STEW (Belgium)

The original recipe for this luscious dish uses egg yolks to thicken the sauce. I use a couple of drops of yellow coloring so the sauce will be the same color without the egg yolks. Frances Nielsen makes this and it is really good.

1 cup finely chopped leeks or
  green onions
½ cup finely chopped celery
½ cup finely chopped onions
½ cup finely chopped carrots
1 tablespoon finely chopped
  parsley
¼ cup (½ stick) margarine
½ teaspoon salt
⅛ teaspoon white pepper
3 to 4 pounds chicken
  breasts, legs, and thighs

1 teaspoon salt
⅛ teaspoon white pepper
½ cup hot fat-free chicken
  broth
½ cup evaporated skimmed
  milk
¼ cup all-purpose flour
2 drops yellow food coloring
Steamed Rice or Homemade
  Noodles (see recipes)

Fry leeks or green onions, celery, onions, carrots, and parsley in margarine in heavy frying pan over moderate heat, stirring frequently, until vegetables are limp but not browned. Spread vegetables evenly over the bottom of a small roaster or shallow casserole. Sprinkle with ½ teaspoon salt and ⅛ teaspoon pepper.

Wash chicken thoroughly under running water. Drain well. Remove all skin and visible fat with a sharp knife. Place chicken pieces evenly over vegetables. Sprinkle with 1 teaspoon salt and ⅛ teaspoon pepper. Pour chicken broth over the chicken and vegetables. Cover tightly and bake 1 hour and 15 minutes or until chicken is very tender. Transfer cooked chicken pieces to platter and keep warm until needed.

Stir evaporated milk, flour, and coloring together until smooth. Pour slowly into the vegetables and liquid remaining in the roaster or casserole. Cook and stir on top of the range about 5 minutes or until sauce is smooth and the starchy taste is gone. Serve hot chicken on a mound of Steamed Rice or Homemade Noodles (see Index) with the sauce poured over it.

Low sodium diets: Omit salt. Use salt-free margarine and low sodium broth.

Yield: 6 servings

COQ AU VIN (France)

This is one of my favorite chicken recipes and I often use it for guests. It freezes well so you can prepare it ahead of time and freeze the leftovers, if there are any.

6 pounds chicken legs, thighs, and breasts
¼ cup vegetable oil
¼ cup (½ stick) margarine
½ cup (1 4-ounce can) drained chopped mushrooms
1 cup sliced green onions with tops
¾ cup pearl onions or coarsely chopped onions
⅓ cup all-purpose flour

2 cups Beaujolais, Burgundy, or Chianti
2 cups hot fat-free chicken broth
Salt to taste
¼ teaspoon pepper
½ teaspoon ground thyme
2 tablespoons chopped parsley
½ teaspoon garlic powder
2 tablespoons tomato puree or sauce

Wash the chicken well. Remove all skin and fat with a sharp knife and set aside to drain.

Combine oil and margarine in a heavy frying pan. Stir over low heat until the margarine is melted. Pour most of the fat mixture into a container. Use as much of the fat mixture as necessary to brown the chicken in batches in the frying pan. Transfer chicken to a small roasting pan as it is browned.

Fry mushrooms and onions in the same pan until onions are limp but not browned, adding more fat, if necessary. (Coarsely chopped onions may be used for all the onions if the others are not available, but the green and pearl onions are characteristic of the French recipe.) Remove mushrooms and onions with a slotted spoon and scatter over the chicken.

Add more fat to the frying pan, if necessary, for a total of ¼ to ⅓ cup fat. Add flour and cook and stir over medium heat until smooth. Add wine and broth to the flour mixture and cook and stir over medium heat until smooth. Add salt, pepper, thyme, parsley, garlic powder, and tomato puree or sauce. Mix and pour over hot chicken. Stir lightly to distribute the sauce.

Cover tightly and bake at 350° F. for 1 to 1½ hours or until the chicken is tender. (Cut the baking temperature to 325° F. if you use a glass roaster.) Serve chicken hot with some of the sauce.

Low sodium diets: Omit salt. Use salt-free margarine and low sodium broth, tomato puree or sauce or fresh tomatoes, and fresh mushrooms.

Yield: 8 to 10 servings

ROAST CHICKEN (Greece)

This recipe was given to me by Anthony P. Angelos, owner-manager of the Oak Lawn Restaurant in Oak Lawn, Illinois. We used to eat there often before we moved to Iowa and we never miss going there now when we return to the Chicago area. The restaurant prepares a great many excellent items, but this was always my favorite. I asked him for the recipe after we moved away from there so I could prepare it myself, and he very graciously gave it to me.

2 2½- to 3-pound broiler-fryer chickens	1½ tablespoons fresh lemon juice
½ cup (1 stick) softened margarine	1½ teaspoons salt
1½ tablespoons leaf oregano	¼ teaspoon white pepper
	Rice Pilaf or Steamed Rice (see recipes)

Wash chicken thoroughly under cold running water. Pat dry with a paper towel or clean cloth. Remove any visible fat with a sharp knife.

Blend margarine, oregano, lemon juice, salt, and pepper together. Rub the seasoned fat well into the skin of each chicken. Put a heaping teaspoonful of the seasoned fat inside each chicken.

Place chickens, breast side up, in a small roaster. Bake uncovered at 400° F. for 1 hour. Turn chickens breast side down. Continue to bake for another ½ to 1 hour or until chickens are golden brown and very tender. Baste every 15 minutes with the remaining seasoned fat, using a pastry brush dipped in the fat or pan juices. (Do not bake at a lower temperature. It just isn't good that way. I tried it and it isn't bad but it is just plain roast chicken and not the good Greek chicken.)

Mr. Angelos roasts the chickens, cuts them into serving-sized portions and refrigerates them until needed. This is an excellent idea for a low cholesterol diet because it gives you time to chill the pan juices and remove the fat from the juices. At serving time, remove the skin from the portions for those on a low cholesterol diet, put chicken portions, bone side down, under the broiler, and reheat to serving temperature. Serve hot chicken with reheated pan juices and Rice Pilaf or Steamed Rice (see Index).

Low sodium diets: Omit salt. Use salt-free margarine.

Yield: 4 ½-chicken servings or 8 ¼-chicken servings

SAVORY BAKED CHICKEN (United States)

3 to 4 pounds chicken breasts, legs, and thighs
1 teaspoon celery salt
¼ teaspoon garlic powder
1 tablespoon Worcestershire sauce
2 tablespoons soy sauce
⅓ cup vegetable oil

Wash chicken thoroughly under cold running water. Pat dry with a paper towel or clean cloth. Remove all skin and visible fat from chicken with a sharp knife. Place chicken in a shallow casserole. Combine celery salt, garlic powder, Worcestershire sauce, soy sauce, and oil. Mix well and pour over chicken pieces. Cover and refrigerate for 1 to 3 hours, turning the chicken in the marinade every ½ hour.

Bake chicken and sauce, covered, at 350° F. for 1 hour, basting the chicken with the sauce at the end of each ½ hour. Uncover the casserole and continue to bake another hour or until the chicken is tender, basting with the pan juices every ½ hour. Serve chicken hot with some of the hot pan juices.

Low sodium diets: This recipe is not suitable.

Yield: 6 to 8 servings

SKILLET BARBECUED CHICKEN (Florida)

Frances Gunsallus fixed this for us one time when we were all visiting her sister, Mary Boineau, in Chicago. Frances said the recipe came from her brother-in-law, John Holton, and it sort of reminds me of John—easygoing but with a punch and very nice.

2 pounds chicken breasts, legs, and thighs
½ cup grape jelly

2 cups Heinz or Kraft barbecue sauce

Wash chicken thoroughly under running water. Pat dry with a paper towel or clean cloth. Remove all skin and visible fat with a very sharp knife.

Place jelly and sauce in an electric skillet. Cook and stir at 200° F. until jelly is melted into the sauce. Add the chicken, cover, and continue to cook for 1 hour. Turn the chicken over occasionally in the sauce while it is cooking. At the end of the hour, remove the cover and let it continue to simmer at 200° F. until the chicken is very tender. Serve hot chicken with some of the sauce.

Low sodium diets: This recipe is not suitable.

Yield: 4 servings

SUNDAY CHICKEN BAKE
(Midwestern United States)

This recipe, which Hazel Gernand has served to us several times, is delicious. She says she got the recipe from her friend Zella Strong. They called it a Sunday bake because you can put it into the oven before you leave for church and it will be done about the time you get home. You can even vary the time a few minutes either way without making much difference in the final results.

1 cup long-grain rice	1 cup skimmed milk
1 10¾-ounce can cream of chicken soup	1 2½- to 3-pound broiler-fryer chicken
1 10¾-ounce can cream of celery soup	1 package dry onion soup mix

Spread rice evenly over the bottom of a 9″ × 13″ cake pan or shallow casserole. Combine soups and milk and stir until it is almost smooth. Pour the soup mix over the rice.

Wash chicken well under running water. Pat dry and cut into serving-sized pieces. Remove any skin or visible fat with a sharp knife and lay the chicken pieces on the rice, sort of nested down into the soup and rice. Sprinkle chicken and rice with onion soup mix. Cover tightly with aluminum foil and bake at 325° F. for 2½ hours. Serve the chicken hot with some of the hot rice.

Low sodium diets: This recipe is not suitable.

Yield: 4 servings

APPLE AND RAISIN STUFFING (Germany)

Elfrieda Schmal from Strawberry Point, Iowa, gave me this heirloom recipe, which she has used for years as a stuffing for goose, chicken, or turkey.

7 cups day-old bread cubes
1 cup finely chopped onions
3 cups pared, cored, and
   diced apples
1 cup raisins
1½ teaspoons salt

⅛ teaspoon pepper
¼ cup sugar
½ teaspoon ground cinnamon
¾ cup (1½ sticks) melted
   margarine
Hot water

Place bread cubes in a bowl. Add onions, apples, and raisins. Sprinkle salt, pepper, sugar, and cinnamon over mixture. Drizzle melted margarine over mixture and toss lightly. Add enough hot water to give a moist consistency. Spread dressing evenly in a 9"-square pan or a 1½-quart casserole that has been well greased with margarine.

Bake at 375° F. for 45 minutes or until browned. (It will take a little longer in the casserole than it will in the flat pan.) Serve hot.

Low sodium diets: Omit salt. Use salt-free margarine.

Yield: 6 to 8 servings

BREAD DRESSING (United States)

¾ cup finely chopped celery
½ cup finely chopped onions
¼ cup (½ stick) margarine
6 cups (about 10 slices) diced
   day-old white bread

1½ cups fat-free chicken
   broth
2 egg whites
¼ teaspoon salt
⅛ teaspoon pepper
½ teaspoon ground sage

Fry celery and onions in margarine over moderate heat, stirring frequently, until onions are golden but not browned. Pour vegetables and margarine over bread cubes. Toss lightly. Combine broth, egg whites, salt, pepper, and sage. Mix to blend and pour over bread. Toss lightly. Spread dressing evenly in an 8"-square pan or a 1-quart casserole that has been well greased with margarine. Bake at 375° F. for 45 minutes or until top is browned. Serve hot.

Low sodium diets: Omit salt. Use salt-free margarine and low sodium broth.

Yield: 4 to 6 servings

CORNBREAD DRESSING
(Southern United States)

1½ cups coarse crumbs from day-old Cornbread (see recipe)
½ cup chopped celery
½ cup chopped onions
¼ cup (½ stick) margarine

1½ cups fat-free chicken broth
2 egg whites
½ teaspoon salt
¾ teaspoon poultry seasoning
3 cups (about 5 slices) cubes from day-old white bread

Prepare cornbread (see Index) the day before it is to be used. Serve part of it hot and reserve the rest for the crumbs needed for the dressing.

Fry celery and onions in margarine until onions are golden but not browned. Combine chicken broth, egg whites, salt, poultry seasoning, and fried vegetables and the margarine in which they were fried. Mix lightly and pour over the cornbread crumbs and the diced bread cubes, which have been placed in a bowl. Toss lightly and spread evenly in an 8″-square pan or a 1-quart casserole that has been well greased with margarine. Bake at 350° F. for about 50 to 60 minutes or until browned. Serve hot.

Low sodium diets: Omit salt. Use salt-free margarine and low sodium broth and Yankee Cornbread (see Index).

Yield: 4 to 6 servings

SKILLET STUFFING (United States)

½ cup chopped onions
¾ cup chopped celery
¼ cup (½ stick) margarine
½ teaspoon poultry seasoning
¼ teaspoon powdered sage
⅛ teaspoon ground nutmeg

⅛ teaspoon salt
½ cup white raisins
½ cup water
2 cups day-old whole wheat
   bread cubes
2 cups day-old white bread
   cubes

Fry onions and celery in margarine over moderate heat in a heavy frying pan, stirring occasionally, until onions are limp but not browned. Add poultry seasoning, sage, nutmeg, salt, raisins, and water. Stir to mix well. Add bread cubes and mix lightly. Cover stuffing and cook over low heat for 45 minutes, adding a little additional water, if necessary.

Low sodium diets: Omit salt. Use salt-free margarine.

Yield: 4 servings

CHICKEN OR TURKEY GRAVY (United States)

BASIC INGREDIENTS	AMOUNTS FOR 2 CUPS GRAVY	AMOUNTS FOR 4 CUPS GRAVY
Fat-free chicken broth, water, or skimmed milk	2 cups	4 cups
Vegetable oil	2 tablespoons	¼ cup
Flour	3 tablespoons	⅓ cup
Salt and pepper	to taste	to taste

Remove cooked turkey from roaster to carving board. Pour the drippings from the pan into another container, leaving the brown particles in the pan. Let the fat rise to the top of the drippings and then skim off as much fat as possible from the drippings. Add enough liquid to the drippings to yield the necessary amount of liquid or save the drippings for another time and use the fat-free broth, water, or skimmed milk.

Pour the oil into the roaster. Put the roaster over low heat, add the flour, and cook and stir over low heat until smooth and bubbling. Add the cool liquid all at once and cook, stirring constantly, over moderate heat, until thickened and smooth, scraping the brown particles from the pan as you stir the gravy. Simmer gently, stirring frequently, for about 5 minutes. Taste for seasoning and add salt and pepper, if desired. Serve hot.

Low sodium diets: Omit salt. Use low sodium broth or water for gravy. Cook chicken or turkey without salt.

QUICK CHICKEN OR TURKEY GRAVY
(United States)

It is important that the broth used in this gravy is well flavored and full bodied. The broth can be made from chicken bouillon cubes, in which case you should be careful not to add salt until you taste it. It can also be made with broth from cooked chicken or drippings from roast chicken with added water, but it must taste good or the gravy will not taste good.

BASIC INGREDIENTS	AMOUNTS FOR 2 CUPS GRAVY	AMOUNTS FOR 4 CUPS GRAVY
Hot fat-free chicken broth	2 cups	4 cups
Thyme (optional)	⅛ teaspoon	¼ teaspoon
Salt and pepper	to taste	to taste
Margarine	2 tablespoons (¼ stick)	¼ cup (½ stick)
All-purpose flour	3 tablespoons	⅓ cup
Cold fat-free chicken broth	⅓ cup	⅔ cup

Place hot chicken broth in small saucepan. Heat to boiling. Add thyme and salt and pepper to taste. Add margarine. Shake flour and cold broth together until smooth in a small jar or container with a tight lid. Add to hot broth and margarine and cook and stir until smooth. Simmer for 5 minutes, stirring frequently, and serve hot.

Low sodium diet: Omit salt. Use salt-free margarine and low sodium broth.

5
Fish

Fish is important in the low cholesterol diet because it is low in calories and contains only a very small amount of cholesterol. If you are used to serving a great deal of fish, I can only say more power to you. Keep up the good work and remember not to use shellfish more often than a four-ounce serving once a week. Never prepare the fish you use with butter, cream, egg yolks, or other saturated fats. If you want to deep-fat fry fish, be sure you fry it in unsaturated fat instead of lard or shortening and serve it with lemon juice, tartar sauce based on salad dressing, or a tomato sauce. Some of the European countries serve fish with melted flavored margarines. I also like the way they serve fish with vinegar in Great Britain and often do so myself.

Fish come in the following forms:

Whole fish are fish as they come from the water. The fish must be scaled and eviscerated; usually, the head, tail, and fins are removed. The fish may then be filleted, cut into steaks or chunks, or cooked whole.

Dressed fish are fish with scales and entrails removed. Usually, the head, tail, and fins are also removed, though sometimes the heads and tails are left on the smaller fish. These are called pan-dressed fish and are ready to cook as purchased, such as trout or catfish. The fish may also be cut into fillets, steaks, or chunks.

Fillets are the sides of fish cut lengthwise from the backbone. They are ready to cook as purchased.

Steaks are cross-sectional slices from large dressed fish, generally cut ⅝ to 1 inch thick. A cross section of the backbone is the only bone in a steak. Steaks are ready to cook as purchased.

Chunks are cross sections of large dressed fish. A cross section of the backbone is the only bone in a chunk. Chunks are ready to cook as purchased.

Sticks and squares are generally cut from frozen fish blocks. They are coated with a batter or breading. They are not recommended for a low cholesterol diet unless you are sure that the coating does not include whole eggs.

Portions are generally individual pieces of fish that have been dipped in a batter or breading and frozen so they can be cooked or reheated without further preparation. They, too, are not recommended for a low cholesterol diet if they are purchased breaded or in a batter. It is much better to purchase them without coating and coat them yourself with egg white or skimmed milk and then dip them in crumbs.

Canned fish includes many varieties of both fish and shellfish. They are ready to use as purchased. The ones packed in water will be lower in calories than the ones packed in oil.

The recipe and type of fish you plan to use will determine the amount of fish you need to purchase. You generally need about 3 ounces of cooked fish per adult, a little less for children, and a little more for hungry men or adolescent boys. The following table will help you decide how much fish to buy per person:

Whole fish: ¾ pound per person
Dressed or pan-dressed fish: ½ pound per person
Fillets or steaks: ⅓ pound per person
Fish portions: ⅓ pound per person
Canned fish: about 2½ to 3 ounces per person

When you are buying fresh fish, it must be really fresh. Fresh whole or dressed fish should have the following characteristics:

Flesh should be firm and not separated from the bones.

Odor should be fresh and mild. A fish that is freshly caught has practically no odor. The fishy odor becomes more apparent when the fish is older.

Eyes should be bright and clear. The eyes become sunken as the fish becomes stale.

Gills should be red and free of slime.

Skin should be shiny with color unfaded. Older fish lose their irridescence and the color fades.

Fish steaks or fillets should have a fresh-cut appearance. They should be firm in texture with no trace of brown or dryness around the edges.

When you are buying frozen fish you should look for the following characteristics:

Flesh should be frozen solid when purchased. There should be no discoloration or freezer burn.

Odor should not be apparent. Fish that is frozen properly should have little or no odor. A strong fish odor means poor quality.

Wrappings should be of moisture-vapor–retardant materials. There should be little or no air space between the fish and the wrapping.

A wide variety of canned fish is available on the market today. The most abundant varieties of canned fish are tuna, salmon, mackerel, and sardines.

Several species of fish are marketed as tuna, all of which are equally desirable. Canned tuna is available in three different packing styles. The pack does not refer to quality but to the size of the pieces in the can.

Fancy or solid pack tuna usually contains large pieces packed in oil. This pack is ideal for cold plates and for dishes in which appearance is important. It is the most expensive pack.

Chunk pack is tuna cut into convenient-sized pieces. It is especially adaptable for salads and other recipes in which chunks are desirable. It is moderately priced.

Flaked or grated tuna contains smaller pieces. It is excellent for sandwiches or canapes in which tuna is blended into a paste. It is generally lower-priced than the other tuna packs.

Canned tuna may be purchased in cans that contain 3¼, 3½, 6½, 7, 9¼, 12½, and 13 ounces.

Five distinct species of salmon are canned on the Pacific Coast. These are usually sold by their names since that indicates the type of meat. The differences affect texture, color, and flavor. The higher-priced varieties are deeper red in color and have a higher oil content. In descending order, according to the way they are generally priced, are red or sockeye, chinook or king, medium red, coho or silver, pink, and chum or keta. Canned salmon may be purchased in cans that contain 3¾, 7¾, and 16 ounces.

Mackerel, which is good in salads or served cold with dressing, is purchased in 15-ounce cans.

Sardines may be purchased in various-sized cans, depending on whether they are packed in this country or abroad. They may be packed in oil, tomato, or mustard sauce.

After fish are purchased, they must be stored correctly to maintain their quality and flavor and to avoid spoilage or food poisoning.

Fresh fish should be placed in the refrigerator in their original wrapper immediately after they are purchased. A storage temperature of 35° to 40° F. is needed to maintain quality. Fresh fish should not be kept in the refrigerator more than a day or two before they are cooked.

Frozen fish should be placed in the freezer in their original wrappings immediately after they are purchased unless you want to thaw and cook them right away. They should be stored at 0° F. or lower to maintain their quality. They should be dated when purchased and not kept frozen over six months.

It is important that frozen fish be thawed correctly and cooked within 24 hours of thawing. The best way to thaw fish is to place the individual packages in the refrigerator, allowing about 24 hours for a 1-pound package. If quicker thawing is necessary, the individual packages may be placed under cold running water, allowing 1 to 2 hours for each 1-pound package. Fish *must not* be refrozen or thawed at room temperature. Fish portions, squares, or sticks should not be thawed before they are cooked. Frozen fillets or steaks may be cooked without thawing if you allow additional cooking time. Fillets or steaks to be breaded or baked should always be thawed before they are used.

Fish is cooked to develop flavor, to soften the small amount of connective tissue, and to make it easier to digest. Fish cooked at too high a temperature or for too long a period of time will be tough and dry and the flavor will be poor.

Fish is a very important part of the diet of many countries where there is an abundant supply of fish. It is generally prepared with other ingredients that are also abundant in the area. The tomato sauces of the Mediterranean countries, the sour cream of the Scandinavian countries, the elaborate sauces of France, and the fish and chips of Great Britain all reflect the use of ingredients that are readily available and enjoyed in those countries. Our own country has regional favorites such as the clam chowders of New England, the cioppino of California, and the salmon dishes of the Northwest. Thanks to modern communications, we have access to the many recipes available to us that use ingredients that are suitable for a low cholesterol diet.

I included the basic methods of preparation for fish in my first low cholesterol cookbook, which I hope you will use along with this one. Therefore, I have included in this book only those recipes that are regional and ethnic and suitable for a low cholesterol diet. I hope you will enjoy trying these recipes and that you will also look to your own ethnic and regional backgrounds for other recipes that are suitable for your low cholesterol diet.

CIOPPINO (California)

Anita Kane knew she couldn't have the original version of this dish, with all of its shellfish, so she created this combination, which we think is luscious. She says that if you like your food really hot you should increase the pepper to 1 teaspoon, but I'm happier with the $\frac{1}{4}$ teaspoon listed in the recipe. I especially like to dunk Italian or French bread in the sauce when we serve it.

1 cup coarsely chopped
onions
1 cup diced celery
½ cup diced fresh green
peppers
¼ cup vegetable oil
2 minced garlic cloves or ½
teaspoon garlic powder
1 29-ounce can tomatoes
1 15-ounce can tomato sauce

1 15-ounce can stewed
tomatoes
1 teaspoon sugar
1 crushed bay leaf
1 teaspoon basil
1 teaspoon leaf oregano
¼ teaspoon black pepper
1 teaspoon salt
1½ cups dry white wine
2 pounds fish fillets, cut into
2-inch pieces

Fry onions, celery, and peppers in oil in heavy 3- to 4-quart pot until vegetables are limp but not browned. Add garlic. Crush tomatoes into small pieces and add tomatoes and juice with tomato sauce, stewed tomatoes, sugar, bay leaf, basil, oregano, pepper, and salt to hot vegetables. Cover and simmer for 30 minutes. Add wine and fish and simmer, covered, for another 20 to 25 minutes or until fish is tender.

Serve hot in shallow bowls with Italian or French bread.

Low sodium diets: Omit salt. Use low sodium tomatoes, tomato sauce, and stewed tomatoes or fresh tomatoes.

Yield: 6 to 8 servings

FILLET OF FISH BONNE FEMME (France)

1½ pounds boneless fish fillets
½ cup (1 4-ounce can) sliced
drained mushrooms
½ cup chopped onions
⅔ cup dry white wine
1 cup fat-free chicken broth
1 tablespoon chopped parsley
2 tablespoons lemon juice

1 teaspoon salt
⅛ teaspoon white pepper
¼ cup (½ stick) margarine
3 tablespoons all-purpose
flour
½ cup evaporated skimmed
milk

Thaw fish, if necessary, and wipe dry. Spread mushrooms and onions on the bottom of a 9″-square stove-top and oven-proof glass pan that has been well greased with margarine. Spread the fish evenly over the mushrooms and onions. Add the wine and broth to the fish and sprinkle evenly with parsley, lemon juice, salt, and pepper. Cut the margarine into slices and place it on top of the fish and seasonings. Bring to a boil over moderate heat; cover tightly with aluminum foil and bake at 350° F. for 10 to 15 minutes or until the fish flakes easily when tested with a fork.

Transfer the fish to a hot oven-proof platter. Pour the liquid and vegetables into a saucepan and cook over moderate heat until the liquid is reduced by half. Mix the flour and milk together until smooth and add to the hot sauce. Cook and stir over moderate heat until the sauce is thickened and the starchy taste is gone. Wipe the fish dry with a paper towel, place evenly on the oven-proof platter, cover with the sauce, and run under the broiler until bubbling hot and lightly browned. Serve hot.

Low sodium diets: Omit salt. Use salt-free margarine and low sodium broth.

Yield: 4 to 6 servings

FISH PIQUANT (Acadiana-Cajun)

The first time I prepared this recipe, it contained ¼ teaspoon cayenne pepper and I spent all afternoon drinking water. The next time I tried it, I used only ⅛ teaspoon pepper and that seems to be about right. I generally serve it with rice and that cuts the strength of the spices a little, but it is still a rather spicy recipe.

1 medium onion	¼ teaspoon garlic powder
1 medium-sized fresh green pepper	¼ teaspoon ground thyme
	⅛ teaspoon cayenne pepper
2 tablespoons vegetable oil	½ teaspoon salt
¼ cup all-purpose flour	1 pound fish fillets, cut about
2 tablespoons margarine	½ to ¾ inch thick
2 cups (1 1-pound can) tomato sauce	

Clean and chop onion and green pepper and fry in oil over moderate heat, stirring frequently, until the onion is limp but not browned. Add the flour and margarine to the vegetables and cook and stir over moderate heat until lightly browned. Add tomato sauce, garlic powder, thyme, cayenne pepper, and salt. Cook and stir until thickened.

Place the fish fillets evenly in the bottom of an 8″-square glass dish. Cover with the hot sauce and bake at 350° F. for 20 to 25 minutes or until the fish flakes easily.

Low sodium diets: Omit salt. Use salt-free margarine.

Yield: 3 to 4 servings

FISH SOUFFLE (Norway)

½ cup (1 stick) margarine
⅓ cup all-purpose flour
1 cup evaporated skimmed
  milk
1½ cups skimmed milk
¼ teaspoon ground nutmeg
½ teaspoon salt
Sprinkle of white pepper

½ cup liquid egg substitute
1 cup finely chopped cold
  poached codfish, whitefish,
  or other firm white fish
½ cup (about 4) egg whites at
  room temperature
½ cup dry bread crumbs
Melted margarine

Stir margarine and flour together over moderate heat until smooth. Add milks, nutmeg, salt, and pepper. Cook and stir over moderate heat until smooth and thickened. Remove from heat and stir into egg substitute. Add flaked fish and cool for 5 minutes. Beat egg whites until foamy but not firm and fold the sauce into the egg whites. Pour into a shallow 2-quart glass casserole that has been well greased with margarine. Sprinkle with crumbs and bake at 350° F. for 45 minutes or until well browned. Serve as soon as possible with hot melted margarine.

Low sodium diets: Omit salt. Use salt-free margarine and fish that has been cooked without salt.

Yield: 4 to 6 servings

GEFILTE FISH (Jewish)

Anita Kane measured everything very carefully the last time she made this dish, and gave me the recipe to share with you. Anita is also on a low cholesterol diet, so we share recipes with each other.

2 pounds fish	2 medium sized onions
2 quarts water	⅓ cup matzo meal or crumbs
2 large onions	⅔ cup liquid egg substitute
1 cup sliced carrots	½ teaspoon pepper
2 teaspoons salt	1 teaspoon salt
1 teaspoon pepper	2 tablespoons sugar
⅓ cup sugar	Paprika

Skin, debone, and cut fish into pieces. (Use 1 pound trout and 1 pound pike or any other combination of available fish.) Place the skin and bones in the bottom of a 6-quart kettle. Cover with 2 quarts water, 2 large onions, carrots, 2 teaspoons salt, 1 teaspoon pepper, and ⅓ cup sugar. Cover and simmer while the fish is being prepared.

Grind the raw fish and 2 medium-sized onions, putting them both through the grinder twice. Add the matzo meal or crumbs, egg substitute, ½ teaspoon pepper, 1 teaspoon salt, and 2 tablespoons sugar to the fish mixture. Place in the mixer bowl and mix at low speed for about 4 minutes or until the fish mixture is beginning to hold its shape. Wet your hands and form balls of the fish mixture. Drop the balls carefully into the simmering stock. It is best to have just 1 layer of the balls, but you may have 2 if necessary. Cover and simmer for 1½ hours. Baste occasionally if any of the balls are out of the liquid. Remove the cooked balls from the hot liquid and place carefully on a large platter. Sprinkle with paprika and garnish with slices of the cooked carrot, if desired.

Low sodium diets: Omit salt.

Yield: 4 servings

HERRING SALAD (Scandinavia)

1 cup chopped marinated
   herring
1 cup chopped beef with fat
   and gristle removed
1½ cups chopped cooked
   potatoes
¼ cup finely chopped onions
¼ cup drained sweet pickle
   relish
¾ cup evaporated skimmed
   milk

1 teaspoon vinegar
1 tablespoon sugar
Salt and pepper to taste
1 cup finely chopped well-
   drained pickled beets
¾ cup finely grated carrots
Sprig of parsley
3 sliced stuffed whole green
   olives

Combine herring (the type you buy already marinated in a jar), beef, potatoes, onions, and pickle relish. Toss lightly. Mix milk, vinegar, and sugar together and pour over the salad. Mix lightly and taste for seasoning. Add salt and pepper, if necessary. (The amount of salt will depend on the saltiness of the herring.) Toss together and press into a 1½-quart bowl that has been rinsed with cold water. Refrigerate for several hours. Turn salad out onto a platter and decorate with alternating stripes of beets and carrots, moving from the top to the bottom. Top with a sprig of parsley and sliced olives. Serve cold.

Low sodium diets: This recipe is not suitable.

Yield: about 8 servings

OVEN-FRIED FISH (United States)

2 pounds fish fillets or steaks
1 cup milk
1 tablespoon salt

1 cup dry bread crumbs
¼ cup (½ stick) melted
   margarine

Thaw fish, if necessary. Separate fish into individual fillets or steaks. Combine milk and salt and dip each piece of fish in the milk and then in the bread crumbs. Place each piece of fish in a baking pan or on aluminum foil that has been well greased with margarine. Pour the melted margarine over the fish.

Bake the fish on the top shelf of the oven at 500° F. for 10 to 15 minutes, depending on the thickness of the fish, or until the fish flakes easily. Serve hot.

Low sodium diets: Omit salt. Use salt-free margarine.

Yield: 4 to 6 servings

PAPRIKA FISH (Hungary)

2 pounds boneless fillet of
  halibut, haddock, or
  whitefish
1 cup chopped onions
½ cup (1 stick) margarine
¾ cup evaporated skimmed
  milk

2 tablespoons paprika
¼ teaspoon pepper
1 teaspoon salt
Boiled potatoes or
  Homemade Noodles (see
  recipe)

Thaw fish, if necessary. Pat dry with a paper towel and set aside until needed.

Fry the onions over moderate heat in as much of the margarine as necessary, stirring frequently, until the onions are golden. Spread the onions in the bottom of a shallow casserole. Place the fish evenly on top of the onions and dot with the remaining margarine. Mix the milk, paprika, pepper, and salt together and pour over the fish. Bake at 375° F., basting frequently with the juice, for 20 to 25 minutes or until the fish flakes easily when tested with a fork. Transfer the fish to a serving platter, pour the sauce over it, and serve hot with plain boiled potatoes or Homemade Noodles (see Index).

Low sodium diets: Omit salt. Use salt-free margarine.

Yield: 6 to 8 servings

SALMON AND POTATO CASSEROLE
(Northwestern United States)

1 1-pound can salmon	1 cup canned drained peas
¼ cup all-purpose flour	Salt and pepper to taste
¼ cup (½ stick) margarine	3 cups mashed potatoes
2½ cups salmon liquid and skimmed milk	½ cup dry bread crumbs
	½ teaspoon paprika

Drain salmon. Discard bones and skin. Break salmon into chunks. Refrigerate salmon and juice separately.

Place flour and margarine in saucepan. Cook and stir over moderate heat until smooth. Add enough skimmed milk to salmon juice to total 2½ cups liquid. Add juice and milk to flour and margarine and cook and stir over moderate heat until smooth and thickened. Add salmon and peas to sauce. Taste for seasoning and add salt and pepper to taste.

Spread mashed potatoes evenly in the bottom of a 2½- or 3-quart casserole. Spread the salmon mixture evenly over the potatoes. Combine the bread crumbs and paprika and sprinkle evenly over the salmon mixture.

Bake, uncovered, at 350° F. for 20 to 25 minutes or until bubbling and lightly browned.

Low sodium diets: Omit salt. Use salt-free margarine and peas, potatoes, and salmon that have been cooked without salt.

Yield: 6 servings

SALMON BISCUIT ROLL
(Northwestern United States)

1 1-pound can salmon	¼ cup finely chopped onions
½ cup chopped celery	2 tablespoons margarine
½ cup chopped fresh green peppers	½ cup chopped stuffed green olives

1 10¾-ounce can cream of
  chicken soup
2 cups all-purpose flour
3 tablespoons instant dry
  milk
4 teaspoons baking powder

1 teaspoon salt
3 tablespoons margarine
¾ cup water
Skimmed milk
1 tablespoon lemon juice

Drain salmon, discarding skin and bones. Break salmon into bite-sized pieces. Refrigerate salmon and juice separately.

Fry celery, green peppers, and onions in 2 tablespoons margarine until onions are transparent but not browned. Add olives and salmon and ¼ cup soup to the vegetables. Set aside until needed.

Stir flour, dry milk, baking powder, and salt together to blend. Cut 3 tablespoons margarine into the flour mixture until it resembles coarse meal. Add water and stir with a fork to form a soft dough. Knead the dough about 10 times on a lightly floured board. Pat or roll dough to form a 9″ × 12″ rectangle. Spread dough with salmon mixture and roll up lengthwise like a jelly roll. Transfer roll to an ungreased cookie sheet with the seam down and bake at 400° F. for 25 to 30 minutes or until lightly browned. Serve hot with a sauce made by heating the remainder of the soup with enough skimmed milk added to the salmon juice to equal ½ cup and lemon juice.

Low sodium diets: Omit salt and olives. Use salt-free margarine, low sodium baking powder, and 1½ cups salmon cooked without salt.

Yield: 6 servings

SALMON FRUIT SALAD
(Northwestern United States)

1 1-pound can salmon
1 peeled and sliced avocado
1 tablespoon lemon juice
2 cups mandarin oranges
1½ cups thinly sliced celery

½ cup toasted slivered
  almonds
⅓ cup salad dressing
Salad greens

Drain salmon and discard bones, skin, and juice. Break salmon into bite-sized chunks. Sprinkle avocado with lemon juice to prevent discoloration. Set aside 6 avocado slices and 6 orange sections for garnish. Cut remaining avocado into 1-inch chunks. Combine salmon, avocado chunks, orange sections, celery, almonds, and salad dressing. Mix lightly and chill. Shape into a mound on salad greens. Garnish with reserved avocado and orange sections. Serve chilled.

Low sodium diets: Use 1½ cups fresh salmon cooked without salt and low sodium salad dressing.

Yield: 6 servings

SEVICHE (Mexico)

This marinated fish is popular in Mexico and South America, where it is generally used as an appetizer.

2 pounds boneless fillet of
  whitefish, halibut, sole, or
  other firm white fish
2 cups lime juice
½ cup finely chopped onions
¼ cup finely chopped green
  chilis
¼ cup finely chopped parsley
¼ teaspoon garlic powder
1 teaspoon salt
⅛ teaspoon cayenne pepper
1 cup peeled, chopped, and
  seeded tomatoes
¼ cup vegetable oil

Thaw the fish, if necessary. Pat dry with a paper towel and cut into thin strips with a very sharp knife. Put fish into a plastic container and cover with lime juice. Refrigerate for 4 to 6 hours. Drain well and discard the lime juice. Combine the onions, chilis, parsley, garlic powder, salt, pepper, tomatoes, and oil and pour over the fish. Toss lightly and refrigerate until serving time.

Low sodium diets: Omit salt.

Yield: 2 pounds fish and sauce

SPAGHETTI WITH TUNA (Italy)

2 6½-ounce cans of tuna
½ cup chopped fresh green
  peppers
½ cup chopped onions
¼ cup vegetable oil
2 cups (1 16-ounce can)
  tomato sauce

½ teaspoon leaf oregano
½ teaspoon basil
½ teaspoon salt
⅛ teaspoon pepper
8 ounces spaghetti

Drain tuna well and set aside for later use. If the tuna is canned in oil, use the oil for frying the green peppers and onions. If not, discard the liquid and fry the vegetables in vegetable oil until the onions are lightly browned. Add the tomato sauce, oregano, basil, salt, and pepper. Simmer, uncovered, for 5 minutes. Add the tuna and simmer for another 5 minutes. Serve hot over hot spaghetti that has been cooked and drained.

Low sodium diets: Omit salt. Use low sodium canned tuna and tomato sauce. Cook the spaghetti without salt.

Yield: about 4 servings

SWEET SOUR FISH (Jewish)

Anita Kane's husband, Rudy, is an avid fisherman and likes to have his catch fixed this way. However, she also uses this recipe for whitefish when she doesn't have any of the fish he has caught in the freezer.

2 to 3 pounds fish steaks
3 or 4 large onions
1 tablespoon mixed spices in
  a tea strainer or white
  cloth bag

1 teaspoon salt
1 teaspoon pepper
½ cup sugar
¾ cup vinegar
2½ cups water

Have fish cut into steaks about 1½ inches thick. Place fish, neatly arranged, in the bottom of a kettle. Cover with sliced onions. Add spices, salt, pepper, sugar, vinegar, and water. Bring to a boil. Reduce heat and simmer, uncovered, for 15 to 20 minutes or until the fish flakes easily. Refrigerate fish and juice until needed. Serve the fish and onions, drained and cold, as an appetizer or main dish. Fish will keep in the refrigerator for 2 to 3 weeks.

Low sodium diets: Omit salt.

Yield: 2 to 3 pounds fish

TUNA AND NOODLES
(Midwestern United States)

This recipe was given to me by Mrs. Hazel Sorensen of Oelwein, Iowa. You will notice there are no mushrooms in it. We like it this way and think you will also. The homemade noodles add a great deal to the recipe although it can be used with the commercial noodles.

8 ounces (⅓ recipe) Homemade Noodles (see recipe)
1 6- to 7-ounce can tuna
½ cup finely chopped celery
½ cup finely chopped onions
¼ cup (½ stick) margarine
2 tablespoons all-purpose flour
2 cups lukewarm fat-free chicken broth
⅛ teaspoon white pepper
Salt

Cook noodles according to directions. Drain well but do not rinse the noodles. Drain and flake the tuna, saving the oil if they are packed in oil. (Try to have the noodles hot and the sauce ready at the same time.) Fry celery and onions in margarine or in part margarine and the rest of the oil drained from the tuna until the onions are soft but not browned. Sprinkle the flour over the celery and onions and cook over medium heat, stirring constantly, until the flour is absorbed by the vegetables. Add the broth and pepper to the vegetables. Cook and stir over medium heat until the sauce is thickened. Test for seasoning and add salt, if necessary. Combine noodles, tuna, and sauce. Mix lightly and place in a 1½-quart casserole that has been well greased with margarine. Bake at 375° F. for 30 to 40 minutes or until lightly browned.

Low sodium diets: Omit salt. Use salt-free margarine and low sodium noodles, tuna, and broth.

Yield: 4 to 6 servings

SAUCES TO SERVE WITH FISH (United States)

There are many different sauces to serve with fish. Many ingredients combine well and any of them are acceptable as long as they don't include any saturated fats. I like the flavored cream sauces used in some countries. The flavored vinegars are also excellent and low in calories. Melted margarine with some lemon juice in it is good, and a tasty salad dressing is excellent with fish. Finally, we mustn't forget that lemon juice is one of the best.

TANGY TARTAR SAUCE (ABOUT 1¼ CUPS)
1 cup salad dressing
1 tablespoon sweet pickle
   relish
1 teaspoon salad mustard
1 tablespoon chopped parsley
1 tablespoon finely chopped
   onions
¼ cup finely chopped celery
1 tablespoon white vinegar

TARTAR SAUCE (ABOUT 1¼ CUPS)
1 cup salad dressing
¼ cup sweet pickle relish
1 tablespoon lemon juice
1 tablespoon finely chopped
   onions
¼ teaspoon salt

TOMATO HORSERADISH SAUCE (ABOUT 1½ CUPS)
¾ cup catsup
¾ cup chili sauce
1 tablespoon lemon juice
1 teaspoon Worcestershire
   sauce
1 teaspoon prepared mustard

QUICK TARTAR SAUCE (ABOUT 1½ CUPS)
1 cup salad dressing
½ cup grated drained
   cucumbers
2 tablespoons lemon or lime
   juice
¼ teaspoon onion salt

Combine all ingredients and refrigerate until needed.

6
Breads

Bread has always been an important part of the cuisine of most countries, and regional and ethnic breads seem to be having a revival these days. The world is becoming smaller each day, and most people are becoming more knowledgeable about the breads of their own heritage and those that come from other regions, nations, and ethnic groups. I'm happy to see that even the large commercial bakeries are once again beginning to bake and sell some of the old-world breads that have more body and character.

Many of these breads are so high in eggs, shortening, and cream that they can't be used on a low cholesterol diet, but many of them can be easily adapted for the low cholesterol diet. This chapter includes some of my favorites, which we have adapted for my husband Chuck's low cholesterol diet. I hope you will use them and enjoy them as much as we do. I also hope that you will work on the breads of your own regional and/or ethnic background and try to adapt them to your use so that you won't lose that priceless part of your culinary heritage.

I have always enjoyed baking bread. I first learned to make

bread when my grandmother broke her hip when I was eighteen years old. My mother had to go away to take care of her, so I stayed home and kept house for my father and younger sister that term and made up the missed months in college by attending summer school the next year. Anyway, it was unthinkable that we shouldn't have homemade bread, so one of our neighbors taught me to make it. The first batch was a bit too sweet, but my father ate it and said the next baking would be better and it was. He was so proud of my bread. I think it was more important to him than the fact that I kept the house clean and washed and ironed and did all the other household chores.

I continued to like to make bread and used to make bread and rolls in my apartment in Chicago before Chuck and I were married. It is so satisfying to make bread. I've read that your hostilities and anxieties are released when you knead bread and I find that true. I also enjoy the smell of baking yeast breads and rolls. Someone should invent a perfume that smells like baking bread. I think it would catch a husband for more girls than some of the French perfumes.

It isn't advisable to buy many of the special breads commercially because you don't know what is in them unless you read the list of ingredients very carefully and that is impossible in most bakeries. You are safe buying Italian and French breads because they generally consist of flour, water, yeast, salt, and a little oil. Many of the light commercial breads are also safe, mostly because they contain nonfat dry milk and oil to cut costs, but you must be careful to read the list of ingredients very carefully.

Making bread isn't all that difficult, but you do have to pay attention to the correct ingredients and temperatures. I use a thermometer every time I make bread to check the temperature of the liquid used to dissolve the yeast. Yeast is a living organism and can be very tricky. It can be frozen safely, but if you dissolve it at the wrong temperature it will release enzymes that can spoil the whole batch of bread. If you let your bread get warmer than 140° F. while it is rising, the yeast will die and that will ruin the bread very quickly. Yeast grows best at a temperature of 78° to 98° F. Active dry yeast may be stored at room temperature, but compressed yeast must be refrigerated until it is used and should not be kept for more than two to three weeks unless it is frozen. If you have frozen the compressed yeast, it should be allowed to come back to room temperature before it is used. Compressed yeast should be allowed to dissolve in liquid that is at about 85° to 87° F., but active dry yeast should be dissolved in liquid that is at about 110° to 115° F. I have given measures for active dry yeast in these recipes because I find that many people these days are buying their active dry yeast in jars instead of in the package and I wanted them to be able to know how much to use. I find that if you don't want to measure it carefully, you can use 1 tablespoon of bulk yeast for each package with good results. Some of the recipes may seem to call for too much yeast, but it is often necessary to increase the amount of yeast because a heavier dough inhibits the growth of yeast and you need more yeast to keep the dough rising well.

Flour is also very important in bread baking. All-purpose and bread flours have the highest gluten content and are generally added first to the liquid so they can be mixed to develop the gluten. Most people use all-purpose flour, so I have used that in all but one recipe. The use of bread flour is an excellent idea because it is high in gluten and can give strength to breads with a higher content of whole wheat or other specialty flours, but it is a little tricky and you have to follow the recipes exactly when you are using it. Bread flour takes more liquid than does all-purpose flour, so it is best to follow the recipe on the container when you first start using it.

Flours are combined and added all at once in hot breads because their leavening is provided by baking powder or baking soda and it is not necessary to knead them to develop the gluten.

White flour may be stored in a cool dry place, but it is important to refrigerate whole grain flours if they are not used within a few days to prevent rancidity. I like to keep an assortment of various kinds of flours on hand. I take them out of the bags they are packed in and put them in empty gallon jars and then keep them in the freezer until I need them. I am convinced that a high-fiber regimen is good for anyone on a low cholesterol diet, so I try to keep graham, whole wheat, and rye flours on hand and use them whenever possible to keep up the fiber content in Chuck's diet. I find that I can use graham flour in most of my regular bread recipes, using about half and half or 60 percent white flour to 40 percent graham flour, at the very least. Most commercial whole wheat breads are 60 percent white flour and 40 percent whole wheat flour. I like the graham flour because it has the same nutrients as the whole wheat flour but is ground finer and thus is easier to use. It can be substituted in equal measure for white flour, but if you are substituting whole wheat flour for white flour you only use ⅞ cup of whole wheat flour for each cup of white flour.

It is important to use the correct proportion of liquid to dry ingredients in all cooked foods, but this is particularly important in breads. If too little liquid is used in yeast breads, the dough will be heavy and the yeast won't grow as well. If too much liquid is used, the dough will be sticky, hard to handle, and will probably fall when baked. It is difficult to specify the exact amount of liquid that is perfect for a certain amount of flour because some flours absorb more liquid than others. That is why most recipes for yeast breads state a standard amount of liquid and a variable amount of flour.

I use instant dry milk in these recipes because it is convenient, fat free, economical, and convenient to use. It is sometimes dissolved in water before the yeast is added in yeast breads or is added along with the flour and other dry ingredients in quick breads. Milk helps soften the texture of yeast breads, gives a browner crust, and helps retain freshness. I like being able to know that I can keep it in a package and don't have to worry about running out of milk if I want to make some bread unexpectedly. It also spares you from scalding milk before you make bread, which saves some time you can use for something else.

Sugar provides food for the yeast and adds flavor and tenderness to breads. However, a large amount of sugar added to yeast breads will retard the development of the yeast and make the dough heavy, so you will probably have to use a larger amount of yeast for those rich sweet breads that most of us like so well.

Salt improves the flavor of breads and helps strengthen the gluten in yeast breads, but it slows down the action of the yeast so you generally add it after the gluten has been well developed in the first flour added to the liquid. Breads made from rye or whole wheat flour or breads high in milk or fat need more salt. If a low sodium bread is being made, a salt substitute should be used instead of eliminating the salt, because the lack of salt can adversely affect the texture of the bread.

Vegetable oil is used in these recipes because it is an unsaturated fat, and it is convenient, easy to measure, doesn't need to be melted, and yields a good product. Margarine is also sometimes used for flavor. Both fats add tenderness, flavor, and a softened texture to the final breads.

Baking soda is a leavening agent that reacts with acids such as lemon juice, vinegar, molasses, sour milk, and buttermilk. I didn't mention sour cream because it is a no-no on a low cholesterol diet, but baking soda is almost always used for leavening with sour cream as well. I have found that many recipes that use sour cream can be adapted by using ⅔ cup buttermilk and ⅓ cup oil or melted margarine for each cup of sour cream in your recipe. This doesn't work for soups and sauces in which sour cream is added last for flavor, but it will often work when you are using the sour cream in a baked product. Some old recipes tell you to dissolve the soda in liquid. This is because soda used to be hard, but now it is soft and smooth and can be added with the dry ingredients.

Baking powder is a dry leavening agent activated by liquid. Therefore, doughs or batters that use baking powder should be baked as soon as possible after it is added unless the recipe states otherwise.

Liquid egg substitute is a great help in baking because we can't use whole eggs and sometimes the egg whites don't give the same results. I have found that I can use egg whites for the whole eggs in place of 1 or 2 eggs, but if the recipe includes more than 2 eggs, I generally have to use the liquid egg substitute. It comes frozen and should be kept that way until you are ready to use it. It can be defrosted in the refrigerator or in warm water if you need it faster. It should be kept refrigerated after it is defrosted and should be used within a few days. The directions generally specify using ¼ cup liquid egg substitute for each egg and I follow that rule exactly. I find that it is important to have the egg substitute at room temperature, so I generally pour out as much as I will need and let it come to room temperature and then return the rest of it to the refrigerator until needed.

I find that I can make a much better bread by using the dough hook on my mixer. If you do not have a dough hook on your mixer, you can mix the liquids and the first amount of flour in the mixer and then put the remaining flour in a bowl, add the light flour and liquid mixture to it, and finish it by hand, using a large wooden spoon or other mixing spoon. As a matter of fact, you can mix the whole dough without a mixer, if you like. Just follow the general directions, beating by hand instead of with the mixer, being sure that you beat it long enough on the first addition of the flour to develop the gluten or that you knead it long enough after all of the flour is added to develop the gluten.

Most mixes can't be used because they contain dried whole egg, but some of them do not, and if the directions tell you to add an egg and fat to the mix, you may be able to use it. Read the ingredients; if they don't include any ingredients that are prohibited, you can use them with a clear conscience.

BARM BRACK (Ireland)

The Irish call this speckled bread, probably because of the raisins in it, and serve it at Halloween. They wrap a ring for marriage, a coin for wealth, and a button for single blessedness in paper and bake them in the bread so the lucky recipients will know their fate for the coming year.

1½ cups very hot water
⅓ cup instant dry milk
½ cup sugar
2 packages (1½ tablespoons) active dry yeast
2 cups all-purpose flour
2 teaspoons salt
¼ cup liquid egg substitute

¼ cup vegetable oil
2 cups all-purpose flour
1¼ cups raisins
¼ cup chopped orange or lemon peel
1 cup all-purpose flour
Margarine
Sugar

Place water, dry milk, and ½ cup sugar in mixer bowl. Mix at low speed to dissolve the sugar. Cool to 110° to 115° F. Add yeast and let stand for 5 minutes. Add 2 cups flour and mix at low speed, using dough hook, for 3 minutes. Add salt, egg substitute, oil, and the second 2 cups of flour and beat at low speed, using dough hook, for another 2 minutes. Add raisins and peel and mix at low speed for 1 minute or until the fruit is distributed in the dough. Turn dough out on a working surface sprinkled with the remaining 1 cup flour and knead, using as much of the flour as necessary, to form a smooth elastic dough. Form dough into a smooth ball and place in a bowl that has been well greased with margarine. Turn the ball over so the top will be greased, cover, and let stand in a warm place until doubled in volume.

Turn dough out onto a lightly floured working surface and knead lightly. Form into a ball and return to the greased bowl, turning the top of the ball over so it will be greased on top. Cover and let stand in a warm place until doubled in volume.

Turn the dough out onto a lightly floured working surface. Knead lightly. Divide into 2 equal parts. Form each half into a ball, cover, and let rest for 10 minutes. Form each ball into a loaf and place in two 9″ × 5″ × 3″ loaf pans that have been well greased with margarine. Cover and let rise in a warm place until doubled in volume.

Bake at 375° F. for about 45 minutes or until browned. As soon as the bread is removed from the oven, turn out on a wire rack and brush heavily with margarine. Sprinkle sugar generously over the top of the loaf and let cool. (The top of the loaf should be sticky and sweet.)

Low sodium diets: Omit salt. Use 1 teaspoon salt substitute and salt-free margarine.

Yield: 2 loaves

BEER BREAD (Milwaukee)

The recipe for this bread comes from Earl Villmow, a retired lieutenant from the Milwaukee fire department. He says that the men make it often in the firehouse. It is delicious served hot with margarine. Be sure to use self-rising flour. The other kind just doesn't work.

| 1 12-ounce can or bottle of beer | 2 tablespoons sugar |
| 2½ cups self-rising flour | |

Combine room temperature beer, sugar, and flour in mixer bowl and mix at low speed until all the flour is moistened and the batter is comparatively smooth. Pour into a 9″ × 3″ × 5″ loaf pan that has been very well greased with margarine. Cover and let stand at room temperature for 25 minutes.

Bake at 425° F. for 30 minutes or until it is nice and brown.

Low sodium diets: This recipe is not suitable.

Yield: 1 loaf

CHALLAH BREAD (Jewish)

1⅓ cups very hot water	¼ cup (½ stick) softened margarine
¼ cup sugar	
2 packages (1½ tablespoons) active dry yeast	3 cups all-purpose flour
	1 cup all-purpose flour
3 cups all-purpose flour	1 egg white
1 cup liquid egg substitute	¼ cup water
2 teaspoons salt	2 teaspoons sesame seeds

Place hot water and sugar in mixer bowl. Mix at low speed to dissolve sugar. Cool to 110° to 115° F. Add yeast. Mix lightly and let stand 5 minutes. Add 3 cups flour to liquid and beat at low speed, using dough hook, for 4 minutes. Add egg substitute, salt, softened margarine, and another 3 cups flour. Mix at low speed, using dough hook, for another 2 minutes or until a smooth dough is formed. Place 1 cup flour on working surface. Turn the dough out onto the flour and knead, using as much of the flour as necessary, to form a smooth dough. Form into a ball and place in a bowl that has been well greased with margarine. Turn the ball over to grease the top. Cover and let stand in a warm place until doubled in volume.

Turn dough out onto a lightly floured working surface. Knead lightly. Form into a ball and return to the bowl, turning the ball over to grease the top of it. Cover and let rise until doubled in volume.

Turn the dough out onto a lightly floured working surface. Divide the dough into 2 equal portions. Round each portion into a ball. Cover with a cloth and let rest 10 minutes. Divide each ball into 3 equal portions and roll each portion gently to form a roll about 14 inches long. Braid 3 rolls to form a loaf, tucking the ends under the end of the loaf. Place the loaves on 1 or 2 cookie sheets that have been lightly greased with margarine. Cover with a cloth and let stand in a warm place until doubled in volume.

Beat egg white and ¼ cup water together. Brush each loaf with the egg white mixture. Sprinkle with sesame seeds.

Bake at 400° F. for 30 minutes or until the loaves sound hollow when tapped and are lightly browned. Transfer loaves from hot pan to wire rack to cool.

Note: This bread makes marvelous French Toast or Bread Pudding (see Index).

Low sodium diets: Omit salt. Use 1 teaspoon salt substitute and salt-free margarine.

Yield: 2 loaves

LIMPA (Sweden)

This orange- and caraway-flavored rye bread is a favorite in the Dakotas and other parts of the Midwest. It is a dark, rather heavy bread and makes excellent sandwiches.

2 cups hot water
⅓ cup molasses
2 ounces compressed yeast
4 cups all-purpose flour
3 tablespoons vegetable oil
2 tablespoons caraway see

1 teaspoon salt
Finely shredded peel of 1
  large orange
2½ cups rye flour
½ cup all-purpose flour
Softened margarine

Place water and molasses in mixer bowl. Mix lightly and cool to about 85° F. Add yeast. Mix lightly and let stand for 5 minutes. Add 4 cups flour and mix at low speed, using dough hook, for 4 to 5 minutes. Add oil, caraway seed, salt, orange peel, and rye flour. Mix at low speed, using dough hook, for another 2 to 3 minutes or until well mixed. Spread ½ cup flour on working surface. Turn the dough out onto the floured working surface and knead lightly, using as much flour as necessary to form a smooth, rather heavy dough.

Form the dough into a ball and place in a bowl that has been well greased with margarine. Turn the ball over so the top will be well greased. Cover with a cloth and let stand in a warm place until doubled in volume. Turn the dough out onto a lightly floured working surface and knead about 10 times. Return the ball of dough to the bowl, turning the ball again to grease the top. Cover and let rise in a warm place until doubled in volume.

Turn the dough out onto a lightly floured working surface. Divide into 3 equal portions. Form into balls and place on baking sheet that has been well greased with margarine. Cover and let rise in a warm place until doubled in volume.

Bake at 350° F. for 45 minutes or until well browned. Remove to a wire rack and brush with softened margarine.

Low sodium diets: Omit salt. Use unsalted margarine and ½ teaspoon salt substitute.

Yield: 3 medium-sized round loaves

ORANGE CINNAMON BREAD (Greece)

3 cups very hot water
¾ cup instant dry milk
½ cup sugar
⅓ cup dry orange drink mix
2 packages (1½ tablespoons) active dry yeast
4 cups all-purpose flour
1 tablespoon salt

½ cup (1 stick) softened margarine
2 teaspoons ground cinnamon
4 cups all-purpose flour
1½ cups all-purpose flour
1 egg white
¼ cup water

Place 3 cups hot water, dry milk, sugar, and orange drink mix in mixer bowl. Mix at low speed to dissolve sugar and drink mix. Cool to 110° to 115° F. Add yeast. Mix lightly and let stand 5 minutes. Add 4 cups flour to liquid. Mix, using dough hook, at low speed for 4 minutes. Add salt, margarine, cinnamon, and another 4 cups flour. Mix, using dough hook, at low speed for 4 minutes.

Place 1½ cups flour on a working surface. Turn dough out onto flour and knead lightly, using as much of the flour as necessary, to form a smooth elastic dough. Form dough into a ball. Place ball of dough in a bowl that has been well greased with margarine. Turn the ball over so that the top of the ball is greased. Cover with a cloth and let stand in a warm place until doubled in volume.

Turn dough out onto a lightly floured working surface. Knead lightly. Form into a ball and return to the bowl, turning over the top of the ball so that it is greased. Cover with a cloth and let stand in a warm place until doubled in volume.

Turn dough out onto a lightly floured working surface. Divide dough into 3 equal portions. Form each portion into a ball and place each ball in a 9″ cake pan that has been well greased with margarine. Cover with a cloth and let stand in a warm place until doubled in volume.

Mix egg white and ¼ cup water together until smooth. Brush the top of each loaf with the mixture, using a pastry brush. Bake at 350° F. for 1 hour or until well browned. Remove loaves from pans and place on wire racks to cool.

Low sodium diets: Omit salt. Use 1½ teaspoons salt substitute and salt-free margarine.

Yield: 3 loaves

PANETTONE (Italy)

I love this bread. Chuck's cousin used to send us a big loaf of it from Milan, Italy, every Christmas. I tried so many times to make it, but it never tasted quite right to us until I finally found a recipe that used aniseed. It is served at Christmas and other holidays, though it will vary greatly from one city to the other.

Some bakers omit the anise and use orange and lemon peel, and others use candied citron along with pignola nuts. Sometimes it is frosted and it is often baked in tall cans so that the finished bread looks like a mushroom.

2½ cups very hot water
½ cup instant dry milk
¾ cup sugar
½ cup instant dry potatoes
4 drops yellow food coloring
2 packages (1½ tablespoons) active dry yeast
4 cups all-purpose flour
¾ cup (1½ sticks) softened margarine

1½ teaspoons salt
2 cups all-purpose flour
½ cup white seedless raisins
½ cup chopped candied fruit
1½ tablespoons aniseed
¾ cup all-purpose flour
Skimmed milk
Softened margarine

Place hot water, dry milk, sugar, instant potatoes, and food coloring in mixer bowl. Mix lightly to dissolve sugar. Cool to 110° to 115° F. Add yeast and let stand 5 minutes. Add 4 cups flour to liquid. Beat, using dough hook, at medium speed, for 4 minutes. Add ¾ cup margarine, salt, and 2 cups flour to batter. Mix at low speed, using dough hook, for 2 minutes or until well mixed. Add raisins, candied fruit, and aniseed to dough. Beat at low speed about 1 minute or until well mixed.

Place ¾ cup flour on working surface. Turn dough out onto flour and knead, using as much flour as necessary, to form a smooth elastic dough.

Form dough into a ball. Place in a bowl that has been well greased with margarine. Turn the ball over to grease the top of it. Cover with a cloth and let stand in a warm place until doubled in volume.

Turn dough out onto a lightly floured working surface. Knead lightly. Form into a ball and return to bowl. Turn over to grease the top of the ball. Cover with a cloth and let stand in a warm place until doubled in volume.

Turn dough out onto a lightly floured working surface. Knead lightly. Divide into 2 equal portions and round each portion into a ball. Place each ball in a 9″ cake pan that has been well greased with margarine. Cover with a cloth and let stand in a warm place until doubled in volume.

Cut a cross on the top of each loaf with a razor blade or very sharp knife as you would a hot cross bun. Brush each loaf with a pastry brush dipped in milk.

Bake at 350° F. for about 1 hour and 15 minutes or until golden brown and firm. Remove from pans, brush with softened margarine, and cool to room temperature.

Low sodium diets: Omit salt. Use ¾ teaspoon salt substitute and salt-free margarine.

Yield: 2 loaves

WHOLE WHEAT BREAD (United States)

This recipe is neither regional nor ethnic because a good whole wheat bread is a part of everyone's heritage. I wanted to include this recipe because it uses bread flour, which makes it easier to produce a good loaf of whole wheat bread. Bread flour is higher in gluten, so you can use a larger percentage of graham flour than you can with the all-purpose flour; therefore, you get a bread that is tastier with a higher fiber content.

2½ cups very hot water
¼ cup sugar
½ cup instant dry milk
2 packages (1½ tablespoons) active dry yeast
2 cups bread flour
¼ cup (½ stick) softened margarine
2 teaspoons salt
4 cups graham flour
½ cup bread flour
Vegetable oil

Place water, sugar, and dry milk in mixer bowl. Mix to dissolve sugar. Cool to 110° to 115° F. Add yeast and let stand 5 minutes. Add 2 cups bread flour and beat at low speed, using dough hook, for 4 minutes. Add softened margarine, salt, and graham flour. Mix at low speed, using dough hook, for 2 minutes or until smooth. Place ½ cup bread flour on working surface. Turn dough out onto flour and knead, using as much of the flour as necessary, to make a smooth elastic dough.

Form the dough into a ball and place in a bowl that has been well greased with margarine. Turn the ball over to grease the top. Cover and let rise in a warm place until doubled in volume.

Turn the dough out onto a lightly floured working surface. Knead lightly. Form into a ball, turning it over to grease the top. Cover and let stand in a warm place until doubled in volume.

Turn the dough out onto a lightly floured working surface. Divide into 2 equal portions. Round each portion into a ball, cover, and let rest for 10 minutes. Form each ball into a loaf and place in two 9″ × 5″ × 3″ loaf pans that have been well greased with margarine. Brush the top of the loaves with a pastry brush dipped in oil. Cover and let rise until doubled in volume.

Bake at 375° F. for 45 minutes or until well browned and the loaves sound hollow. Transfer to a wire rack and cool to room temperature.

Note: This recipe uses bread flour (not all-purpose flour) and graham flour (not whole wheat flour).

Low sodium diets: Omit salt. Use 1 teaspoon salt substitute and salt-free margarine.

Yield: 2 loaves

CHRISTMAS STOLLEN (Germany)

⅓ cup instant dry milk
½ cup sugar
1 cup hot water
1 ounce compressed yeast
2 cups all-purpose flour
1 teaspoon salt
½ cup liquid egg substitute
1 teaspoon ground cinnamon

¼ teaspoon ground mace
¼ teaspoon ground cardamom
¼ cup vegetable oil
2½ cups all-purpose flour
1 cup mixed diced candied fruit
¾ cup raisins

1 cup all-purpose flour ¼ cup cinnamon sugar
¼ cup (½ stick) softened
margarine

TOPPING
1¾ cups powdered sugar   1 to 2 tablespoons skimmed
2 tablespoons (¼ stick)   milk
softened margarine   ¼ cup chopped pecans
1½ teaspoons vanilla   Candied red and green
cherries

Place dry milk, sugar, and water in a mixer bowl. Mix at low speed to dissolve sugar. Cool to 85° to 87° F. Add yeast and let stand for 5 minutes. Add 2 cups flour to liquid. Mix at low speed, using dough hook, for 2 minutes. Add salt, egg substitute, cinnamon, mace, cardamom, oil, and 2½ cups flour to batter. Mix at low speed, using dough hook, for 2 minutes. Add fruit and raisins and mix at low speed for another 2 minutes. Turn the dough out onto a working surface that has been sprinkled with 1 cup flour. Knead, using as much of the flour as necessary, to form a smooth elastic dough. Form dough into a ball. Place ball in a bowl that has been well greased with margarine. Turn the ball over to grease the top, cover, and let rise in a warm place until doubled in volume.

Turn dough out onto a lightly floured surface. Knead lightly. Divide dough into 2 equal portions. Round each portion into a ball, cover, and let rest on the working surface for 10 minutes. Flatten each portion into an oval about ½ to ¾ inch thick. Brush each oval with half the ¼ cup of margarine. Sprinkle each oval with 2 tablespoons cinnamon sugar over the margarine. Fold lengthwise, not quite in half, and place on a greased cookie sheet. It should resemble a very large Parkerhouse roll. Pinch the ends together. Cover with wax paper and a cloth and let rise again until doubled in volume.

Bake at 350° F. for 40 to 45 minutes or until browned and the stollen sounds hollow when the bottom is tapped. Brush lightly with softened margarine and let cool on a wire rack.

Combine powdered sugar, 2 tablespoons margarine, vanilla,

and skimmed milk and mix until smooth. Spread the top of each of the cooled stollen with ½ of the frosting. Sprinkle chopped pecans on top of the frosting. Decorate with candied red and green cherries. Cut each stollen into 12 equal slices and serve with margarine.

Low sodium diets: Omit salt. Use ½ teaspoon salt substitute and salt-free margarine.

Yield: 2 stollen

NUT ROLLS (Hungary)

1¾ cups very hot water
¾ cup instant dry milk
¼ cup sugar
½ cup instant dry potatoes
2 drops yellow food coloring
1 package (2¼ teaspoons) active dry yeast
2 cups all-purpose flour
2 cups all-purpose flour

½ cup (1 stick) softened margarine
1 teaspoon salt
¾ cup all-purpose flour
Vegetable oil
½ cup (about 4) egg whites
¾ cup sugar
¾ cup ground (not chopped) nuts

Place hot water in mixer bowl. Add dry milk, ¼ cup sugar, dry potatoes, and food coloring. Mix to dissolve sugar. Cool to 110° to 115° F. Add yeast and let stand 5 minutes. Add 2 cups flour to the liquid and mix, using dough hook, for 4 minutes. Add the remaining 2 cups flour, margarine, and salt to the batter. Mix at medium speed, using dough hook, for 2 minutes or until the dough comes away from the sides of the bowl.

Spread ¾ cup flour on a working surface. Turn the dough out onto the flour and knead, using as much flour as necessary, to form a smooth elastic dough. Form the dough into a ball and place in a bowl that has been well greased with margarine. Brush the top of the dough with a pastry brush dipped in oil. Cover and let stand until doubled in volume. Place the dough on a lightly floured working surface. Knead lightly. Divide the dough into 3 equal portions and form each portion into a ball. Cover with a cloth and let rest for 10 minutes.

While the dough is resting, beat egg whites at high speed until stiff. Beat ¾ cup sugar into the egg whites, a little at a time, to form a meringue. Add ground nuts and beat at low speed only until blended. Set aside for later use.

Roll out each ball, 1 at a time, to form a rectangle about 11″ × 15″. Spread ⅓ of the filling on each roll, keeping the filling about 1 inch from the outside of the dough. Roll the dough loosely lengthwise. Pinch the ends together and place on a lightly greased cookie sheet with the open side down. Cover and let rise until doubled in volume.

Bake at 350° F. for 35 to 40 minutes or until browned. Serve warm, if possible.

Low sodium diets: Omit salt. Use ½ teaspoon salt substitute.

Yield: 3 rolls

HOT CROSS BUNS (England)

1¼ cups very hot water
⅓ cup instant dry milk
½ cup sugar
3 packages (6¾ teaspoons) active dry yeast
2 cups all-purpose flour
1 teaspoon salt
1½ teaspoons ground cinnamon
1 teaspoon ground nutmeg
½ cup (1 stick) softened margarine
2½ cups all-purpose flour
½ cup chopped candied fruit
½ cup raisins
Vegetable oil
Plain powdered sugar frosting (optional)

Place water, dry milk, and sugar in a mixer bowl. Mix at low speed to dissolve the sugar. Cool to 110° to 115° F. Add yeast and let stand for 5 minutes. Add 2 cups flour and beat at low speed, using dough hook, for 4 minutes. Add salt, cinnamon, nutmeg, margarine, and 2 cups of the remaining 2½ cups flour. Beat at low speed about 2 minutes. Add fruit and raisins and beat 1 minute at low speed. Place the remaining ½ cup flour on a working surface. Turn the dough out onto the flour and knead lightly, using as much of the flour as necessary, to form a smooth elastic dough. Form the dough into a ball and place in a bowl that has been well greased with margarine. Brush the top of the dough with oil. Cover and let stand in a warm place until doubled in volume.

Turn dough out onto a lightly floured working surface. Knead lightly and form into a ball. Return to greased bowl. Brush the top of the ball lightly with oil. Cover and let rise again until doubled in volume.

Turn dough out onto a lightly floured working surface. Knead lightly. Divide dough into 2 equal portions and form into balls. Cover lightly with a cloth and let rest for 10 minutes. Roll each portion into a roll and divide each roll into 9 equal portions. Roll each portion into a ball and place on cookie sheets that have been lightly greased with margarine. Cover and let rise until almost doubled in volume. Cut a cross in the top of each roll with a razor or very sharp knife. Cover again and let rise until doubled in volume.

Bake at 400° F. for 18 to 20 minutes or until browned. Transfer rolls from cookie sheets to a wire rack to cool. Rolls may be frosted on top or in the cross with a plain powdered sugar frosting, if desired.

Low sodium diets: Omit salt. Use ½ teaspoon salt substitute and salt-free margarine.

Yield: 1½ dozen

KRINGLA (Norway)

This recipe is based on one from Therese Ballantine, who learned to make Kringla as a girl growing up in a Norwegian community in Minot, North Dakota. Kringla, which is really neither bread nor cookie, is generally served hot or lukewarm with coffee or tea. Some cooks brush them with milk or sprinkle them with sugar before they are baked; other cooks frost them with simple icing after they are baked. We like them best served plain with margarine and coffee, and we even like them served very cold.

2 tablespoons lemon juice	2 teaspoons vanilla
Skimmed milk	4 cups all-purpose flour
1¼ cups sugar	1 teaspoon soda
¾ cup (1½ sticks) margarine	1 teaspoon baking powder
2 egg whites	

Place lemon juice in a measuring cup and add enough milk to total ¾ cup liquid. Set aside for later use.

Cream sugar and margarine together until light and fluffy. Add egg whites, milk, and vanilla and mix at low speed to blend. Stir flour, soda, and baking powder together to blend and add all at once to the creamed mixture. Mix 2 minutes at low speed or until well blended. Cover with plastic and refrigerate overnight.

The next day divide dough into 2 equal portions. Roll each piece of dough out on a floured board to form an oblong about 12″ × 4″. Cut the dough with a sharp knife into 24 equal slices, each ½″ × 4″. Roll each piece in your hands to form a roll about 8 inches long and shape into a figure eight or a wreath and place on a cookie sheet that has been lightly greased with margarine.

Bake at 400° F. 10 to 12 minutes or until lightly browned. Remove from baking sheet to wire rack while still warm.

Low sodium diets: This recipe is not suitable.

Yield: about 4 dozen

KOLACHES (Czechoslovakia)

These always look very pretty on a tea table, but they taste so good that they never last long.

2 cups very hot water
¾ cup sugar
⅓ cup instant dry milk
2 packages (1½ tablespoons)
    active dry yeast
3 cups all-purpose flour
½ cup liquid egg substitute

½ cup (1 stick) softened
    margarine
2 teaspoons salt
3½ cups all-purpose flour
Vegetable oil
2 cups cherry, strawberry,
    or apricot jam, or
    poppyseed or prune filling

Place water, sugar, and dry milk in mixer bowl. Mix at low speed to dissolve sugar. Cool to 110° to 115° F. Add yeast and let stand 5 minutes. Add 3 cups flour and beat at low speed, using a dough hook, for 4 minutes. Add liquid egg substitute, margarine, salt, and 2 cups of the remaining 3½ cups all-purpose flour. Beat at low speed for 1 minute or until well combined. Place the remaining 1½ cups flour on a working surface. Turn the dough out onto the flour and knead lightly, using as much of the flour as necessary, to make a smooth elastic dough. Shape the dough into a ball and place in a bowl that has been well greased with margarine. Brush the top of the dough with a pastry brush dipped in oil, cover, and let rise until doubled in volume.

Turn dough out onto a lightly floured working surface. Knead lightly. Divide the dough into 2 equal portions. Form each portion into a ball. Cover with a cloth and let rest for 10 minutes. Form each ball into a roll and cut each roll into 12 equal portions. Form each portion into a ball and place about 1½ inches apart on a cookie sheet that has been lightly greased with margarine. Flatten each roll with the palm of your hand.

Cover and let rise until doubled in volume. Press down the center of each roll with the end of a rolling pin. Fill the center of each roll with about 1 tablespoon jam or filling. Cover and let rolls rise again until doubled in volume.

Bake at 350° F. for about 25 minutes or until lightly browned. Transfer hot rolls from the cookie sheet to a wire rack to cool.

Low sodium diets: Omit salt. Use ½ teaspoon salt substitute and salt-free margarine.

Yield: 2 dozen

BAGELS (Jewish)

Sorry, you can no longer have bagels with cream cheese and
smoked salmon. However, they are good with margarine and
smoked salmon or toasted and served with jelly and margarine.
Frances Nielsen makes these frequently, and they are extra good
when eaten fresh with jelly and margarine.

3 cups very hot water	8 cups all-purpose flour
⅓ cup sugar	1 teaspoon salt
3 packages (2 tablespoons	Hot water
plus 1 teaspoon) active dry	Sugar
yeast	1 egg white
	¼ cup water

Place 3 cups water and ⅓ cup sugar in mixer bowl. Mix lightly
to dissolve sugar. Cool to 110° to 115° F. Add yeast and let stand
for 5 minutes. Add 6 cups flour and salt to liquid and beat at low
speed, using dough hook, for about 6 minutes. Place the remaining 2 cups flour on a working surface. Turn the dough out onto
the flour and knead lightly, using as much of the flour as necessary, to make a smooth, elastic, moderately heavy dough. Round
into a ball. Cover and let rest for 15 minutes. Divide dough into 2
equal portions. Round into balls. Cover and let rest for 15 minutes. Shape each ball into a roll about 12 inches long. Cut each
roll into 12 equal portions. Roll each portion into a ball. Punch a
hole in the center of each roll with a floured finger. Pull gently to
enlarge the hole, working each bagel into a uniform doughnut-
shaped roll. Cover and let rest on a lightly floured surface for 15
minutes.

Put hot water in a shallow pan, adding 1 tablespoon of sugar
for each gallon of water. Bring to a boil. Reduce heat and simmer.
Drop bagels carefully into the pot. Simmer 3½ minutes on each
side. Remove from pot and drain. Place bagels on an ungreased
cookie sheet. Beat egg white with ¼ cup water and brush the
bagels with the mixture. Bake at 375° F. about 35 minutes or
until browned. Transfer bagels from pans while still hot to racks
for cooling. Serve warm or cold or split and toasted.

Low sodium diets: Omit salt. Use ½ teaspoon salt substitute.

Yield: 2 dozen

ONION ROLLS (New York)

1½ cups very hot water
2 tablespoons sugar
3 tablespoons instant dry
  milk
1 package (2¼ teaspoons)
  active dry yeast

2 cups all-purpose flour
2 teaspoons salt
2 tablespoons vegetable oil
1 cup finely chopped onions
1½ cups all-purpose flour
½ cup all-purpose flour

Place water, sugar, and dry milk in mixer bowl. Mix lightly to
dissolve sugar. Cool to 110° to 115° F. Add yeast and let stand for
5 minutes. Add 2 cups flour and beat at low speed, using dough
hook, for 4 minutes. Add salt, oil, onions which have had as much
liquid as possible pressed out of them, and 1½ cups flour. Mix at
low speed for 2 minutes, using a dough hook. Spread ½ cup flour
on working surface. Turn dough out onto flour and knead lightly,
using as much of the flour as necessary, to form a smooth elastic
dough. Form dough into a ball and place in a bowl that has been
well greased with margarine. Turn the ball over to grease the
top. Cover and let stand in a warm place until doubled in volume.

Turn dough out onto a lightly floured working surface, knead
lightly, and return to greased bowl. Turn the ball over to grease
the top of it. Cover and let rise in a warm place until doubled in
volume.

Turn dough out onto lightly floured working surface. Knead
lightly. Divide into 2 equal portions. Round each portion into a
ball. Cover and let rest for 10 minutes. Form each portion into a
roll about 9 inches long. Cut each roll into 9 equal pieces. Round
each piece into a ball and place all of the balls in a 9″ × 13″ cake
pan that has been well greased with margarine. Cover and let
rise until doubled in volume.

Bake at 400° F. for about 20 minutes or until well browned. Remove from heat. Let stand in pan for 3 minutes. Turn out onto wire rack to finish cooling.

Low sodium diets: Omit salt. Use 1 teaspoon salt substitute.

Yield: 1½ dozen rolls

SCHNECKEN (Germany)

1 cup very hot water
½ cup sugar
¼ cup instant dry milk
2 packages (1½ tablespoons) active dry yeast
2 cups all-purpose flour
2 cups all-purpose flour
¼ cup (½ stick) softened margarine
1 teaspoon salt

2 egg whites
1 cup all-purpose flour
2 cups brown sugar
1½ teaspoons ground cinnamon
¾ cup (1½ sticks) melted margarine
½ cup seedless raisins
½ cup chopped nuts

Place water, sugar, and dry milk in mixer bowl. Mix lightly to dissolve sugar. Cool to 110° to 115° F. Add yeast and let stand for 5 minutes. Add 2 cups flour and beat at low speed, using dough hook, for 4 minutes. Add another 2 cups flour, softened margarine, salt, and egg whites. Mix at low speed, using dough hook, for another 3 minutes. Place 1 cup flour on working surface. Turn dough out onto flour and knead, using as much of the flour as necessary, to form a smooth elastic dough. Shape dough into a ball and place in a bowl that has been well greased with margarine. Turn the ball over to grease the top of it, cover with a cloth, and let rise in a warm place until doubled in volume.

While dough is rising, combine brown sugar, cinnamon, and melted margarine. Put a scant 2 teaspoons of the mixture into the bottom of each of 2 dozen muffin tins. Set aside for later use.

Roll dough out on a lightly floured working surface to form a 10″ × 18″ rectangle. Spread the remaining sugar mixture evenly over the rectangle, leaving about a ½-inch border without the sugar mixture. Sprinkle raisins and nuts over the rectangle. Roll into a long roll like cinnamon rolls and cut the roll crosswise into 24 ¾-inch slices. Place each slice, cut side down, in one of the muffin cups. Cover and let rise until doubled in volume.

Bake at 375° F. for 20 to 25 minutes or until well browned. Turn out onto a tray or working surface as soon as they come out of the oven. Serve warm, if possible.

Low sodium diets: Omit salt. Use ½ teaspoon salt substitute and salt-free margarine.

Yield: 2 dozen

STICKY BUNS (Pennsylvania Dutch)

These buns are based on a recipe from Anita Kane. They are wonderful with hot coffee, tea, milk, or alone for that matter. They freeze well and can be reheated by wrapping them loosely in aluminum foil and placing them in a preheated 350° F. oven for 15 to 20 minutes.

1¼ cups very hot water
¼ cup sugar
½ cup instant dry milk
2 packages (1½ tablespoons) active dry yeast
3 cups all-purpose flour
1 egg white
¼ cup vegetable oil
1 cup all-purpose flour
1 teaspoon salt

½ cup all-purpose flour
1 cup (2 sticks) margarine
1⅓ cups brown sugar
4 tablespoons corn syrup
¾ cup brown sugar
1 tablespoon cinnamon
¼ cup vegetable oil
1 cup chopped nuts or raisins (optional)

Place hot water, sugar, and dry milk in mixer bowl. Mix lightly to dissolve sugar. Cool to 110° to 115° F. Add yeast and let stand for 5 minutes. Add 3 cups flour and beat at low speed, using dough hook, for 4 minutes. Add egg white, ¼ cup vegetable oil, 1 cup flour, and salt. Beat for 2 minutes at medium speed. Spread ½ cup flour on working surface. Turn dough out onto flour and knead, using as much of the flour as necessary, to form a smooth elastic dough. Round dough into a ball and place in a bowl that has been well greased with margarine. Roll the dough over in the bowl so the top will be greased. Cover with a cloth and let stand in a warm place until doubled in volume.

While the dough is rising, prepare 4 9″ cake pans by spraying each of them with vegetable spray. Put ¼ cup (½ stick) margarine, ⅓ cup brown sugar, and 1 tablespoon syrup in each pan. Cook and stir over low heat until the mixture is smooth and melted. Set the pans aside in a warm place. (One way to do it is to preheat your oven to 150° F. Turn off the oven and keep the pans in there until needed.)

When the dough has doubled in volume, turn it out onto a lightly floured working surface. Divide it into 4 equal portions and round each portion into a ball. Cover and let rest for 10 minutes.

While the dough is resting, combine ¾ cup brown sugar and cinnamon. Mix well and set aside. Roll each portion of dough out to form an 8″ × 12″ rectangle. Spread each portion with about 1 tablespoon oil and then sprinkle it with ¼ of the cinnamon mixture. Sprinkle with ¼ of the nuts or raisins and roll lengthwise to form a roll about 12 inches long. Cut roll into 9 or 10 equal pieces, just over 1 inch thick. Put the rolls, cut side down, in the cake pans, using each roll for a cake pan. Cover and let rise until doubled in volume.

Bake at 375° F. for 20 minutes. Remove from oven. Cool in pans for 3 minutes and then turn out onto wire racks that have a big piece of wax paper under them. Take any of the syrup left in the pan or any that dribbles down onto the wax paper and put it back on the rolls. Serve warm, if possible.

Low sodium diets: Omit salt. Use ½ teaspoon salt substitute and salt-free margarine.

Yield: 36 or 40

CINNAMON ROLLS (Midwestern United States)

1¼ cups very hot water
1 cup sugar
⅓ cup instant dry milk
2 ounces compressed yeast
2 cups all-purpose flour
2 cups all-purpose flour
½ cup (1 stick) softened margarine
½ cup liquid egg substitute

1½ teaspoons salt
1½ cups all-purpose flour
Vegetable oil

TOPPING
¼ cup (½ stick) softened margarine
¾ cup brown sugar
¾ cup sugar
1 teaspoon ground cinnamon

Place water, 1 cup sugar, and dry milk in mixer bowl. Mix to dissolve sugar. Cool to lukewarm, 85° to 87° F., and add yeast. Let stand for 5 minutes. Add the first 2 cups of flour and beat for 4 minutes, using a dough hook. Add the next 2 cups of flour, ½ cup margarine, egg substitute, and salt and beat about 2 minutes or until well blended. Place 1½ cups flour on a working surface and turn the dough out onto the flour. Knead, using as much of the flour as necessary, to form a smooth elastic dough. Shape the dough into a ball and place in a bowl that has been well greased with margarine. Brush the top lightly with oil using a pastry brush. Cover with a cloth and let stand in a warm place until doubled in volume.

Turn dough out onto a lightly floured working surface. Knead 2 minutes and return to bowl. Brush top of the dough with oil. Cover with a cloth and let rise again until doubled in volume.

Turn dough out onto a lightly floured working surface. Roll into a ball. Cover with a cloth and let stand for 10 minutes.

For the topping, heavily grease an 18″ × 12″ cookie sheet or two 9″ × 13″ cake pans with ½ the margarine. Mix brown sugar and ¾ cup sugar and sprinkle ½ the sugar mixture over the margarine in the baking pan. Roll the dough out to form a 9″ × 16″ rectangle. Spread the remaining margarine evenly over the dough. Sprinkle with the sugar mixture and then with the cinnamon. Roll into a long roll and cut the roll like a jelly roll into 24 pieces. Place the rolls cut side down on the sugar mixture, spacing them evenly. Cover with a cloth and let rise until doubled in volume.

Bake at 375° F. for 30 to 35 minutes or until golden brown. Turn rolls out upside down immediately and serve warm, if possible.

Variation: Whole Wheat Cinnamon Rolls. Substitute 2 cups of graham flour for the second 2 cups of all-purpose flour in the recipe.

Low sodium diets: Omit salt. Use ¾ teaspoon salt substitute and salt-free margarine.

Yield: 2 dozen

BAKED BROWN BREAD (New England)

This bread is baked in a loaf instead of steamed in a mold, but the flavor and texture closely resemble that of the steamed bread.

1 cup skimmed milk	½ teaspoon salt
1 tablespoon vinegar	1½ teaspoons baking soda
1½ cups all-purpose flour	1 cup light molasses
1 cup whole wheat flour	1 egg white
½ cup sugar	2 tablespoons vegetable oil

Combine milk and vinegar and set aside for later use.

Stir flours, sugar, salt, and soda together until well blended.

Combine molasses, egg white, vegetable oil, and milk mixture. Beat together until well blended. Stir milk mixture into flour mixture and beat about 1 minute by hand. Pour batter into a 9″ × 5″ × 3″ loaf pan that has been well greased with margarine.

Bake about 1 hour in a 350° F. oven or until a cake tester comes out clean. Cool 20 minutes in the pan and then turn out onto a wire rack.

Low sodium diets: This recipe is not suitable.

Yield: 1 loaf

BRAN NUT COFFEE CAKE (United States)

TOPPING
¼ cup Bran Buds or All Bran
2 tablespoons sugar
¼ cup brown sugar
1 tablespoon all-purpose
 flour
1 teaspoon ground cinnamon
2 tablespoons margarine
⅓ cup chopped nuts

BATTER
¾ cup (1½ sticks) margarine
¾ cup sugar
1 teaspoon vanilla
2 egg whites
1½ cups all-purpose flour
¼ cup instant dry milk
1 tablespoon baking powder
½ teaspoon salt
¾ cup Brand Buds or All
 Bran
¾ cup water

Combine ¼ cup bran, 2 tablespoons sugar, brown sugar, 1 tablespoon flour, cinnamon, 2 tablespoons margarine, and chopped nuts. Work together to form a coarse crumb. Set aside for later use.

For batter, cream together ¾ cup margarine, ¾ cup sugar, and vanilla until light and creamy. Add egg whites and beat at medium speed until blended. Stir 1½ cups flour, dry milk, baking powder, and salt together to blend. Add all at once with the ¾ cup bran and water to the creamed mixture. Mix at low speed only until the flour is moistened. Spread evenly in a 9″ × 13″ cake pan that has been well greased with margarine. Sprinkle the topping evenly over the batter and bake at 350° F. for about 25 to 30 minutes or until the coffee cake is lightly browned and has pulled away from the sides of the pan. Serve hot, if possible.

Low sodium diets: Omit salt. Use salt-free margarine and low sodium baking powder.

Yield: 1 9″ × 13″ coffee cake

COFFEE CAKE (Jewish)

This is another basic recipe that can be used in a variety of ways. The topping can be omitted and ½ cup of raisins or nuts stirred into the batter. The topping can be swirled through the dough instead of layered, or different toppings can be used. It can be baked in a 9″ tube pan, in a flat 9″ square pan, or it can be baked in muffin tins for individual coffee cakes.

¼ cup brown sugar
½ cup finely chopped pecans
1 teaspoon cinnamon
½ teaspoon vanilla
¾ cup (1½ sticks) margarine
1 cup sugar

1 cup buttermilk
2 egg whites
1 teaspoon vanilla
2½ cups all-purpose flour
1 teaspoon salt
1 teaspoon baking powder
1 teaspoon baking soda

Combine brown sugar, pecans, cinnamon, and ½ teaspoon vanilla and set aside.

Cream margarine and sugar together until light and fluffy. Add buttermilk, egg whites, and 1 teaspoon vanilla. Mix at low speed for ½ minute. Stir flour, salt, baking powder, and soda together to blend. Add to creamed mixture and mix at medium speed for 1 minute.

Spoon ½ of the batter into a 9″ loaf pan that has been well greased with margarine. Spoon ½ of the brown sugar mixture over the batter. Spread the remaining batter over the brown sugar mixture and top with the remaining mixture.

Bake at 350° F. for about 55 minutes or until a cake tester comes out clean. Serve warm, if possible.

Low sodium diets: This recipe is not suitable.

Yield: 1 9″ loaf

SNICKERDOODLE COFFEE CAKE
(Pennsylvania Dutch)

TOPPING

½ cup brown sugar

2 tablespoons (¼ stick) margarine

2 tablespoons all-purpose flour

1 teaspoon ground cinnamon

CAKE

2¼ cups cake flour

1 tablespoon baking powder

2 tablespoons instant dry milk

¼ teaspoon salt

¾ cup washed and drained raisins

½ cup chopped nuts

½ cup (1 stick) softened margarine

¾ cup sugar

2 egg whites

1 teaspoon vanilla

⅔ cup water

Combine brown sugar, 2 tablespoons margarine, 2 tablespoons flour, and cinnamon. Mix to blend. Set aside.

Stir cake flour, baking powder, dry milk, salt, raisins, and nuts together to blend well and set aside.

Cream ½ cup margarine and sugar together until light and fluffy. Combine egg whites, vanilla, and water. Mix with a fork to blend well. Add all at once with the flour mixture to the creamed mixture. Beat at low speed for about 1 minute to blend well. Spread evenly in a 9″ × 13″ cake pan that has been well greased with margarine. Spread the topping evenly over the batter and bake at 375° F. for 20 to 25 minutes or until the cake springs back when touched in the center. Serve hot, if possible.

Low sodium diets: Omit salt. Use salt-free margarine and low sodium baking powder.

Yield: 1 9″ × 13″ coffee cake

BAKING POWDER BISCUITS (United States)

2 cups all-purpose flour
3 tablespoons instant dry
  milk

4 teaspoons baking powder
1 teaspoon salt
3 tablespoons margarine
¾ to 1 cup water

Stir flour, dry milk, baking powder, and salt together to blend well. Cut margarine into the flour mixture until it resembles coarse meal. Add as much of the water as necessary to form a soft dough. (The amount of water will depend on the flour.) Turn the dough out onto a lightly floured working surface and knead it 10 times. Pat or roll the dough out about ½ inch thick. Cut into biscuits with a 2-inch cutter that has been dipped in flour. Place the biscuits on an ungreased cookie sheet and bake at 400° F. for 15 to 20 minutes or until golden brown. Place them close together for soft biscuits and farther apart for crustier biscuits. Serve hot.

Low sodium diets: Omit salt. Use salt-free margarine and low sodium baking powder.

Yield: 10 to 12

SCONES (England)

If you'd like these scones to taste more the way they probably did when our ancestors made them, use brown sugar instead of white and substitute 1 cup of graham flour for 1 cup of the all-purpose flour. I think you'll like the variation as well as this version.

2 cups all-purpose flour	½ cup (1 stick) margarine
1 tablespoon baking powder	½ cup water
½ teaspoon salt	2 egg whites
⅓ cup sugar	½ cup raisins
⅓ cup instant dry milk	

Stir flour, baking powder, salt, sugar, and dry milk together to blend well. Rub or cut the margarine into the flour mixture as you would for baking powder biscuits until you have a coarse crumb. Stir the water and egg whites together with a fork. Add to the flour mixture and stir with a fork to form a soft dough. Add the raisins. Turn the dough out onto a floured working surface and knead about 10 times. Form the dough into a 9-inch round on a cookie sheet that has been well greased with margarine. Cut the dough into 8 equal pie-shaped wedges. Separate the wedges if you like the scones crusty or leave them together if you prefer a softer scone.

Bake at 400° F. for about 25 minutes or until well browned. Serve hot, if possible, with margarine, honey, orange marmalade, or other jam or jelly.

Low sodium diets: Omit salt. Use salt-free margarine and low sodium baking powder.

Yield: 8 scones

GINGERBREAD (Scandinavia)

This doesn't taste like American gingerbread, but it is very good. It tastes more like a bread than a cake even though it does contain 2 cups of sugar.

	1 teaspoon baking soda
½ cup liquid egg substitute	1 teaspoon baking powder
2 cups brown sugar	½ teaspoon salt
3 cups all-purpose flour	1 cup buttermilk
2 teaspoons cinnamon	⅔ cup (1⅓ sticks) softened
1 tablespoon ground ginger	margarine
1 teaspoon cardamom	Dry bread crumbs

Place liquid egg substitute and sugar in mixer bowl. Mix at medium speed until light and foamy.

Stir flour, cinnamon, ginger, cardamom, soda, baking powder, and salt together. Add all at once with buttermilk and softened margarine to creamy mixture. Beat 2 minutes at medium speed.

Spread the batter evenly in a 9″ × 13″ cake pan that has been well greased with margarine and dusted with bread crumbs.

Bake at 350° F. for about 30 minutes or until a cake tester inserted in the center comes out clean.

Serve warm, if possible, with margarine and jam or jelly or Lemon Sauce (see Index).

Low sodium diets: This recipe is not suitable.

Yield: 1 9″ × 13″ gingerbread

CORN BREAD (Northern United States)

This is our favorite corn bread recipe and I make it at least a couple of times a month. I like it with soup or salad or just with a meal. I generally make it in an 8″ pan because I like it thicker, but it is thinner and crustier in a 9″ pan.

1 cup cornmeal	⅓ cup instant dry milk
1 cup all-purpose flour	1 cup water
4 teaspoons baking powder	1 egg white
⅓ cup sugar	¼ cup vegetable oil
¼ teaspoon salt	

Place cornmeal, flour, baking powder, sugar, salt, and dry milk in mixer bowl and mix at low speed to blend well. Beat water, egg white, and oil together with a fork and add all at once to the dry mixture. Beat at low speed only until the flour is moistened. Pour into an 8″- or 9″-square pan that has been well greased with margarine.

Bake at 400° F. for about 25 minutes for a 9″ pan or 30 to 35 minutes for an 8″ pan. Serve hot, if possible, with honey, sorghum, jam, or jelly and margarine.

Low sodium diets: Omit salt. Use low sodium baking powder.

Yield: 1 8″ or 9″ square

CORN BREAD (Southern United States)

This is a true Southern corn bread that is meant to be baked in a hot iron skillet. The oil is heated in the skillet before it is poured into the batter and the skillet is then put back onto the heat so it will be really hot when the batter is poured into it. The corn bread is baked until it is golden brown, crusty, and utterly delicious.

2 cups cornmeal
½ cup all-purpose flour
2 teaspoons baking powder
½ teaspoon baking soda

2 tablespoons sugar
1 teaspoon salt
2 cups low-fat buttermilk
½ cup liquid egg substitute
⅓ cup vegetable oil

Place cornmeal, flour, baking powder, soda, sugar, and salt together in mixer bowl. Mix at low speed for 1 minute to blend. Mix buttermilk and egg substitute together and add to cornmeal mixture. Mix at low speed only until the cornmeal is moistened. Add oil, which has been warmed in the skillet. Pour the batter into the hot skillet.

Bake at 450° F. for about 20 minutes or until the corn bread is browned. Serve hot with margarine.

Low sodium diets: This recipe is not suitable.

Yield: 1 10″ round

LIGHT BRAN MUFFINS (United States)

I am so convinced that a high fiber diet helps bring down your cholesterol level that I want to include as many recipes with a high fiber content as possible. This is one of our favorites, which Chuck likes best when ½ cup chopped dates or nuts are added. I especially like them with ½ cup raisins added.

⅓ cup sugar	2 cups Bran Buds or All
⅓ cup vegetable oil	Bran
⅓ cup instant dry milk	1½ cups all-purpose flour
2 egg whites	4 teaspoons baking powder
½ teaspoon salt	½ cup chopped dates, nuts, or
1¼ cups water	raisins (optional)

Place sugar, oil, dry milk, egg whites, salt, and water in mixer bowl. Mix at low speed until well blended. Stir bran, flour, baking powder, and dates, nuts, or raisins together to blend. Add all at once to liquid and mix at low speed only until the flour is moistened.

Fill muffin tins that have been well greased with margarine or lined with liners about ⅔ full of batter. (It is important to work as quickly as possible here.)

Bake at 400° F. for 20 to 25 minutes or until muffins are lightly browned and firm in the center.

Low sodium diets: Omit salt.

Yield: 1 dozen

GOLDEN BRAN MUFFINS (United States)

½ cup (1 stick) margarine
⅓ cup sugar
2 egg whites
¾ cup All Bran or Bran Buds
1¼ cups water
2 cups all-purpose flour

4 teaspoons baking powder
½ teaspoon salt
⅓ cup instant dry milk
1 cup raisins or chopped nuts
or ½ cup chopped candied
fruit (optional)

Cream margarine and sugar together until light and fluffy. Add egg whites, bran, and water. Mix at low speed to blend and let stand for 10 minutes. Stir flour, baking powder, salt, dry milk, and raisins, nuts, or candied fruit together. Add to creamed mixture and mix at low speed only until flour is moistened.

Place about ¼ cup mixture in each of 12 paper-lined muffin cups and bake at 400° F. for 20 to 25 minutes or until lightly browned and center springs back when touched. Serve warm, if possible.

Low sodium diets: Omit salt. Use salt-free margarine and low sodium baking powder.

Yield: 1 dozen

CORNMEAL MUFFINS
(Midwestern United States)

This was my mother's favorite recipe; she used to make it when we were children. I remember that she especially liked to serve these muffins with bean soup on cold winter days.

¼ cup (½ stick) margarine
¼ cup sugar
½ cup liquid egg substitute
1 cup water

1 cup all-purpose flour
1 cup cornmeal
⅓ cup instant dry milk
1 tablespoon baking powder
½ teaspoon salt

Cream margarine and sugar together until light and fluffy. Combine egg substitute and water and set aside. (It is important that the water and egg substitute be at room temperature.) Stir flour, cornmeal, dry milk, baking powder, and salt together to blend well. Add flour mixture and liquid at the same time to the creamed mixture and beat at low speed only until the flour is moistened. Fill muffin cups about ⅔ full of batter. (Grease muffin cups well with margarine or line them with paper liners.)

Bake at 375° F. for about 25 minutes or until browned. Serve hot, if possible, with margarine, jam, or jelly.

Low sodium diets: Omit salt. Use salt-free margarine and low sodium baking powder.

Yield: 1 dozen

SPOON BREAD (Southern United States)

½ cup white cornmeal
1 teaspoon sugar
½ teaspoon salt
¾ cup boiling water
¼ cup (½ stick) softened margarine
⅔ cup skimmed milk
⅓ cup liquid egg substitute
2 teaspoons baking powder

Place cornmeal, sugar, and salt in mixer bowl. Add boiling water. Mix at low speed until smooth. Add margarine and mix at low speed until margarine is blended into the batter. Cool to room temperature. Add milk and egg substitute. Mix only to blend. Add baking powder. Mix lightly and pour into an ungreased 1-quart casserole.

Bake at 325° F. for 30 to 35 minutes or until a silver knife inserted in the center comes out clean. Serve hot.

Low sodium diets: Omit salt. Use salt-free margarine and low sodium baking powder.

Yield: 3 to 4 servings

TOASTED GARLIC BREAD (Italy)

½ cup (1 stick) softened   1-pound loaf French or
  margarine   Italian bread sliced into 16
½ teaspoon garlic powder   slices

Combine margarine and garlic powder and mix to blend well.
(Any leftover mixture may be kept in the refrigerator until
needed.) Brush each slice of bread with the garlic mixture and
place on a cookie sheet. The slices may be shingled, if necessary.
Heat in a 400° F. oven for about 15 minutes or until the edges are
toasted and golden brown. Serve hot.

Low sodium diets: Use salt-free margarine.

Yield: about 8 servings

7
Salads

Salads, an important part of the low cholesterol diet, add both texture and good nutrition to your menus. They are low in calories unless you add a lot of high-calorie dressing to them. They are also filling and add fiber as well as vitamins and minerals to your diet. Since they are so important, they should be fresh, crisp, colorful, and tasty. Generally, they should be served chilled and should be as attractive as possible.

In many countries salads are not served with the entree as they are here. Rather, they are served as a separate course or as part of a smorgasbord or buffet. Some countries use salads such as the famous Greek salad or the tomato and meat salads of Italy and Spain as a main course. Tossed or green salads are always appropriate with Italian, Greek, Spanish, and Hungarian meals, but they don't seem to serve salads in Great Britain very often. I was there once for three weeks and the only salad I had while I was there was one prepared specially for me by some friends in Ireland when I was staying at their home.

I love the custom of serving chilled cooked vegetables with a dressing as they do in some parts of Europe and in South America. Once, when I was visiting friends in Buenos Aires, the cook served a big dish of cooked marinated vegetables and my hostess told me she couldn't get her to serve fresh vegetables. She didn't think they were good for the digestion and absolutely refused to prepare them because she felt they would make our hostess sick.

A good tossed salad begins with clean, crisp, cold greens. Greens lose texture and nutrients from day to day, even when properly refrigerated. Salad greens are fragile and must be stored carefully. It is best not to wash them until shortly before they are to be used. Everyone has a different idea about the best way to keep greens fresh. Some cooks like to wash them and wrap them in a damp towel and put them in the vegetable section of the refrigerator. Others, including myself, like to clean them and put them in a plastic container in the refrigerator. If they are wilted, you can often soak them for a short time in clear cool water to revive them and then pat them dry and refrigerate them until you need to use them. Salad dressings shouldn't be added until just before you want to serve a green salad and the dressings should be light and not overpowering.

I am so pleased that manufacturers are finally putting information on salad dressings that indicates the amount of cholesterol in the dressing. We have always known that we could use the vinegar and oil dressings made with an approved oil, but it is nice to know that my favorite salad dressing, Miracle Whip, is so low in cholesterol that I can use it freely without worrying about the cholesterol content. Now all I have to worry about is the calories. I have included some of my favorite dressings in this chapter, but feel free to use any dressings you like in the salad recipes, as long as the cholesterol count listed on the label is low and the dressing doesn't include any cheese, cream, or other forbidden goodies.

I am also happy to include in this chapter a recipe for Creamless Cheese made from skimmed milk and instant dry milk. It really is good and I hope you'll try it. Chuck and I both missed cream cheese, which is a no-no on a low cholesterol diet, and we were pleased when I found the recipe for cheese made from skimmed milk. It really isn't hard to do and the cheese is a good substitute in many recipes that call for cream cheese. We like it in salads, for dips, or served with fresh fruit. I even used it in cream cheese and jelly sandwiches. It just proves that you can come up with a pretty good substitute for almost any item you are missing on your low cholesterol diet.

I hope you will enjoy the salads in this chapter and will use some of these techniques to adapt your own favorite salads to your low cholesterol diet.

CRANBERRY RELISH (New England)

This was a great favorite of my grandfather, William Hall. My mother always made it for him during the holiday season. He thought it tasted like fresh strawberries and I agree with him.

1 pound fresh cranberries	1 large tart red apple
1 navel orange	1¾ cups sugar

Wash cranberries, discarding any soft or discolored berries. Drain well. Grind coarsely and place in a mixing bowl. (I use my food processor for this.) Wash orange and peel and keep the orange peel, discarding the white membrane and any seeds. Cut orange into chunks and grind coarsely with the peel. Add to cranberries. Wash apple and remove the core and any bruised spots. Grind coarsely and add with sugar to the cranberry mixture. Mix lightly to blend. Cover and refrigerate at least 24 hours before serving.

Low sodium diets: May be used as written.

Yield: 3 to 4 cups

FRIJOLE SALAD (Southwestern United States)

1 cup rinsed and drained
  kidney beans
⅔ cup Basic French Dressing
  (see recipe)
4 cups shredded cabbage
½ cup thinly sliced sweet
  onions or green onions and
  tops

1 cup diced drained fresh
  tomatoes
½ cup peeled and thinly
  sliced cucumbers

Combine well-drained beans and French Dressing (see Index). Cover and refrigerate overnight. Just before serving, place cabbage in mixing bowl and place beans, onions, tomatoes, and cucumbers on top. Toss lightly or toss at the table just before serving.
Note: Lettuce may be substituted for cabbage, if desired.

Low sodium diets: Use beans cooked without salt and low sodium salad dressing.

Yield: 6 to 8 servings

GARDEN COTTAGE CHEESE (United States)

¼ cup chopped radishes
¼ cup finely chopped onions
½ cup finely chopped celery
¼ cup finely chopped fresh
  green peppers
1 cup thinly sliced
  cucumbers

1 teaspoon salt
2 tablespoons Salad Dressing
  (see recipe)
1½ pounds low fat cottage
  cheese

Combine radishes, onions, celery, green peppers, and cucumbers. Toss lightly. Add salt to Salad Dressing (see Index) and mix well. Add well-drained cottage cheese to vegetable mixture. Refrigerate until served. Drain off any liquid before serving.

Notes: This should be prepared as close to serving time as possible. Use any variety of fresh vegetables you prefer—chives, well-drained chopped tomatoes, slivers of fresh cauliflower, grated carrots, etc.

Low sodium diets: Omit salt. Use low sodium salad dressing.

Yield: about 5 cups

KIM CHE (Korea)

Dr. Crockett sent this recipe, which he says is hot and smelly but a very good appetizer when served cold and in small portions. It will keep for several days in the refrigerator and is, in fact, better the second day.

½ medium-sized head of cabbage	½ teaspoon salt
¼ cup rock salt	2 teaspoons sugar
2 medium-sized carrots	2 tablespoons vegetable oil
3 green onions	2 tablespoons sesame oil
1 to 4 chopped garlic cloves	½ teaspoon cayenne pepper or paprika

Cut cabbage into bite-sized pieces and sprinkle with rock salt. Let stand for ½ hour or until the cabbage is wilted. Place cabbage in a colander and rinse well to remove all of the salt. While the cabbage is wilting, clean carrots and shred coarsely and chop onions. Drain the cabbage well and place in a mixing bowl. Add the carrots and onions to the cabbage. Combine garlic, salt, sugar, oils, and pepper or paprika. Mix with a fork and add to the vegetables. Mix well to coat the vegetables with the dressing and refrigerate for a minimum of 24 hours until needed. Serve chilled in small portions or use as part of a relish or appetizer tray.

Low sodium diets: Omit salt. Wash the cabbage very well to remove all of the rock salt.

Yield: 1½ to 2 cups

MACARONI SLAW (Germany)

This recipe, which was given to me by Elfrieda Schmal, combines two of the favorite dishes for picnics. It is excellent not only for picnics but for buffets and cold suppers as well.

2 cups uncooked macaroni
3 cups finely shredded
  cabbage
1 cup coarsely shredded
  carrots

½ cup finely chopped fresh
  green peppers
½ cup finely chopped onions
1 cup Cole Slaw Dressing
  (see recipe)
Parsley

Cook macaroni according to directions on the package. Rinse under cold water and drain very well.

Combine cabbage, carrots, green peppers, onions, and Cole Slaw Dressing (see Index). Toss lightly. Add drained macaroni and toss lightly again. Refrigerate until served. Just before serving, drain off any liquid, place in a bowl, and garnish with parsley.

Low sodium diets: Cook macaroni without salt and use low sodium Cole Slaw Dressing (see Index).

Yield: about 2 quarts

RED CABBAGE SALAD (Germany)

This recipe comes from Sara Seedorf of Arlington, Iowa, who told me she got it from a very old German-American cookbook that had been in her family a long time. Sara and her sister, Hazel Oldfather, recently made several trips to Germany and report that they really enjoyed the food, including the many different ways they served red cabbage.

½ medium-sized head of red
  cabbage
¼ cup vegetable oil
1 teaspoon sugar
1 peeled and diced tart apple

2 tablespoons vinegar
¼ cup dry red or white wine
1 teaspoon caraway seed
Salt and pepper to taste
Imitation bacon bits

Shred red cabbage as you would for cole slaw and set aside. Combine oil, sugar, apple, vinegar, and wine. Cook and stir over moderate heat until the sugar is dissolved. Pour hot over the shredded cabbage. Add caraway seed, salt, and pepper. Toss lightly to coat the cabbage with the hot dressing. Sprinkle with imitation bacon bits and serve at room temperature.

Low sodium diets: Omit salt. Garnish with parsley instead of bacon bits.

Yield: 4 to 6 servings

CUCUMBER SALAD (Hungary)

Frances Sonitzky, who gave me this recipe, says it is a basic Hungarian dish. You should prepare it to suit your own taste using these approximate measures. You may want to use more onion or more or less sugar, and you may want to add just a whisper of white pepper. Frances says she especially likes this salad because it can be prepared several hours before it is served without loss of flavor.

2 medium-sized cucumbers
¾ teaspoon salt
2 tablespoons finely chopped
  onions
4 teaspoons sugar

2 tablespoons white vinegar
2 tablespoons evaporated
  skimmed milk
Paprika

Slice cucumbers as thin as possible. Sprinkle with salt and let stand at room temperature for 1 or 2 hours. Drain well and squeeze as much of the juice out of the cucumbers as possible between the palms of your hands. Add onions, sugar, vinegar, and milk. Taste and add additional seasonings if desired. Refrigerate until ready to serve. Sprinkle with paprika and serve chilled.

Low sodium diets: Omit salt.

Yield: 2 to 4 servings

CUCUMBERS WITH CREAMY DRESSING
(Poland)

2 large cucumbers	1 teaspoon salt
Boiling water	1 tablespoon sugar
Very cold water	Dash of white pepper
½ cup evaporated skimmed milk	1 teaspoon chopped fresh dill or dill weed
1 tablespoon white vinegar	Chopped chives or parsley

Wash cucumbers well. Do not peel them if they are fresh and tender, but do peel them if they are older with tough skins. Slice cucumbers as thin as possible. (A food processor is a big help here.) Cover cucumbers with boiling water and let stand 10 minutes. Drain well and immerse in very cold water. Drain well and refrigerate for 30 minutes. Drain well again.

Combine milk, vinegar, salt, sugar, pepper, and dill and pour over cucumbers. Mix well and refrigerate until served. Garnish with chopped chives or parsley.

Low sodium diets: Omit salt.

Yield: 2 to 4 servings

POTATO SALAD (India)

3 medium-sized Idaho
  potatoes
1 tablespoon chopped green
  onions
½ cup finely chopped celery
1 cored and chopped
  medium-sized tart red
  apple

¾ cup drained pineapple
  chunks
½ cup Salad Dressing (see
  recipe)
½ teaspoon salt
⅛ teaspoon white pepper

Wash potatoes and cook in their skins until tender. Cool potatoes, peel and chop potatoes, and place in a bowl. Add onions, celery, apple, and pineapple. Mix Salad Dressing (see Index), salt, and pepper together and mix into potatoes and fruit. Refrigerate at least 1 hour before serving.

Low sodium diets: Omit salt. Use low sodium salad dressing.

Yield: 4 to 6 servings

POTATO SALAD (Italy)

This recipe is a favorite of Frances's daughter, Neta Kallhauge. She likes to serve it in the summer for picnics or buffet suppers.

2 pounds (6 medium) red
  potatoes
½ cup chopped chives or
  green onions
¼ cup finely chopped celery
2 tablespoons chopped
  pimientos

Salt and pepper to taste
½ cup Italian-style vinegar
  and oil dressing
Chopped parsley
Vinegar and oil dressing

Wash the potatoes well. Cover them with boiling water and cook about 20 minutes or until tender. Drain them in a colander and peel them as soon as you can handle them. Slice the potatoes about ¼ inch thick and layer them with the chives or onions, celery, and pimientos, sprinkling each layer with salt and pepper to taste and Italian dressing. Toss lightly and sprinkle with parsley. We prefer this salad warm, though it can be served at room temperature. If it is necessary to refrigerate the salad, it should be allowed to return to room temperature before it is served. (Do *not* try to reheat it in your microwave. I tried it once and it was a disaster.) Vinegar and oil dressing should be served with the salad for those who prefer salad with more dressing.

Low sodium diets: Omit salt. Use low sodium vinegar and oil dressing.

Yield: 6 to 8 servings

GRATED POTATO SALAD (Iowa)

Gladys Thomas first developed this potato salad when she and her husband, Art, had a restaurant in Elkader, a beautiful town surrounded by hills just northeast of Wadena. It proved to be so popular that now it is used by many people in this area.

4 large russet potatoes
1 cup salad dressing
¼ cup finely chopped onion
¼ cup finely chopped celery
¼ cup chopped pimiento
¼ cup finely chopped pickles
Chopped whites of 4 hard-
  cooked eggs
½ teaspoon salt
Sprinkle of white pepper
Salad Dressing (see recipe)

Cook potatoes in their skins about 20 minutes or until tender. Cool to room temperature, peel, and grate coarsely. (You should have about 4 to 5 cups grated potato.)

Place Salad Dressing (see Index) in a mixing bowl. Add onion, celery, pimiento, pickles, egg whites, salt, and pepper. Mix together. Add potatoes and mix gently to coat the potatoes with dressing. Sprinkle with salt and pepper and mix lightly. Taste for seasoning and add more salt and pepper, if desired. You may also need to add a little more dressing, depending on the amount of potatoes you use. Place salad in a bowl, cover, and refrigerate for at least 2 hours before serving.

Low sodium diets: Omit salt. Use low sodium salad dressing.

Yield: 6 to 8 servings

TOMATO SALAD (Germany)

3 medium (about 1 pound)
  ripe red tomatoes
½ cup finely chopped onions
1 tablespoon chopped parsley
½ teaspoon salt

Sprinkle of pepper
¼ cup salad dressing
2 tablespoons evaporated
  skimmed milk
Imitation bacon bits

Wash and core tomatoes and cut into about 1-inch cubes. Place tomatoes in a colander and allow them to drain for 15 to 20 minutes. Place the drained tomatoes in a salad bowl. Sprinkle onions, parsley, salt, and pepper over tomatoes. Toss lightly and refrigerate for 1 hour or until served. Combine salad dressing and milk and refrigerate until later. Just before serving, add dressing to tomato mixture. Toss gently. Sprinkle with imitation bacon bits and serve cold.

Low sodium diets: Omit salt and imitation bacon bits.

Yield: about 6 servings

SUMMER SALAD (Italy)

This is one of Chuck's favorite salads, which he likes to make with the very first ripe tomatoes from the garden.

3 medium (about 1 pound)   ½ cup Italian-style vinegar
  ripe red tomatoes   and oil dressing
1 medium sweet onion   Chopped parsley
1 medium fresh green
  pepper

Wash and core tomatoes. Cut each into about 8 wedges. Place tomatoes in a colander and allow them to drain for 15 to 20 minutes. Place drained tomatoes in the bottom of a salad bowl. Peel onion and cut it into thin slices. Wash green pepper, remove the core, and slice into thin julienne strips. Place onion slices and green pepper strips on tomatoes. Add dressing and toss lightly. Refrigerate for about 1 hour before serving. Toss lightly and serve with some of the dressing for each salad. Garnish with parsley and serve cold.

Low sodium diets: Use low sodium salad dressing.

Yield: about 6 servings

PIQUANT SALMON SALAD (Italy)

1 1-pound can salmon   ¼ cup chopped stuffed green
4 ounces rotini   olives
¾ cup Italian-style vinegar   1 cup drained cooked peas
  and oil dressing   2 medium-sized ripe red
¼ cup finely chopped onions   tomatoes

Drain salmon, remove skin and bones, and break into bite-sized pieces. Refrigerate salmon until needed.

Cook rotini according to package directions. Drain well but do not rinse. Pour salad dressing over rotini and toss to coat each piece well with dressing. Add salmon, onions, olives, and peas to the rotini. Toss lightly and serve immediately or refrigerate until needed. Garnish with tomatoes that have been cut into wedges just before serving the salad.

Note: Rotini is a form of spaghetti. If it is unavailable, shell macaroni or another shape of pasta may be used.

Low sodium diets: This recipe is not suitable.

Yield: 6 to 8 servings

TUNA AND BEAN SALAD (Italy)

This salad is good on an antipasto tray. It can be served at room temperature or chilled and looks good on a buffet in a pretty glass bowl or on lettuce when used for individual salads.

4 cups (2 16-ounce cans) washed drained kidney or white beans
½ cup Italian-style vinegar and oil dressing
1 6- to 7-ounce can tuna
½ cup thinly sliced celery
¼ cup minced onions
1 tablespoon chopped parsley
2 tablespoons chopped pimiento

Place drained beans in mixing bowl. Add dressing and mix well to coat all the beans with dressing. Drain the tuna well and add to the beans along with the celery, onions, parsley, and pimiento. Mix lightly and serve immediately or refrigerate until serving time.

Low sodium diets: Use 4 cups beans cooked without salt and low sodium tuna and salad dressing.

Yield: 6 to 8 servings

APPLE SALAD (Midwestern United States)

Kathryn Knochel gave me this recipe, which is sweet and yet tart, a perfect accompaniment for chicken, turkey, or very lean ham.

1 3-ounce package lemon-
  flavored gelatin
1¾ cups boiling water
1 cup Creamless Cheese (see
  recipe)

1½ cups cored and chopped
  tart red apples
½ cup finely chopped celery
½ cup chopped English
  walnuts

Dissolve gelatin in boiling water and cool to room temperature. Stir Creamless Cheese (see Index) into the gelatin. Add apples, celery, and nuts. Pour into a 1½-quart glass bowl. Refrigerate until firm.

Low sodium diets: Use low sodium Creamless Cheese (see Index).

Yield: 4 to 6 servings

PINEAPPLE CHEESE SALAD
(Midwestern United States)

1 3-ounce package lemon-
  flavored gelatin
1 cup boiling water
¾ cup pineapple juice
½ cup Creamless Cheese (see
  recipe)

1 tablespoon chopped
  pimientos
1 cup drained crushed
  pineapple

Dissolve gelatin in water. Add pineapple juice and refrigerate until syrupy but not thickened. Stir cheese into the thickened gelatin, add pimientos and pineapple, and pour into a 1-quart glass bowl or mold. Refrigerate until firm.

Low sodium diets: Use low sodium pineapple. Do not use fresh pineapple because there is an enzyme in fresh pineapple that will prevent the gelatin from becoming firm.

Yield: 4 to 6 servings

SPICY PEACH SALAD
(Midwestern United States)

2 cups (1 16-ounce can) sliced
   peaches
Water
¼ cup white vinegar
½ cup sugar

1 stick cinnamon
¼ teaspoon whole cloves
1 3-ounce package orange-
   flavored gelatin

Drain peaches well and refrigerate until needed. Add enough water to the juice to yield 2 cups liquid. Add vinegar, sugar, cinnamon, and cloves. Cover and simmer for 10 minutes. Strain and add hot liquid to the gelatin. Stir until the gelatin is thoroughly dissolved. (If the peaches were canned in heavy syrup, use only ¼ cup sugar.) Cool to room temperature. Pour into a 1½-quart glass bowl, add the reserved chilled peach slices, and refrigerate until firm.

Low sodium diets: May be used as written.

Yield: 4 to 5 servings

CREAMLESS CHEESE (United States)

Chuck really missed cream cheese and I missed being able to use it in salads, dips, and as a sandwich spread. This version is really very simple to make and I think you'll like it as well as we do.

2 quarts skimmed milk
1 cup instant dry milk

¼ cup buttermilk
1 teaspoon salt

Combine skimmed milk, dry milk, and buttermilk. Pour into a stainless steel pan or bowl. Cover tightly and let stand at room temperature for 24 to 48 hours or until it has formed a soft curd and looks like a soft yogurt.

Line a colander with a square of muslin or old linen dish towel. Pour the milk mixture into the cloth and let it drain for 1 hour. Place the colander and the cloth with the curd in it in a cake pan to collect the drippings, place the whole thing in a plastic bag, and refrigerate it for 24 hours. Collect the drippings at the end of 12 hours and then return it to the refrigerator for the rest of the time. At the end of 24 hours, turn the curd into another clean cloth inside the colander and let it drain for another 12 hours. Turn the drained curd into a bowl and stir the salt into it. Place the cheese in a container. Cover tightly and refrigerate until needed.

This cheese forms an excellent base for recipes that specify cream cheese. It makes good dips, is good in salad dressings and salads, and is good with jelly or olives for a sandwich spread.

Note: If the cheese is still too soft, turn it into another clean cloth and let it stand for another 3 hours.

Low sodium diets: Omit salt.

Yield: about 2½ cups

Salad Dressings

BASIC FRENCH DRESSING (France)

¾ cup vegetable oil
¼ cup white vinegar
1 teaspoon salt
1 teaspoon sugar
1 teaspoon paprika
½ teaspoon dry mustard
Dash of pepper

Combine oil, vinegar, salt, sugar, paprika, mustard, and pepper in a 1-pint jar. Shake vigorously until well mixed. Refrigerate until needed. Shake well before using.

Low sodium diets: Omit salt.

Yield: about 1 cup

COLE SLAW DRESSING (United States)

1¼ cups Salad Dressing (see recipe)
1 cup sugar

½ cup white vinegar
2 tablespoons celery seed
4 teaspoons salt

Combine Salad Dressing (see Index), sugar, vinegar, celery seed, and salt and mix well. Refrigerate until needed.

Low sodium diets: Omit salt. Use low sodium salad dressing.

Yield: about 2 cups

CREAMY GARLIC DRESSING (United States)

1½ cups Salad Dressing (see recipe)
1 cup evaporated skimmed milk

½ to 1½ teaspoons garlic powder

Combine Salad Dressing (see Index) and milk and mix until smooth. Add garlic powder, ½ teaspoon at a time, until it is the strength you desire. The amount of garlic powder will depend on the strength of the powder and how well your family likes garlic. (Do not use garlic salt for seasoning.)

Creamy Onion Variation: Substitute onion powder for garlic powder. (Be careful to use onion powder and not onion salt.)

Low sodium diets: Use low sodium salad dressing.

Yield: about 2 cups

MAYONNAISE (France)

½ cup liquid egg substitute
¾ teaspoon salt
½ teaspoon dry mustard
¼ teaspoon paprika

½ teaspoon sugar
2 tablespoons white vinegar
1 cup vegetable oil

Place egg substitute, salt, mustard, paprika, sugar, vinegar, and ½ cup oil in blender or food processor. Cover and beat on medium-high speed just until blended. Pour the remainder of the oil slowly into the blender or food processor while it is running. If necessary, stop and use a rubber spatula to push the mixture down to keep it running into the blades. Keep mayonnaise refrigerated until needed.

Low sodium diets: Omit salt.

Yield: 1½ cups

HERB DRESSING (Italy)

2 teaspoons chopped parsley
½ teaspoon chopped basil
½ teaspoon leaf oregano
¼ cup water

¾ cup vegetable oil
¼ cup white vinegar
1 teaspoon sugar
¼ teaspoon salt

Place parsley, basil, oregano, and water in a 1-pint jar. Let rest for 10 to 15 minutes. Add oil, vinegar, sugar, and salt and shake vigorously. Refrigerate until needed. Shake well before using on tossed green or fresh vegetable salads.

Low sodium diets: Omit salt.

Yield: about 1¼ cups

SALAD DRESSING (United States)

This dressing is particularly good on potato, kidney bean, or pea salad and it mixes well with ground meats for sandwiches.

1 cup liquid egg substitute	1 cup sugar
1 cup water	2 teaspoons salt
1 cup white vinegar	⅛ teaspoon white pepper
2 teaspoons dry mustard	2 tablespoons cornstarch
	2 cups vegetable oil

Beat egg substitute, water, and vinegar together until smooth. Place in the top of a double boiler over simmering water. Combine mustard, sugar, salt, pepper, and cornstarch, mix well, and beat into the liquid. Cook, stirring occasionally, until the starchy taste is gone. (You can cook this over moderate heat if you like, but you must watch it carefully and stir it constantly if you do.) Transfer sauce to mixer bowl and cool to room temperature.

Add the oil very slowly to the cooked sauce, beating at high speed, until all the oil has been absorbed. Place in a 1-quart jar or other container and refrigerate until needed.

Low sodium diets: Omit salt.

Yield: about 1 quart

TOMATO SOUP DRESSING (United States)

Anita Kane, who sent me this recipe, says she likes this dressing particularly well on tossed green salads or lettuce, and we do too.

2 tablespoons grated onion	½ cup vinegar
1 minced garlic clove	2 tablespoons dill vinegar
¼ cup sugar	Dash of tabasco sauce
½ teaspoon salt	1 10¾-ounce can tomato soup
½ cup vegetable oil	

Combine onion, garlic, sugar, salt, oil, vinegar, dill vinegar, tabasco sauce, and soup and beat at medium speed until thick and well blended. (A food processor or blender does this more efficiently than a mixer.) Refrigerate until needed. Shake well before using on tossed green salads or lettuce.

Note: If you can't get dill vinegar at your store, soak 1 tablespoon dill seed in ¼ cup white vinegar for a couple of days, drain well, and use the vinegar as directed above.

Low sodium diets: This recipe is not suitable.

Yield: about 2½ cups

VINAIGRETTE DRESSING (France)

This is the dressing Frances Nielsen makes that we like so well. She uses it on tossed green salads and fresh vegetables such as sliced tomatoes or cooked and chilled green beans, Brussels sprouts, broccoli, etc.

2½ cups vegetable oil	1 teaspoon paprika
1¼ cups white, brown, wine, or tarragon vinegar	2 tablespoons chopped parsley
⅔ cup powdered sugar	2 garlic cloves
1½ tablespoons soy sauce	⅓ cup finely chopped onions

Combine oil, vinegar, sugar, soy sauce, paprika, parsley, and garlic. Mix well and serve over greens or other vegetables. Refrigerate when not in use, but bring back to room temperature before using. Add the onions to the sauce just before it is used. Onions may be left in the sauce up to 1 week before it is used, but after that the onions will lose their quality.

Low sodium diets: Omit soy sauce.

Yield: about 1 quart

8

Vegetables

Fruits and vegetables are the guys in the white hats when you are on a low cholesterol diet. Any and all are welcome, with the exception of coconut, and they can do no wrong as long as you don't add any saturated fats such as butter, cream, or bacon when you are preparing them. They are low in calories and high in vitamins, minerals, fiber, and taste appeal.

I never completely understood Frances's enthusiasm for the first spring vegetables until I discovered that, in Europe, those vegetables are greeted with festivals in many areas. I only knew that to Frances and Chuck the first asparagus, the first little new potatoes, and the first strawberries are eagerly awaited and enjoyed to the utmost. Here, in Iowa, as in New England, we always hope to have creamed new potatoes and peas for the fourth of July. In fact, Chuck always plants some potatoes that are considered early potatoes so he will have some for that very important date. If the whole hill isn't ready, he goes out to "snitch" some potatoes by pulling some little potatoes out of each hill, using his fingers to find them without disturbing the rest of the potatoes in the hill. Frances always enjoys that and thinks that snitching them is great fun.

It is important to me that vegetables be fresh. I like my green beans fresh from the garden and think they should be cooked or frozen within a couple of hours of picking. I marvel at how people can buy and use those tired-looking green beans you see at the supermarket when you know they have probably been picked and stored for several days before they are sold. I think it is far better to buy frozen vegetables if you can't get fresh ones from your own garden, from a vegetable market, or from a supermarket whose staff really cares about the quality of the vegetables.

Most people also agree that vegetables should be cooked in a small amount of water and only until they are tender, not until they are completely exhausted. However, since any vegetables can be used freely on a low cholesterol diet, you can feel free to cook them any way, as long as they appeal to you and your family. They can be braised, boiled, stir fried, baked, used in salad, served plain or with seasoned margarines. The most important thing is that they be served in whatever form they will be enjoyed so that you and your family can take advantage of the many good qualities of the vegetables.

Most sections of the United States and other countries have an amazing variety of vegetables and vary their preparation in countless ways. I haven't even included a good sampling here— just a few of our favorites, which I hope you will also enjoy. I hope that these will inspire you to seek out other ways to prepare vegetables to add a little more interest to your meals, along with all the fiber, vitamins, and minerals.

BRAISED BEETS AND CELERY
(Midwestern United States)

My cousin's wife, LaVerle Sniffin, served this to us one day when they invited us for Sunday dinner. I loved it and even Chuck, who generally hates beets, told me later that he liked it.

3 tablespoons minced onions	½ teaspoon salt
3 tablespoons margarine	⅛ teaspoon pepper
2 cups cooked diced beets	1½ tablespoons vinegar
2 cups cooked celery	

Fry onions in margarine in a heavy frying pan over medium heat until soft but not browned. Add drained beets and celery, salt, pepper, and vinegar. Heat thoroughly, stirring occasionally, and serve hot.

Low sodium diets: Omit salt. Use salt-free margarine and beets and celery that have been cooked without salt.

Yield: 4 to 6 servings

BAKED BEANS (Sweden)

4 cups (2 16-ounce cans) beans in tomato sauce
1 large tart red apple, washed, cored, and diced
¼ cup raisins
½ cup chopped onions
½ cup chopped very lean ham
¾ cup brown sugar
¼ cup drained sweet pickle relish
1 teaspoon salad mustard
¾ cup catsup

Combine beans, apple, raisins, onions, ham, brown sugar, pickle relish, mustard, and catsup. Mix well and pour into a shallow casserole. Bake, uncovered, at 250° F. for 1½ to 2 hours or until beans are dry and lightly browned. Serve hot or at room temperature.

Low sodium diets: This recipe is not suitable.

Yield: 6 to 8 servings

BAKED BEAN SANDWICH (New England)

This sandwich is surprisingly good and is high in protein as well as in fiber. The amount of salad dressing depends on the dryness of the beans, but you should aim for a smooth, not a sloppy, filling. Some people like to add a little mustard, but I generally have mustard in my baked beans so I don't add any to the filling.

4 cups dry baked beans
   without bacon or other fat
   meat
1 cup finely chopped celery
½ cup finely chopped fresh
   green peppers

½ cup finely chopped onions
½ cup drained pickle relish
Salad dressing
Lettuce (optional)

Place baked beans, celery, green peppers, onions, and pickle relish in a mixing bowl. Mix with a spoon, adding salad dressing, if necessary. Serve on whole wheat, rye, or pumpernickel bread that has been spread with softened margarine. Lettuce is optional.

Low sodium diets: Use low sodium baked beans and salad dressing and omit pickle relish.

Yield: about 5 cups filling

SWEET LIMA BEANS (Germany)

Gladys Thomas, who is a full-time nursing home administrator and is active in many other organizations, says this recipe is a favorite of her family. However, it does take time, so they sometimes have to wait until she has the time to prepare it.

2⅓ cups (1 pound) dried lima
   beans
Water
2 tablespoons grated onion

2¾ cups (1 pound) brown
   sugar
Salt and pepper to taste

Look over beans, discarding any dark or discolored ones. Cover beans with water and let stand overnight. During the next morning, add water to cover beans generously and cook, covered, over low heat until tender. Drain well.

Add onion, brown sugar, salt, and pepper to beans. Mix lightly and place in a casserole. Cover and bake at 300° F. for about 6 hours or until beans are browned and glazed. (It may be necessary to remove the cover for the last hour of baking time to glaze the beans properly.) Beans should retain their shape and not be mushy. Serve warm, if possible.

Low sodium diets: Omit salt.

Yield: 6 to 8 generous servings

THREE-BEAN BAKE (Minnesota)

My cousin's wife, Glenda Thronson, brought this along to a family reunion in Minnesota. It is rather like baked beans and yet not really, because of the meat in it and the variety of beans. We all enjoyed it very much.

1½ pounds lean ground beef	½ cup finely chopped onions
4 cups (2 16-ounce cans) kidney beans	1 cup brown sugar
	1 cup catsup
4 cups (2 16-ounce cans) meatless beans in tomato sauce	2 tablespoons vinegar
	1 tablespoon salad mustard
	1 teaspoon salt
2 cups (1 16-ounce can) cooked dried lima beans	⅛ teaspoon pepper

Fry meat in its own fat in a heavy frying pan over moderate heat, stirring constantly, until browned and well broken up. Drain well and discard the liquid. Wash and drain the kidney beans and combine with the browned meat, meatless beans and tomato sauce, drained lima beans, onions, brown sugar, catsup, vinegar, mustard, salt, and pepper. Mix lightly and place in a shallow casserole. Bake at 350° F. for 1 hour. Serve hot or lukewarm.

Low sodium diets: Omit salt. Use low sodium beans or beans cooked without salt and low sodium catsup.

Yield: about 12 servings

EGGPLANT AND NOODLES (Italy)

1 1-pound eggplant
½ cup coarsely chopped
  onions
½ cup coarsely chopped fresh
  green peppers
1 minced garlic clove
¼ cup vegetable oil

2 cups (1 16-ounce can)
  Italian plum tomatoes
¼ cup chopped parsley
¾ teaspoon salt
⅛ teaspoon pepper
1 teaspoon sugar
4 ounces dry noodles
Hot beef broth

Wash eggplant and remove ends. Cut into 1-inch cubes without removing the skin. Fry over moderate heat with onions, green peppers, and garlic in vegetable oil, stirring occasionally, in a heavy frying pan, until eggplant is transparent and tender. Add tomatoes, parsley, salt, pepper, and sugar. Cook and stir over moderate heat until hot. Add noodles and simmer, stirring occasionally, 5 to 8 minutes or until noodles are tender, adding hot broth ¼ cup at a time, if the mixture becomes too dry. Serve hot.

Low sodium diets: Omit salt. Use low sodium tomatoes or fresh tomatoes. Use low sodium beef broth.

Yield: 4 to 6 servings

RATATOUILLE (the Mediterranean)

1 1-pound eggplant
2 6- to 8-inch zucchini
Vegetable oil
¾ cup coarsely chopped
  onions
¾ cup coarsely chopped fresh
  green peppers

1 minced garlic clove
2 cups (1 16-ounce can)
  chopped canned tomatoes
  and juice
¾ teaspoon salt
⅛ teaspoon pepper
1 teaspoon sugar
1 tablespoon chopped parsley

Wash eggplant and zucchini. Remove ends and cut eggplant into ¾-inch cubes. Cut zucchini into ¼- to ½-inch slices. Fry eggplant and zucchini in as much oil as necessary in a heavy frying pan over moderate heat, stirring occasionally, for about 10 minutes or until eggplant is transparent. Transfer eggplant and zucchini to a casserole, using a slotted spoon.

Fry onions, peppers, and garlic in the same frying pan used for the eggplant and zucchini, adding more oil, if necessary, until the onions are transparent. Transfer to the casserole with a slotted spoon and sprinkle over the eggplant and zucchini. Pour tomatoes and juice over the vegetables. Sprinkle salt, pepper, sugar, and parsley over the tomatoes and mix lightly.

Bake, uncovered, at 350° F. for 1 hour or until vegetables are almost dry, stirring every 15 minutes during the baking time. Serve hot as a vegetable or lukewarm as an appetizer.

Low sodium diets: Omit salt. Use low sodium canned tomatoes or fresh tomatoes.

Yield: 6 to 8 servings

FRIED OKRA (Southern United States)

1 pound fresh or frozen okra   ½ teaspoon salt
½ cup white cornmeal   ⅛ teaspoon pepper
⅓ cup all-purpose flour   Vegetable oil

Thaw okra, if necessary, and cut into 1-inch pieces. Dredge in a mixture of cornmeal, flour, salt, and pepper. Fry in vegetable oil on a griddle or in a heavy frying pan for about 10 minutes or until golden brown. Serve hot.

Low sodium diets: Omit salt.

Yield: 6 servings

PASTA SHELLS AND PEAS (Italy)

8 ounces pasta shells	2 tablespoons vegetable oil
2 cups (1 16-ounce can)	2 tablespoons margarine
canned peas	¼ cup finely chopped parsley
1 cup minced onions	½ teaspoon salt
2 minced garlic cloves	Sprinkle of black pepper

Cook shells according to package directions. Drain well and rinse with cold water. Drain peas and set both aside for later use.

Fry the onions and garlic in the oil and margarine until onions are transparent but not browned. Combine drained shells and peas, onions, garlic and the fat in which they were cooked, parsley, salt, and pepper. Cover and bake at 350° F. for 20 minutes. Serve hot.

Low sodium diets: Omit salt. Use salt-free margarine, pasta cooked without salt, and 1 pound frozen peas cooked without salt instead of the canned peas.

Yield: 6 servings

PICKLED VEGETABLES (Greece)

This recipe is one of Dr. Crockett's favorites. The vegetables are usually served cold or at room temperature as an appetizer or vegetable.

2 cups small pickling onions	1 teaspoon sweet basil
3 cups fat-free chicken broth	1 teaspoon salt
1 cup dry white wine	6 sprigs fresh parsley
1 cup olive oil	1 pound whole mushrooms
½ cup lemon juice	2 whole fresh green peppers
2 sliced garlic cloves	2 whole fresh sweet red
1 tablespoon pickling spices	peppers
1 teaspoon tarragon	1 medium crookneck squash
	1 medium zucchini

Peel onions, cover with boiling water, and simmer 1 minute. Drain and set aside for later use.

Combine broth, wine, and oil. Bring to a boil and add lemon juice, garlic, pickling spices, tarragon, basil, and salt. Cover and simmer 10 minutes. Add onions and parsley. Cover and simmer 10 minutes. Add mushrooms and simmer, uncovered, for another 10 minutes. Add peppers, which have been washed, seeded, and cut into julienne strips, and squash, which have been washed but not peeled and cut into about 1-inch cubes. Simmer another 10 to 15 minutes. Remove from heat and refrigerate at least 24 hours before serving.

Low sodium diets: Omit salt. Use low sodium broth.

Yield: about 6 cups

BRAISED SAUERKRAUT (Germany)

3½ cups (1 29-ounce can)
  sauerkraut
2 chicken bouillon cubes
Hot water
½ cup chopped onions

2 tablespoons vegetable oil
2 tablespoons brown sugar
2 tablespoons all-purpose
  flour

Drain sauerkraut well and discard the juice. Place sauerkraut and bouillon cubes in a saucepan, adding just enough hot water to cover; cover and simmer over low heat for 1 hour. Drain kraut, discard liquid, and return the kraut to the saucepan. While the kraut is cooking, fry onions in vegetable oil over low heat, stirring occasionally, until onions are golden. Add onions and oil to the kraut. Combine sugar and flour and sprinkle over the kraut. Cook and stir over moderate heat until sugar and flour are absorbed into the kraut. Serve hot.

Low sodium diets: This recipe is not suitable.

Yield: 4 to 6 servings

STIR-FRIED VEGETABLES (China)

This recipe, from my friend Jean Smith of Clancy, Montana, adds fiber, flavor, and texture to your lunch or dinner—you can't do much better than that.

3 tablespoons margarine
4 cups shredded cabbage
2 cups bias-cut celery
1 cup chopped onions

1 cup chopped fresh green
   peppers
¾ teaspoon salt
Soy sauce

Melt margarine over low heat in deep pan. Add cabbage, celery, onions, and green peppers. Sprinkle with salt. Cook and stir vegetables over high heat for 5 minutes. Cover and cook 3 to 5 minutes over low heat or until vegetables are crisp-tender. Serve immediately with soy sauce.

Low sodium diets: Omit salt and soy sauce. Use salt-free margarine and ⅛ teaspoon white pepper.

Yield: 4 to 6 servings

WHITE SAUCE (United States)

BASIC INGREDIENTS	AMOUNTS FOR THIN SAUCE	AMOUNTS FOR MEDIUM SAUCE	AMOUNTS FOR THICK SAUCE
Margarine	2 tablespoons (¼ stick)	¼ cup (½ stick)	6 tablespoons (¾ stick)
All-purpose flour	2 tablespoons	¼ cup	6 tablespoons
Instant dry milk	⅔ cup	⅔ cup	⅔ cup
Warm water	2 cups	2 cups	2 cups
Salt	¼ teaspoon	¼ teaspoon	¼ teaspoon
Pepper (optional)	Sprinkle	Sprinkle	Sprinkle

Stir margarine and flour together in a small saucepan over low heat until the margarine is melted and the margarine and flour mixture is smooth. Stir the dry milk into the warm water and add all at once to the flour mixture. Cook and stir over moderate heat until the sauce is smooth and thickened. Continue to cook over low heat, stirring frequently, for about 3 minutes or until the starchy taste is gone. Add salt and pepper, stir well, and use as desired.

Variation: Veloute Sauce. Substitute 2 cups chicken, beef, or fish bouillon for the warm water.

Low sodium diets: Omit salt. Use salt-free margarine. Use low sodium bouillon when preparing the veloute sauce.

Yield: 2 cups

WHITE SAUCE MADE WITH A WHIP
(United States)

I remember the first time Frances Nielsen showed me how to make this sauce. I didn't think it would work, and it won't unless you use a whip. However, it is faster and much simpler than the standard method for making white sauce, and it gives a smoother product. This recipe is for 1 cup, but you can increase it as much as you like, as long as you keep the basic ingredients in proportion.

INGREDIENTS	THIN	MEDIUM	THICK
All-purpose flour	1 tablespoon	2 tablespoons	3 tablespoons
Softened margarine	1 tablespoon	2 tablespoons	3 tablespoons
Instant dry milk	⅓ cup	⅓ cup	⅓ cup
Salt	¼ teaspoon	¼ teaspoon	¼ teaspoon
Pepper (optional)	Sprinkle	Sprinkle	Sprinkle
Boiling hot water	1 cup	1 cup	1 cup

Stir flour, margarine, dry milk, salt, and pepper together to blend well. Stir all at once into the rapidly boiling water, using a whip. (A spoon will not give you a smooth white sauce.) Cook, stirring frequently, over low heat for about 3 to 5 minutes or until the starchy taste is gone.

Variation: Velouté Sauce. Substitute 1 cup chicken, beef, or fish bouillon for the hot water.

Low sodium diets: Omit salt. Use salt-free margarine. Use low sodium bouillon when preparing the velouté sauce.

Yield: 1 cup

DRESSING FOR FRESH VEGETABLES
(Missouri)

My friend Beatrice Eskew of Gainesville, Missouri, uses this dressing for the wonderful fresh vegetables they grow in their garden.

½ cup vinegar	Salt and pepper to taste
1 cup honey	Fresh tomatoes, cucumbers,
2 cups water	celery, lettuce, zucchini, etc.

Combine vinegar, honey, and water. Mix well to dissolve the honey. Keep refrigerated until used. Add salt and pepper to fresh vegetables according to taste. Add the dressing just before serving or pass the dressing at the table along with the fresh vegetables.

Low sodium diets: Omit salt.

Yield: about 3½ cups

9

Potatoes and Potato Substitutes

Potatoes and potato substitutes are complex carbohydrates that we need for complete nutrition. Potatoes, rice, and bulgur are all cholesterol-free, and noodles and dumplings may also be cholesterol-free if they are prepared with liquid egg substitute and/or egg whites.

All countries have some source of carbohydrates that are an accepted part of their daily diet. It is only here in America and in some of the European countries that potatoes are a part of every-day meals. Potatoes can be prepared in many ways; all ways are acceptable if they are prepared without added saturated fat. Please don't feel you need to be restricted to the recipes in this chapter; this is really only a sampling of the many ways in which potatoes and potato substitutes can be prepared.

Potatoes are a source of vitamin C and fiber as well when you eat the potato skins. Yams provide a very good source of vitamin A and also provide fiber. Brown rice will provide some of the B vitamins, though polished rice provides only carbohydrate unless it is served with other foods to enrich the nutritional value of the combination.

Pasta is also a good source of carbohydrate without cholesterol if it is made at home with liquid egg substitute or if you purchase the commercial type, which is made with very little egg content. Some pasta recipes using a fatty sauce can be very high in cholesterol, but if you are careful to use homemade sauce that you have prepared without saturated fats, it can be a wonderful addition to your menus. I would have hated to think that we couldn't have any pasta and sauce in our home, so one of the first recipes I really worked on when we found out about Chuck's high cholesterol count was spaghetti sauce.

My grandfather wanted potatoes three times a day, generally fried with bacon fat and served every morning with bacon and eggs. My brother-in-law loved those rich Italian sauces made with fat meat, and my uncle loved his eggs bathed in bacon fat and his cheese with every meal. These were all part of the workingman's diet and they enjoyed every bite of them, but I wonder how they would have felt about them then if they had known that it was going to give them arteriosclerosis or hardening of the arteries that would eventually kill all three of them.

Potatoes can be prepared in many ways that will provide a good healthy meal without increasing the cholesterol count. They don't need to be fried in bacon fat. They can be fried in vegetable oil if you must have them fried, and baked potatoes are luscious with cottage cheese or yogurt. Have you tasted them with the new product called Butter Buds? They are really good. Just remember that it isn't the baked potato itself that is harmful; it is all that goop you put on it that makes it high in calories and high in cholesterol.

I also wish that we in this country would take better advantage of bulgur and brown rice, which are very good for you. I didn't include any recipes for the preparation of brown rice in this chapter because the directions for preparation are on every package and the brown rice can be substituted for white rice in most recipes. All it needs is longer preparation time than the white rice. Bulgur also may be substituted for white rice in most recipes for rice, taking only a little longer cooking time than the white rice.

COLCANNON (Ireland)

In Ireland, it is customary to make a dent in the top of each serving of Colcannon and put a pat of margarine into the dent before it is served.

4 medium-sized white
  potatoes
Boiling water
½ teaspoon salt
¼ cup (½ stick) margarine
½ teaspoon salt

⅛ teaspoon white pepper
¼ cup evaporated skimmed
  milk
2 cups shredded cabbage
½ cup boiling water
½ teaspoon salt

Wash and peel potatoes and cut into quarters. Cover with boiling water and ½ teaspoon salt and simmer about 15 minutes or until tender. Drain well. Cover with a clean cloth and let them rest for 5 minutes to let any excess moisture escape. Add margarine, ½ teaspoon salt, pepper, and milk to potatoes and beat until light and fluffy.

While the potatoes are cooking, place the cabbage, ½ cup boiling water, and ½ teaspoon salt in a covered saucepan and simmer for 12 minutes or until tender. Drain well and beat into the hot mashed potatoes. Serve hot.

Low sodium diets: Omit salt. Use salt-free margarine.

Yield: 4 to 6 servings

MASHED POTATOES WITH APPLESAUCE
(Holland)

2 cups hot mashed potatoes
¼ cup (½ stick) margarine
2 cups unsweetened
  applesauce

2 tablespoons sugar
½ teaspoon nutmeg
½ teaspoon salt

Prepare mashed potatoes as you would ordinarily for your family. While the potatoes are still hot in the mixer bowl or pan, add margarine and beat until margarine is absorbed. Add applesauce, sugar, nutmeg, and salt and mix well. Taste for seasoning and add more, if desired. If you are using sweetened applesauce, omit the sugar until you have tasted it to be sure you need it. You don't want it too sweet. The tartness of the applesauce along with the bland mashed potatoes is the secret of the success of this dish, which is a favorite supper dish in Holland. Serve hot or put into a 1½-quart casserole, swirling the top of the mixture to look pretty, and refrigerate until needed. When you want to serve it, put it into a 400° F. oven for about 30 minutes or until the potatoes and applesauce are lightly browned and serve hot.

Low sodium diets: Omit salt. Use salt-free margarine.

Yield: about 4 servings

POTATOES ANNA (France)

Frances Nielsen sometimes fixes potatoes this way when we aren't cutting calories. They are delicious and look pretty on the platter.

6 medium-sized white potatoes	**½ cup (1 stick) margarine**
	1 teaspoon salt
	⅛ teaspoon white pepper

Peel potatoes and slice them about ¼ inch thick. Wash the slices well in cold water; drain and pat dry with a clean dish towel. Grease the bottom and sides of a 1½-quart casserole very heavily with part of the margarine. Arrange a layer of potatoes in the bottom of the casserole; sprinkle with salt and pepper and dot with margarine. Repeat until the dish is full, leaving a little of the margarine to place on top of the potatoes. Cover tightly with a lid or aluminum foil and bake at 350° F. for 1 hour or until the potatoes are tender. Turn carefully out onto a warm dish and serve hot. The potatoes should be molded and lightly browned.

Low sodium diets: Omit salt. Use salt-free margarine.

Yield: 6 servings

POTATOES COOKED IN BROTH (Belgium)

6 medium-sized white
  potatoes
Hot fat-free chicken broth
⅛ teaspoon thyme

1 tablespoon chopped parsley
Salt to taste
2 tablespoons melted
  margarine

Peel potatoes and cut lengthwise into quarters. Place in a saucepan and cover with hot broth. Add thyme, parsley, and salt to taste and simmer over low heat for 15 to 20 minutes or until the potatoes are tender. Drain potatoes well and serve sprinkled with the melted margarine.

Low sodium diets: Omit salt. Use low sodium broth.

Yield: 6 servings

POTATO PANCAKES (Germany)

This is another of Frances Nielsen's specialties that she generally makes for Chuck and Ed Gernand when she is visiting us. She always makes an extra-large batch so we can have some to freeze, though once in a while they are so hungry for them that there aren't any left. Ed likes his potato pancakes served with cream-style corn, but Chuck likes them with the traditional applesauce.

2 cups grated white potatoes
½ cup grated onions
⅓ cup all-purpose flour
½ teaspoon baking powder
½ teaspoon salt

⅛ teaspoon pepper
2 tablespoons chopped
  parsley
¼ cup liquid egg substitute
Vegetable oil

Peel potatoes and grate them coarsely. Squeeze as much juice as possible from them with your hands and then roll them in a clean linen towel to squeeze out the very last bit of juice. Put the potatoes in a mixing bowl and add onions, flour, baking powder, salt, pepper, parsley, and egg substitute, in that order. Mix well and then fry them in one of the two following ways:

1. Heat ½ inch oil in heavy frying pan until there is a haze above it. Drop ¼ cup batter into the hot oil, using the back of a spoon to form a 3-inch round. Fry the pancake over moderate heat until it is brown and crisp on the bottom. Turn and continue to fry until it is crisp on the other side. Transfer to a paper towel and keep warm until all the pancakes have been cooked. Serve hot.

2. Heat a heavy frying pan with a thin coating of oil over moderate heat for two minutes. Drop about ¼ cup pancake batter onto the hot oil. Spread with the back of a spoon to form about a 4- to 4½-inch pancake. Fry 6 to 7 minutes on one side or until browned. Turn and fry on the other side until browned. Remove to a paper towel and keep hot until served.

Low sodium diets: Omit salt.

Yield: 6 to 8

POTATO PIE (Germany)

This potato pie recipe from Hazel Gernand was originally topped with cubed bacon or salt pork. We certainly can't have that, but Chuck and I both like it with imitation bacon bits for flavor instead of bacon or salt pork.

4 cups mashed potatoes
1 cup chopped onions
¼ cup (½ stick) margarine
⅓ cup evaporated skimmed
  milk

Salt and pepper to taste
⅓ cup imitation bacon bits
1 unbaked 9-inch pie crust

Prepare mashed potatoes as you ordinarily would for your family, using as much seasoning and milk and margarine as you generally do. While the potatoes are cooking, fry the onions until transparent but not browned in as much of the margarine as necessary. Beat the onions with all the margarine into the hot mashed potatoes along with the milk. Taste for seasoning and add salt and pepper as desired. Beat the bacon bits into the potato mixture and spread it evenly in the pie crust, making swirls in it to make it look attractive. Bake at 350° F. for about 1 hour or until the crust is done and the potatoes are browned. Cut into wedges like pie and serve hot.

Low sodium diets: Omit salt and bacon bits. Use salt-free margarine and increase the onions to 1½ cups.

Yield: 4 to 6 servings

YAM SOUFFLE (Southern United States)

3 large fresh yams ½ teaspoon salt
Boiling water ½ cup sugar
½ teaspoon salt ½ cup chopped walnuts
½ cup dry sherry ½ cup liquid egg substitute
½ cup (1 stick) margarine

Peel yams and cut into cubes. Cover with boiling water and ½ teaspoon salt. Bring to a boil and simmer 20 to 25 minutes or until tender. Drain well and allow them to stand, covered with a clean cloth, for 5 minutes to dry as much as possible. Place yams in mixer bowl and mix at medium speed until mashed and smooth. (You should have about 4 cups mashed yams.) Add sherry, ½ teaspoon salt, sugar, walnuts, egg substitute, and margarine. Mix at moderate speed until well blended. Place mixture in a 1½-quart casserole, swirling the top to look attractive. Bake at 350° F. for 30 to 45 minutes or until browned. Serve hot.

Note: The yams may be prepared ahead of time and refrigerated until needed. Bake refrigerated yams about 1 hour at 350° F. or until browned and serve hot.

Low sodium diets: Omit salt. Use salt-free margarine.

Yield: 6 to 8 servings

FRIED CORNMEAL MUSH (New England)

The Italians call this polenta, the Rumanians call it mamaliga, and my mother called it cornmeal mush. I used to serve Chuck polenta with meat sauce and my mother cornmeal mush out of the same crockpot, and I'm sure that an Indian woman living here many years ago would have eaten it with the same delight as they did.

2 tablespoons margarine	1 teaspoon salt
3 cups boiling water	All-purpose flour
1 cup cornmeal	Margarine
	Warm maple syrup

Grease the inside of a crockpot heavily with 2 tablespoons margarine, leaving any unused margarine in the crockpot. Turn the crockpot to high and add the boiling water. Pour the cornmeal slowly into the hot water with one hand while stirring constantly with the other hand. Add the salt and stir until smooth and thickened and then cover the crockpot and cook on high for 2 to 3 hours or on low for 4 to 6 hours, stirring occasionally.

When the mush is cooked, pour it into a 9″ × 5″ × 3″ loaf pan that has been well greased with margarine. Press plastic wrap on top of the mush after it has cooled slightly. Refrigerate for at least 4 hours or overnight, until firm. Turn out onto a working surface and slice carefully into about ½-inch-thick slices. Dip each slice in flour and fry until golden brown on both sides in hot margarine in a heavy frying pan or on a 375° F. grill. Serve hot with warm syrup.

Low sodium diets: Omit salt. Use salt-free margarine.

Yield: 4 to 6 servings

BULGUR PILAF
(Turkey and other Middle Eastern Countries)

I think that bulgur, or cracked wheat, which is available in

health stores and some supermarkets, is greatly underrated. It is
an excellent source of fiber; it can be substituted for rice in most
recipes; it is excellent served with creamed dishes or sauces; and
it has a sweet nutty flavor that I find very appealing.

1¼ cups bulgur
¼ cup finely chopped onions
¼ cup (½ stick) margarine

3 cups fat-free chicken or
  beef broth
Salt and pepper to taste

Fry bulgur and onions in margarine in a heavy saucepan over
moderate heat, stirring constantly, until onions are golden. Add
broth. Taste for seasoning and add salt and pepper, if necessary.
Bring to a boil. Cover and simmer 15 minutes or until tender,
stirring occasionally. Serve hot as a meat accompaniment.

Low sodium diets: Omit salt. Use salt-free margarine and low
  sodium broth.

Yield: about 4 servings

ANDALUSIAN RICE (Spain)

⅓ cup chopped onions
¼ cup vegetable oil
1½ cups long-grain rice
3 cups hot fat-free chicken
  broth
1 crushed bay leaf

1 tablespoon chopped parsley
Salt and pepper to taste
1 cup hot cooked drained
  peas
⅓ cup chopped drained
  pimientos

Fry onions in oil in heavy saucepan until onions are tender but
not browned. Add rice to onions and cook and stir over moderate
heat for 3 minutes. Add broth, bay leaf, and parsley to rice. Cover
and simmer over low heat for 16 minutes or until rice is tender.
Taste for seasoning and add salt and pepper to taste along with
peas and pimientos. Cover with a napkin or other cloth for 3 to 5
minutes to let the rice fluff and to get rid of any excess moisture.
Serve hot.

Low sodium diets: Omit salt. Use low sodium broth and peas cooked without salt.

Yield: 6 to 8 servings

RICE PILAF (Greece)

½ cup (1 4-ounce can)   1 cup long-grain rice
  drained sliced mushrooms   2 cups fat-free beef broth
½ cup chopped onions   Salt and pepper to taste
¼ cup vegetable oil

Fry mushrooms and onions in oil in heavy saucepan over moderate heat, stirring frequently, until onions are transparent but not browned. Add rice and broth; cover and simmer 16 minutes or until rice is tender. Taste for seasoning and add salt and pepper, if necessary. Remove from heat and cover with a cloth. Allow rice to fluff and dry for 3 to 5 minutes and serve hot.

Low sodium diets: Omit salt. Use fresh mushrooms and low sodium broth.

Yield: 4 to 6 servings

RICE AND NOODLE PILAF (Greece)

½ cup finely chopped onions   1 4-ounce can sliced
½ cup (1 stick) margarine   mushrooms
1 cup long-grain rice   2½ cups fat-free beef broth
1 cup very fine noodles   Salt and pepper to taste

Fry onions in margarine in saucepan over moderate heat, stirring frequently, until onions are transparent. Add rice and noodles and cook, stirring frequently, until noodles are lightly browned. Add mushrooms with juice, beef broth, and salt and pepper to taste. Mix well and pour into a casserole. Cover and bake at 350° F. for 1 hour. Stir the mixture at the end of ½ hour. Serve hot.

Low sodium diets: Omit salt. Use salt-free margarine, low sodium broth, and fresh mushrooms.

Yield: 4 to 6 servings

STEAMED RICE (United States)

1 cup long-grain rice   ½ teaspoon salt
2 cups cold water   1 tablespoon vegetable oil

Place rice, water, salt, and oil in a heavy saucepan. Cook and stir over moderate heat until the water starts to boil. Reduce heat to low and simmer, covered, for 16 minutes. Taste the rice and, if it isn't tender, cook for another 2 or 3 minutes. Remove from heat, fluff with a fork, cover with a clean cloth to let the rice become dry and fluffy, and let rest for 5 minutes. Serve hot.

Note: This recipe may be increased as much as desired as long as the same proportions of 2 cups liquid to 1 cup of long-grain rice are maintained. The amount of salt will vary according to the liquid used. A tablespoon of oil is sufficient for up to 6 cups of rice, beyond which it should be increased to 2 tablespoons oil, which will be sufficient for almost any amount of rice and liquid. The vegetable oil is necessary for the prevention of a large amount of foam, which might cause the rice to boil over onto the stove.

Low sodium diets: Omit salt.

Yield: 4 to 4½ cups

HOMEMADE NOODLES (United States)

Many nationalities use homemade noodles. The Italians call them fettucini, the Polish call them kluskis, and the Chinese, German, and many other nationalities also feature them. They are all based on the same simple recipe of flour and eggs. Commercial noodles are good, but they never provide quite the same texture and taste as the ones you have made yourself.

2½ cups all-purpose flour	¼ cup water
1 teaspoon salt	1 tablespoon vegetable oil
¾ cup liquid egg substitute	½ cup all-purpose flour

Place 2½ cups flour and salt in mixer bowl. Mix at low speed to blend. Beat the egg substitute, water, and oil together with a fork until smooth and add all at once to the flour. Beat at low speed, using a dough hook, for about 2 minutes or until smooth. Place the ½ cup flour on a working surface. Turn the noodle dough out onto the flour and knead lightly, using as much of the flour as necessary to make a smooth elastic dough. Roll the dough into a ball and let it rest on the floured surface, covered with a cloth, for about 30 minutes at room temperature.

Divide dough into 3 equal portions and roll each into a very thin rectangle with a rolling pin on a floured surface. Sprinkle the surface of the dough lightly with flour as you roll it to keep it from sticking to the rolling pin. The dough can be cut with a dough cutter, as I prefer, or rolled up like a jelly roll (sprinkle flour lightly on it before you roll it) and cut into strips as wide or narrow as you like. Shake out the strips and put them on a floured towel if they are not to be used immediately. They will dry sufficiently in a few hours to be stored in an airtight container. (My mother used to cover the back of a chair with a clean towel and hang the noodles over the towel to dry. If the room is sufficiently warm and dry, they will be ready in 2 or 3 hours.)

Noodles can be frozen without drying them first. Place them in layers, with wax paper between the layers, in an airtight wrapper in the freezer. *Do not defrost the noodles before cooking them;* cook them from the frozen state. Drop them into boiling liquid just as you would fresh noodles, stir until they are separated, and then cook them until tender.

To Cook Noodles: Drop noodles carefully into rapidly boiling salted water or broth. Add 1 tablespoon vegetable oil to prevent the pot from boiling over, return to a boil, and cook for 10 to 20 minutes, depending on the thickness of the noodles. Test noodles after 10 minutes.

Drain noodles well. Toss with a little margarine and serve hot or prepare as directed in specific recipes.

Low sodium diets: Omit salt.

Yield: 1½ pounds uncooked noodles or about 12 servings

GREEN NOODLES (Italy)

1 10-ounce package frozen chopped spinach
½ cup liquid egg substitute
1 teaspoon salt
2 tablespoons vegetable oil
¼ cup juice from cooking spinach
2½ cups all-purpose flour
½ cup all-purpose flour

Cook frozen spinach according to package directions. Drain well, reserving cooking juice. Cool spinach and then squeeze as much juice as possible out of the spinach by pushing against the side of the drainer with the back of a spoon. Combine spinach, egg substitute, salt, oil, and ¼ cup juice from cooking spinach in a blender or food processor. Beat until smooth and well blended. Place 2½ cups flour in mixer bowl. Add spinach mixture and beat at low speed, using dough hook, for 2 or 3 minutes or until smooth. Place ½ cup flour on a working surface. Turn the noodle dough out onto the flour and knead, using as much of the flour as necessary, to form a smooth elastic dough. Roll the dough into a ball and let it rest, covered with a cloth, for about 30 minutes at room temperature.

Divide dough into 3 equal portions and roll each out to form a very thin rectangle with a rolling pin on a floured surface. Sprinkle the surface of the dough lightly with flour as you roll it to keep it from sticking to the rolling pin. The dough can be cut with a noodle cutter (as I do it) or it can be rolled up like a jelly roll (sprinkling flour lightly on it before you roll it) and cut into narrow or wider strips as you prefer. Shake out the strips and put them on a floured towel if they are not to be used immediately. They will dry sufficiently in a few hours to be stored in an airtight container.

Noodles can also be frozen without drying them first. Place them in layers, with wax paper between the layers, in an airtight wrapper in the freezer. *Do not defrost the noodles before cooking them;* cook them from the frozen state. Drop them into boiling liquid just as you would fresh noodles, stir until they are separated, and cook them until tender.

To Cook Noodles: Drop noodles carefully into rapidly boiling salted water or broth. Add 1 tablespoon vegetable oil to the pot to prevent them from boiling over, return to a boil, and cook for 10 to 20 minutes, depending on the thickness of the noodles. Check noodles after 10 minutes to see if they are done. Thick noodles may even need 25 minutes to become tender.

Drain noodles well; toss with a little margarine and serve hot or prepare them as directed in specific recipes.

Low sodium diets: Omit salt.

Yield: 1¾ pounds uncooked noodles or about 12 servings

NOODLES WITH COTTAGE CHEESE (Hungary)

4 ounces dry noodles
¾ cup chopped onions
¼ cup (½ stick) margarine
½ cup evaporated skimmed milk
1 tablespoon flour

1 cup drained low fat cottage cheese
½ teaspoon salt
⅛ teaspoon white pepper
2 tablespoons imitation bacon bits
Paprika

Cook noodles according to package directions. Rinse well with cold water and drain well.

Fry onions in margarine over moderate heat, stirring frequently, until onions are soft but not browned. Mix skimmed milk and flour together until smooth. Add to onion mixture and cook and stir until slightly thickened. Cool for 5 minutes. Combine sauce, cottage cheese, salt, pepper, and bacon bits with noodles and pour into 1-quart glass casserole that has been well greased with margarine. Sprinkle with paprika and bake at 350° F. for about 20 minutes or until lightly browned. Let rest 3 to 5 minutes and then serve hot.

Low sodium diets: This recipe is not suitable.

Yield: 4 servings

MATZO BALLS (Jewish)

These matzo balls that Frances Nielsen makes are so light and good that we like them not only for soup but with chicken and other entrees as well.

¼ cup (½ stick) melted margarine	2 teaspoons salt
¾ cup liquid egg substitute	¼ cup cold fat-free chicken broth
1 cup matzo meal	Boiling fat-free chicken broth or salted water

Combine melted margarine and egg substitute. Mix lightly to blend. Add matzo meal and salt and mix lightly. Add cold chicken broth and mix lightly. (The whole secret of matzo balls is to treat them with a light hand.) Refrigerate for 1 hour.

Form mixture into balls, using about 1½ tablespoons of the mixture for each ball. Drop into boiling chicken broth or salted water. Cover and simmer 30 to 40 minutes. Serve hot in soup or hot as an accompaniment for chicken or other entrees.

Low sodium diets: Omit salt. Use low sodium broth.

Yield: 5 servings

FRIED MATZOS (Jewish)

Anita Kane says that her family likes these matzos served as a potato substitute, though they can also be served with cinnamon sugar or fruit as a dessert.

2 whole pieces matzo   **Pepper to taste (optional)**
½ cup liquid egg substitute   **Margarine**
½ teaspoon salt

Break matzos into about 1-inch pieces. Place in a colander. Pour very hot water over the matzos to soften them. Drain well.

Beat the liquid egg substitute, salt, and pepper together to blend. Place matzos in a bowl and pour the liquid egg substitute mixture over them. Put matzos into a frying pan in which margarine has been melted. Toss the matzos in the frying pan until somewhat dry. Serve hot.

Low sodium diets: Omit salt. Use salt-free margarine.

Yield: 2 servings

10

Cakes, Cookies, and Frostings

I have always thought that a beautiful cake was a work of art. As for cookies, I love each and every one of them. I think a lot of other people must feel the same way because most ethnic groups and regions in our own country have certain cakes and cookies that are forever associated with that particular spot. Many of these recipes are suitable for a low cholesterol diet, either as they are written or with slight changes, and I have included some of them in this chapter. Hopefully, you will find other recipes that you can use with only a little change or none at all.

Because of the saturated fat content of most mixes and bakery goods, it is not advisable to use them. Therefore, it is a good idea to have your own file of favorite cake and cookie recipes that are suitable for your low cholesterol diet.

I have discovered that most people like something new and different when they are eating cakes or cookies. Of course, there are diehards who will only eat angel food cake or devil's food cake, but they are in the minority. One of the most popular desserts I have ever served in my own home is what I call a "tasting." It all came about because I had to serve a group of people in my home unexpectedly. I didn't have enough of any one dessert in the freezer to serve them, but I did have a variety of different cakes I had been testing while working on a large-quantity ethnic cookbook. I cut each of the cakes into small pieces so that everyone could have several pieces of different kinds of cakes and they loved it. They could go back for more cake if they liked any one kind in particular, and I was surprised at how interested even the men were in the different kinds of cakes and their backgrounds. It worked out so well with cakes that I have also had successful tastings using different kinds of cookies from different countries. Of course, someone who is serving or pouring coffee should be prepared to tell everyone about the different cakes and their backgrounds and ingredients. There is only one drawback to this sort of entertaining: you have to spend a lot of time copying recipes for people.

Many recipes are suitable for a low cholesterol diet, but many are not. Now that liquid egg substitute is available we can make a greater variety of cakes and cookies than we could with only egg whites. It has been my experience that if a cake or cookie recipe requires 1 or 2 eggs, I can generally use 1 or 2 egg whites with no difficulty. But if a recipe needs 3 or more eggs, you almost always have to use liquid egg substitute. I substitute ¼ cup of liquid egg substitute for each egg in a recipe or an equivalent measure if the ingredients list measures of eggs. You will also find that in certain recipes I have specified the amount of egg whites. This is because egg whites have a high percentage of moisture and, if enough of the egg whites aren't used, the final cake or cookie will tend to be dry and hard. I'm sorry to say that I have been unable to use liquid egg substitute for recipes such as jelly roll, cassata, genoise, and most tortes in which the leavening depends on air beaten into the eggs. The liquid egg substitute works best when baking soda or baking powder is used for the leavening in cakes and the eggs are used for texture and flavor.

The fat in a cake or cookie recipe is important for tenderness and flavor. When I am trying to adapt a recipe I generally substitute margarine when the fat is creamed and oil when the fat is melted or softened and added to the batter as is without being creamed. It takes a little more margarine than shortening to get the same results, but oil can be substituted on an equal-volume basis for melted fat in a recipe. You can always add a little butter flavoring if the butter flavor is important to you in the cake or cookie.

Sour cream is generally ⅓ fat and ⅔ milk, so for 1 cup sour cream in a recipe I use ⅓ cup vegetable oil and ⅔ cup buttermilk or sour milk. The buttermilk or sour milk is necessary because most recipes that use sour cream also use soda, which depends on the acid in the sour milk or buttermilk to complete its leavening action. Of course, this works well for baked goods but doesn't do a thing for baked potatoes.

Chocolate is a no-no on a low cholesterol diet because of the cocoa butter, but 3 tablespoons of cocoa and 1 tablespoon of margarine may be substituted for 1 ounce of chocolate in almost all recipes except hot chocolate, in which the extra fat isn't necessary anyway. The cocoa can be added with the flour in a cake or cookie recipe and the fat added to the fat in the recipe, though I generally just forget about the added fat if I think the recipe is rich enough. Who needs those extra calories, anyway?

Most European cakes use all-purpose flour instead of cake flour, which helps explain the heavier texture of many of their cakes. I like that texture very much and really prefer it to the lighter texture of most cake mixes. I have tried testing foreign cakes with cake flour and the final results just aren't the same. I also almost never sift flour. I combine the flour with the other ingredients and stir them together, which blends them and lightens the mixture. That is what the sifting does so we might as well do it the easiest way.

Of course, when you are preparing low cholesterol cakes and cookies, you need to follow all the basic rules for good baking:

1. Recipes should be read and understood thoroughly before starting to prepare anything. All ingredients and equipment should be on hand and accounted for. I like to get everything out and measure it so that when I start mixing I can get right to it. It is often also a good idea to start preheating the oven before you start preparation, depending on how long the recipe will take to prepare and how long it takes your oven to preheat.

2. Regulation measuring cups and spoons should be used and cakes and cookies should be baked at a specified temperature for a specified time. The size of the pans should also not be changed unless the quantities are also changed.

3. All ingredients should be at room temperature unless otherwise specified in the recipe. This is particularly true of liquid egg substitute. You can have a spectacular failure if you use the egg substitute while it is still icy. I did it and it wasted a lot of time and ingredients.

4. Ingredients should not be deleted or substitutions made unless the ratio for the substitutions is understood.

5. Flour should not be sifted unless sifted flour is included in the recipe, since sifted and unsifted flour have different measures.

6. It is presumed in these recipes that an oven will be preheated when the cakes or cookies are put into the oven. The oven door should not be opened until the end of the baking time. If the cake is not done, it should be baked another 5 minutes and then tested again.

7. Follow the recipe exactly as it is written the first time you prepare it. If you want to experiment later, well and good, but do follow everything exactly at first so you will have a solid basis from which to work.

8. If you want to bake your cake in a different size pan, remember to fill the pan ⅔ full. This is also a good point to remember if you want to make cupcakes instead of a cake. The baking time will need to be varied according to the size of the pans.

9. If you are baking a single cake, put it in the center of the rack in the center of the oven. If you are baking layers, place them on the same rack, if possible, being careful that they do not touch each other so that there is room for the hot air to circulate.

Most of the directions for baking cakes should also be used when baking cookies, but there are several other points to remember when you are baking cookies.

1. Cookies should not be overbaked. Overbaked cookies will lose their flavor rapidly. Most cookies are transferred from the hot pans to racks to cool because if they are left on the hot pans they will continue to cook and may overcook.

2. Instructions should be followed for greasing cookie sheets. Some cookie recipes have enough fat in them that it is not necessary to grease the pans, but many others do not. Remember when greasing the pans to use only margarine since oil doesn't do a very good job and you don't want to use butter or shortening even here.

3. Cookies should always be put onto cool pans. If the pans are hot, the cookies will start baking before they are put into the oven and it is hard to control the exact baking times.

4. Cookies may be baked on cookie sheets lined with aluminum foil instead of greased pans to make the cleanup easier, but the dough should not be put onto the aluminum foil and then onto hot pans and baked.

5. Cookies on a cookie sheet should be of uniform size so they will bake evenly. If there is not enough dough left for a full pan of cookies, place them on a smaller pan or put them in the center of the cookie sheet.

6. Baking soda and sugar encourage cookies to spread. Flour and baking powder encourage them to rise instead of spreading. If cookie dough is too soft to roll and cut, it can be formed into a roll and chilled. It can then be sliced and baked.

DEVIL'S FOOD CAKE (Denmark)

This cake tastes like the old-fashioned sour cream devil's food cakes. It is especially good if you sprinkle each layer with chocolate liqueur before frosting it. I like to soak it with the liqueur, frost it, and then let it stand overnight before serving it.

⅔ cup cocoa
2 cups all-purpose flour
2 cups sugar
1 teaspoon baking soda
1 teaspoon salt

½ cup (4 medium) egg whites
1¾ cups low fat buttermilk
1 teaspoon vanilla
⅓ cup vegetable oil

Place cocoa, flour, sugar, soda, and salt together in mixer bowl. Mix at low speed for 1 minute or until well blended.

Combine egg whites, buttermilk, vanilla, and oil and beat

together until well blended. Add buttermilk mixture to flour mixture and beat at medium speed for 2 minutes.

Pour batter into a 9″ × 13″ cake pan that has been well greased with margarine. Bake at 350° F. for 30 to 35 minutes or until a cake tester inserted in the center of the cake comes out clean. Or, pour ⅓ of the batter into each of 3 9″ cake pans that have been well greased with margarine and lined with a circle of wax paper on the bottom of each pan. Bake at 350°F. for 20 to 25 minutes or until a cake tester inserted in the center of the cake comes out clean. Let layers cool in the pan for 10 minutes. Remove from pans. Remove wax paper and let cool to room temperature before frosting the layers.

Low sodium diets: This recipe is not suitable.

Yield: 1 9″ × 13″ cake or 3 9″ layers

DUNDEE CAKE (England)

½ cup (1 stick) margarine
½ cup sugar
⅔ cup liquid egg substitute
1½ cups all-purpose flour
1 teaspoon baking powder
½ teaspoon ground allspice
½ teaspoon ground cinnamon
½ teaspoon ground nutmeg
½ cup chopped candied fruit
½ cup washed and drained currants
½ cup washed and drained seedless raisins
12 almond halves

Grease a no-stick 9″ loaf pan well with margarine. If the loaf pan is not lined with no-stick material, grease well with margarine, line with wax paper, and grease well again with margarine. Set aside for later use.

Cream margarine and sugar together until light and fluffy. Add liquid egg substitute and mix 2 minutes at medium speed. Stir flour, baking powder, allspice, cinnamon, and nutmeg together to blend. Add flour mixture to creamed mixture and beat at low speed for 1 minute. Add candied fruit, currants, and raisins to dough. Mix lightly. Spread batter evenly in prepared loaf pan. Place almond halves on top of the dough so they are about ¾ inch apart. There should be 1 almond half for each slice.

Bake at 350° F. for 1 hour or until a cake tester comes out clean and the cake is lightly browned. Cool in the pan for 10 minutes and then remove the cake from the pan to cool. It is not customary to frost this cake.

Low sodium diets: Use salt-free margarine and low sodium baking powder.

Yield: 1 9″ loaf

HONEY CAKE (Jewish)

This rich, luscious cake doesn't need a frosting. It is best sliced thin and served with wine, lemonade, coffee, or tea. It is a favorite recipe from Anita Kane of Shorewood, Wisconsin, who has given me many good recipes.

1 cup sugar
⅓ cup liquid egg substitute
½ cup vegetable oil
⅔ cup honey
2 tablespoons brandy
2 cups flour
2 teaspoons baking powder
½ teaspoon baking soda
⅛ teaspoon salt
¾ cup washed and drained raisins
¾ cup chopped nuts
⅓ cup hot coffee

Beat sugar, liquid egg substitute, and oil together until smooth and creamy. Add honey and brandy and beat at low speed to blend. Stir flour, baking powder, soda, and salt together. Add with raisins and nuts to creamed mixture. Mix at medium speed until well blended. Add hot coffee to batter and mix at low speed until coffee is absorbed.

Spread dough evenly in a wax paper–lined metal 9″ × 9″ cake pan. (A no-stick pan needs only to be well greased with margarine.)

Bake 1 hour at 350° F. or until a cake tester inserted in the center of the cake comes out clean. The cake should be browned on the edges and light brown on the top. Let the cake cool for 10 minutes on a wire rack and then turn out to finish cooling. It is not customary to frost this cake.

Low sodium diets: This recipe is not suitable.

Yield: 1 9″-square cake

HONEY CAKE (Lithuania)

1½ cups liquid egg substitute
   at room temperature
1 cup sugar
1 cup vegetable oil
1 cup slightly warm honey
2 teaspoons vanilla

2 cups all-purpose flour
1 teaspoon baking soda
½ teaspoon baking powder
½ teaspoon salt
½ teaspoon ground cloves

Place liquid egg substitute, sugar, and oil together in mixer bowl. Mix at medium speed until smooth and creamy. Add honey and vanilla and beat at medium speed until smooth.

Stir flour, soda, baking powder, salt, and cloves together to blend. Add to creamed mixture and beat at medium speed for 1 minute. Pour batter into a 10″ tube pan that has been well greased with margarine.

Bake at 350° F. for 1 hour or until a cake tester inserted in the cake comes out clean. Leave in the pan for 15 minutes and then turn out onto a rack to finish cooling. This cake may be frosted if desired, but it is generally sliced and served plain with ice cream or fruit.

Low sodium diets: This recipe is not suitable.

Yield: 1 10″ tube cake

LIGHT APPLESAUCE CAKE
(Midwestern United States)

1 cup sugar
½ cup (1 stick) margarine
1 egg white
1 cup applesauce
3 tablespoons white vinegar

2 cups all-purpose flour
1 teaspoon baking soda
1 teaspoon salt
2 teaspoons pumpkin pie
  spice

Cream sugar and margarine together until light and fluffy. Add egg white and mix well. Add applesauce and vinegar and beat ½ minute at low speed.

Stir flour, soda, salt, and pumpkin pie spice together to blend. Add to creamed mixture. Beat 2 minutes at medium speed. Pour batter into a 9″-square cake pan that has been well greased with margarine.

Bake about 50 minutes at 325° F. for a glass pan or 350° F. for a metal pan or until a cake tester inserted in the center comes out clean.

Low sodium diets: This recipe is not suitable.

Yield: 1 9″-square cake

MADEIRA CAKE (England)

This is a rather plain but rich cake, almost like a pound cake. It is called Madeira Cake because it is often served with Madeira. I like to serve it with fresh fruit or make jam sandwiches out of it, as they do in England. It is almost never frosted.

1 cup (2 sticks) softened
  margarine
1 cup sugar
2 teaspoons lemon flavoring

1 cup liquid egg substitute
1¾ cups all-purpose flour
1 teaspoon baking powder
½ teaspoon salt

Cream margarine, sugar, and flavoring together until light and fluffy. Add liquid egg substitute, ¼ cup at a time, beating well after each addition. Beat 2 minutes at medium speed after all the egg substitute has been added.

Stir flour, baking powder, and salt together to blend. Add to batter and beat 1 minute at medium speed. Spread batter evenly in a 9″ loaf pan that has been well greased with margarine.

Bake at 350° F. for 1 hour or until a cake tester inserted in the center of the cake comes out clean and the cake is lightly browned. Cool 10 minutes in the pan, remove from the pan, and continue to cool on a wire rack.

Low sodium diets: Omit salt. Use salt-free margarine and low sodium baking powder.

Yield: 1 9″ loaf cake

MOCK ANGEL FOOD CAKE (United States)

This cake sounds impossible, but it isn't and it is good. It really does taste like angel food cake.

2 cups sugar	¾ cup (about 6 medium) egg
2 cups cake flour	whites
1 cup boiling water	½ teaspoon cream of tartar
2 teaspoons baking powder	1 teaspoon vanilla
⅛ teaspoon salt	½ teaspoon almond flavoring

Place sugar and flour in a bowl and stir to blend well. Pour boiling water over the mixture and let it set overnight.

The next day, mix the baking powder and the salt into the flour mixture. Beat the egg whites at high speed until foamy. Add the cream of tartar and continue to beat until stiff. Fold the egg mixture into the flour mixture. Add the extracts and mix lightly.

Rinse a 9″ × 13″ cake pan with water. Pour the batter into the pan and bake 35 to 45 minutes at 300° F. or until the cake springs back when the center is touched. Invert the cake to cool. When cooled, frost with 7-minute frosting.

Low sodium diets: This recipe is not suitable.

Yield: 1 9″ × 13″ cake

ORANGE ALMOND CAKE (Greece)

This is a very rich cake and should be cut and served in small diamonds. I generally serve it along with another not-so-sweet dessert for those who prefer less sweetness. Do not cut the amount of syrup used to soak the cake. A friend of mine makes the cake and uses only about half the syrup. It is good that way, but it is not a Greek cake.

3 cups sugar
3 cups water
¼ cup dry orange drink mix
1 teaspoon almond flavoring
1½ cups (3 sticks) margarine
1 cup sugar
2 tablespoons dry orange drink mix
1 teaspoon almond flavoring

1½ cups uncooked instant cream of wheat
2 cups liquid egg substitute
1½ cups all-purpose flour
1 tablespoon baking powder
½ teaspoon salt
¾ cup orange juice
2 tablespoons grated orange rind (optional)
1½ cups chopped almonds

Combine 3 cups sugar, water, and ¼ cup orange drink mix. Simmer, uncovered, for 15 minutes. Remove from heat and add 1 teaspoon almond flavoring. Set aside for later use.

Cream margarine, 1 cup sugar, 2 tablespoons dry orange drink mix, and 1 teaspoon almond flavoring together until light and fluffy. Gradually add uncooked cream of wheat to creamed mixture, beating at low speed. Slowly pour liquid egg substitute into batter, beating at low speed. Beat another minute at medium speed after egg substitute has been added. Stir flour, baking powder, and salt together to blend. Add flour mixture, orange juice, and rind to batter. Beat 1 minute at medium speed or until well blended. Add almonds.

Spread batter evenly in a 9″ × 13″ cake pan that has been well greased with margarine. Bake at 350° F. for about 50 minutes or until a cake tester comes out clean. Remove from oven and pour cooled syrup over the hot cake. Let cool to room temperature. Cut cake diagonally to form rather small diamonds, about 1½ inches. Serve at room temperature.

Low sodium diets: Omit salt. Use salt-free margarine and low sodium baking powder.

Yield: 1 9″ × 13″ cake

RHUBARB CAKE BAKE
(Midwestern United States)

Lois Erickson gave me this recipe after she served it at a cookout at her home in the country. Chuck says that he can't decide which he likes best, this dessert or rhubarb pie.

5 cups rhubarb, cut into 1-inch pieces	¼ teaspoon salt
	¼ cup brown sugar
1 3-ounce package strawberry-flavored gelatin	1 egg white
	About ¾ cup skimmed milk
	⅓ cup (⅔ stick) softened
¾ cup (1½ sticks) margarine	margarine
2 cups all-purpose flour	½ cup all-purpose flour
1 tablespoon baking powder	1½ cups sugar

Combine rhubarb and gelatin. Toss together and set aside for later use.

Combine ¾ cup margarine, 2 cups flour, baking powder, salt, and brown sugar. Blend well together. Place egg white in a measuring cup and add enough milk to total 1 cup liquid. Add milk mixture to flour mixture and mix only until all the flour is moistened. Spread batter evenly on the bottom and sides of the cake pan, which has been well greased with margarine. Use the back of a tablespoon to push the batter about 1½ inches up against the sides of the pan. Spread the rhubarb and gelatin mixture evenly over the batter.

Combine ⅓ cup margarine, ½ cup flour, and sugar and spread evenly over the rhubarb mixture.

Bake at 350° F. for 50 to 60 minutes or until cake portion springs back when touched. Cut into 3″ × 4″ pieces and serve lukewarm, if possible.

Low sodium diets: Omit salt. Use salt-free margarine and low sodium baking powder.

Yield: 1 9″ × 13″ cake

PLUM KUCHEN (Germany)

Other fruits may be used in this recipe when plums are not in season. Adjust the amount of sugar according to the tartness of the fruit used. We particularly like fresh peaches, which require less sugar, and cherries, which require more sugar.

½ cup hot water
¼ cup sugar
2 tablespoons instant dry milk
1 package (2¼ teaspoons) active dry yeast
2 cups all-purpose flour
¼ cup liquid egg substitute
½ teaspoon salt
½ teaspoon lemon flavoring

½ teaspoon ground cardamom
¼ cup (½ stick) margarine
2½ pounds fresh prune plums
½ cup sugar
1 tablespoon cornstarch
½ teaspoon ground cinnamon
2 tablespoons melted margarine
3 tablespoons powdered sugar (optional)

Combine water, ¼ cup sugar, and dry milk. Stir to dissolve sugar. Cool to 100° to 115° F. Add yeast. Mix lightly and set aside for 10 minutes.

Add flour, egg substitute, salt, lemon flavoring, cardamom, and margarine to yeast mixture. Mix at low speed using a dough hook, or mix by hand with a wooden spoon, about 3 minutes or until the dough forms a ball and leaves the sides of the mixer.

Turn dough out onto a lightly floured working surface and knead lightly. Round into a ball and place in a bowl that has been well greased with margarine. Turn the ball to coat the top of it with margarine. Cover and let stand until doubled in volume.

Turn dough out onto a lightly floured surface. Knead lightly. Round into a ball and return to the bowl. Cover and let stand until doubled in volume.

While dough is rising, wash, pit and quarter plums and set aside for later use. Stir ½ cup sugar, cornstarch, and cinnamon together and set aside for later use.

Lightly knead dough, which has risen for the second time, and form into a ball. Cover the ball with a cloth and let stand for 10 minutes on a lightly floured working surface. Roll dough, using a rolling pin, into an oblong to fit comfortably on a 12″ × 18″ cookie sheet with raised sides. Place the plums evenly in rows on the dough with cut sides up. Leave about ½-inch width along the sides of the dough without any fruit. Sprinkle the sugar mixture evenly over the plums. Dribble the melted margarine over the sugar mixture. Cover with wax paper and let rise in a warm place for about ½ hour.

Bake at 400° F. for 25 to 30 minutes or until the fruit is soft and the crust is lightly browned. Sprinkle lukewarm kuchen with powdered sugar and serve warm, if possible.

Low sodium diets: Omit salt. Use ¼ teaspoon salt substitute and salt-free margarine.

Yield: 1 12″ × 18″ kuchen

WHITE CAKE (United States)

This is a good basic white cake. The batter can be baked in layers, as cupcakes, or in a 9″ × 13″ pan. It can be frosted in a variety of ways and is suitable for a birthday or other special occasion.

¾ cup (1½ sticks) margarine
2½ cups sugar
1 teaspoon vanilla
1 teaspoon almond flavoring
¾ cup (about 6) egg whites

3⅓ cups cake flour
½ teaspoon salt
1 tablespoon baking powder
⅓ cup instant dry milk
1½ cups water

Grease 3 9″ layer cake pans well with margarine and line with wax paper circles. Set aside for later use.

Cream margarine, sugar, and flavorings together until light and fluffy. Add egg whites, which must be at room temperature for the proper volume in the finished cake, ¼ cup at a time, beating well after each addition. Stir flour, salt, baking powder, and dry milk together to blend. Add alternately with water, beating only until smooth after each addition. Place ⅓ of the batter in each of the 3 prepared layer pans.

Bake at 375° F. for 30 minutes or until cake pulls away from the side of the pan and is lightly browned. Let cake layers cool in the pan for 10 minutes, then turn out onto a wire rack to cool. Frost cake at room temperature.

Low sodium diets: Omit salt. Use salt-free margarine and low sodium baking powder.

Yield: 3 9″ layers

WHITE FRUIT CAKE (United States)

I have been making this cake since before Chuck and I were married. I like it because it is so versatile. You can use any combination of fruit and nuts as long as they total 3 pounds. I often use white raisins in the cake or candied pineapple or even mixed chopped candied fruit. I like to make it and then soak it in rum, wine, or brandy. When it is well soaked, I wrap it in aluminum foil and freeze it. Then I have an extra-special dessert in the freezer for holidays or other occasions.

8 ounces whole Brazil nuts

8 ounces whole pecans

8 ounces whole English walnuts

8 ounces whole red candied cherries

8 ounces whole green candied cherries

8 ounces whole pitted dates

¼ cup sugar

¼ cup flour

1¼ cups (about 10) egg whites

¼ cup vegetable oil

2 cups sugar

2 cups all-purpose flour

1½ teaspoons baking powder

2 teaspoons vanilla

½ cup light rum

Place nuts, cherries, and dates in a large mixing bowl. Do not chop them. Sprinkle the nuts and fruit with ¼ cup sugar and ¼ cup flour. Mix well. Place egg whites and oil in a bowl and mix well. The whites should be a little foamy but not whipped, and the oil should have been beaten into the whites. Stir the 2 cups flour, 2 cups sugar, and baking powder together and add with the vanilla and rum to the egg white mixture. Mix at low speed about 1 to 2 minutes or until smooth. Pour the batter over the nuts and fruit mixture and mix well, using a large spoon or your hands.

Spread an equal amount of batter in each of 2 well-buttered no-stick 9″ × 5″ loaf pans. (If the pans are not lined with no-stick material, grease well with margarine, line with brown paper, and grease well again with margarine.) Place the pans on the middle shelf of the oven and bake at 300° F. for 2 hours or until a cake tester comes out clean. Put a shallow pan (I use an old aluminum foil pie tin) with boiling water in it on the lower shelf of the oven. Pour more hot water into the pan if it becomes dry. The steam in the oven will prevent the formation of a hard crust on the cake and ensure even baking.

Cool in the pans for 10 minutes; run a spatula around the edges and transfer the cakes to a wire rack for cooling. Cakes can be soaked in wine, brandy, rum, or fruit juice and wrapped in heavy aluminum foil before they are refrigerated or frozen.

Low sodium diets: Use low sodium baking powder.

Yield: 2 9″ loaf cakes

ALMOND COOKIES (China)

1½ cups (3 sticks) margarine
1 cup sugar
1 egg white
1½ teaspoons almond
  flavoring

3 cups all-purpose flour
1 teaspoon baking soda
½ teaspoon salt
3 dozen almond halves

Cream margarine and sugar together until light and fluffy. Add egg white and flavoring. Beat 1 minute at low speed.

Stir flour, soda, and salt together and add to creamed mixture. Beat ½ minute at moderate speed.

Form balls of dough, using about 1½ tablespoons to form each ball. Place balls on cookie sheets that have been lightly greased with margarine. Make a depression in the center of each ball of dough. Press an almond half into each depression.

Bake at 350° F. about 15 minutes or until lightly browned. Remove cookies from hot pan to a wire rack to cool while still hot.

Low sodium diets: This recipe is not suitable.

Yield: about 3 dozen cookies

APPLESAUCE COOKIES (United States)

½ cup (1 stick) margarine
½ cup brown sugar
½ cup sugar
1 cup applesauce
2 cups all-purpose flour
½ teaspoon ground cinnamon

½ teaspoon ground nutmeg
1 teaspoon baking powder
1 teaspoon baking soda
2 cups rolled oats
1½ cups washed and drained
  raisins

Cream margarine and sugars together until light and fluffy. Add applesauce to creamed mixture and beat 1 minute at medium speed.

Stir flour, cinnamon, nutmeg, baking powder, and soda together. Add to creamed mixture and beat 1 minute at medium speed. Add oats and raisins and mix just to blend.

Drop dough by heaping tablespoonfuls onto cookie sheets that have been lightly greased with margarine. Press each cookie with the bottom of a glass that has been dipped in water and then in sugar until the dough is about ¼ inch thick.

Bake at 375° F. for about 15 minutes or until lightly browned. Transfer cookies from cookie sheets to wire racks while the cookies are still warm.

Low sodium diets: This recipe is not suitable.

Yield: 3 dozen

CARDAMOM SLICES (Lithuania)

1 cup sugar	1½ teaspoons baking powder
¾ cup (1½ sticks) margarine	1 teaspoon ground
1 teaspoon vanilla	cardamom
¾ cup (about 6) egg whites	½ cup chopped nuts
3 cups all-purpose flour	Powdered sugar (optional)

Cream sugar, margarine, and vanilla together until light and fluffy. Add egg whites and beat until smooth.

Stir flour, baking powder, and cardamom together to blend. Add to creamed mixture. Beat ½ minute at medium speed. Add nuts to dough and beat until nuts are well mixed into dough.

Divide the dough into 2 equal portions. Roll out each portion on a lightly floured working surface to form a roll about 12 inches long. Place the two rolls crosswise on a 12″ × 18″ cookie sheet that has been well greased with margarine or place each roll on a smaller cookie sheet greased with margarine.

Bake at 350° F. for 30 minutes or until lightly browned. Remove rolls from the oven and cool only until they can be handled. Cut rolls crosswise into ½-inch slices, about 25 per roll. Place slices flat on ungreased cookie sheets and bake at 250° F. for about 1 hour or until hard and lightly browned. Sprinkle with powdered sugar, if desired. (I never do, but a lot of people like them that way.) Keep cookies in an airtight tin until cookies are to be served.

Low sodium diets: Use salt-free margarine and low sodium baking powder.

Yield: about 50 slices

DOUBLE PEANUT COOKIES
(Southern United States)

1 cup (2 sticks) margarine	¼ cup skimmed milk
2 cups sugar	2¼ cups all-purpose flour
1 cup smooth peanut butter	1 teaspoon salt
½ cup (about 4 medium) egg whites	1 teaspoon baking soda
	2 cups chopped peanuts

Cream margarine, sugar, and peanut butter together until light and fluffy. Add egg whites and milk to creamed mixture. Beat at low speed for 1 minute or until well blended.

Stir flour, salt, and soda together. Add to creamed mixture and beat 1 minute at low speed or until well blended. Add peanuts and beat at low speed only until peanuts are mixed into the dough.

Drop dough by heaping tablespoonfuls onto cookie sheets that have been lightly greased with margarine.

Bake at 350° F. for 15 to 20 minutes or until lightly browned. Transfer cookies from sheets to racks while cookies are still warm.

Low sodium diets: This recipe is not suitable.

Yield: about 5 dozen

FUDGE BROWNIES (United States)

2½ cups sugar	½ cup (about 4) egg whites
2½ cups all-purpose flour	⅓ cup light corn syrup
¾ cup cocoa	2 teaspoons vanilla
1 teaspoon baking powder	1 cup chopped nuts
1 cup (2 sticks) softened margarine	

Place sugar, flour, cocoa, and baking powder in mixer bowl. Mix at low speed to blend. Add margarine, egg whites, syrup, and vanilla. Mix at low speed until well blended. Add nuts. Spread evenly in an 11″ × 15″ jelly roll pan that has been well greased with margarine. The dough will be very stiff.

Bake at 350° F. for 30 minutes. Place pan of brownies on wire rack to cool. Cut into squares after the brownies are cool or they may be frosted and then cut into squares.

Low sodium diets: Use salt-free margarine and low sodium baking powder.

Yield: 1 11″ × 15″ pan of brownies

GINGER COOKIES (England)

Margaret Foxwell, who lives a few miles out in the country from us, gave me this recipe. These Cornish cookies have been a favorite in her husband's family since they came to Iowa from Cornwall in the early nineteenth century. I'm not all that fond of ginger, so I make them with cinnamon instead of ginger, but the traditional cookies are always made with ginger.

2 cups brown sugar
1 cup (2 sticks) margarine
½ cup (about 4) egg whites
½ cup dark molasses

1 teaspoon vinegar
4½ cups all-purpose flour
1 tablespoon soda
2 teaspoons ground ginger
Sugar

Cream brown sugar and margarine together until light and fluffy. Add egg whites, molasses, and vinegar. Mix at medium speed until smooth.

Stir flour, soda, and ginger together to blend. Add to creamed mixture and mix at low speed about 1 minute or until blended.

Form balls, using about 1½ tablespoons of dough. Place balls on cookie sheets that have been lightly greased with margarine. Flatten the cookies, using the bottom of a glass that has been dipped in water and then in sugar.

Bake at 350° F. for 12 to 15 minutes or until cookies are lightly browned and the tops are almost firm. Transfer cookies from pan to a wire rack to cool while the cookies are still warm.

Low sodium diets: This recipe is not suitable.

Yield: about 4½ dozen

GRANDMA'S COOKIES
(Midwestern United States)

We named these cookies Grandma's Cookies because my grandmother always baked them in special shapes for holidays when we were children. They are firm enough to use for Christmas tree ornaments and they don't break easily. The flavor is excellent and we always looked forward to them at any holiday.

⅔ cup (1⅓ sticks) margarine
1 cup sugar
1 teaspoon vanilla
1 egg white
⅔ cup buttermilk
3 cups all-purpose flour

¼ teaspoon ground nutmeg
¼ teaspoon salt
½ teaspoon baking soda
½ cup chopped nuts
  (optional)

Cream margarine and sugar together until light and fluffy. Add vanilla, egg white, and buttermilk. Mix at low speed until smooth. Stir flour, nutmeg, salt, and baking soda together to blend. Add to creamed mixture and mix at medium speed until smooth. Add nuts and mix lightly.

Place dough on lightly floured working surface. Roll to about ¼-inch thickness and cut with a floured 3-inch cutter. Place cookies on a cookie sheet that has been lightly greased with margarine.

Bake at 375° F. for about 15 minutes or until lightly browned. Transfer cookies from hot pans to a wire rack to cool. Cookies may be frosted, if desired, with a plain powdered sugar frosting.

This cookie dough can be the basis for a great variety of cookies. Ground raisins may be used instead of the nuts or both nuts and raisins may be omitted and more spices added. Coloring may be added, such as yellow for pumpkins for Halloween, and the dough may be cut into a variety of shapes. The yield given is for 3-inch cookies, but a greater yield will result from the use of smaller, differently shaped cookie cutters.

Low sodium diets: This recipe is not suitable.

Yield: about 2½ dozen

MANDEL BREAD (Jewish)

The recipe for these cookies came from Anita Kane of Shorewood, Wisconsin. They are hard cookies, good for dunking, and they keep well for a long time in an airtight container.

½ cup (1 stick) margarine	½ teaspoon baking powder
½ cup sugar	⅛ teaspoon salt
⅓ cup liquid egg substitute	½ cup chopped almonds
½ teaspoon vanilla	About 1 cup Solo apricot
1 teaspoon almond flavoring	filling
2 cups all-purpose flour	Cinnamon sugar

Cream margarine and sugar together until light and fluffy. Add liquid egg substitute, vanilla, and almond flavoring. Mix well. Stir flour, baking powder, and salt together. Add to creamed mixture and mix at low speed only until well blended. Add chopped almonds and mix until almonds are mixed into the dough.

Shape dough on a lightly floured board into 2 equal rolls that are 9 to 10 inches long. Place on an ungreased cookie sheet at least 3 to 4 inches apart. Make a groove about ½ inch deep down the center of each roll. Spread the apricot filling evenly in the groove. Sprinkle with cinnamon sugar.

Bake at 350° F. about 25 minutes or until lightly browned. Remove from oven and cool only until they can be handled. Slice each roll into 12 diagonal slices. Spread evenly on cookie sheet and return to oven for another 5 minutes.

Low sodium diets: Omit salt. Use salt-free margarine and low sodium baking powder.

Yield: 24 slices

MARGARINE COOKIES (United States)

This is my version of the well-known butter cookies. They can be decorated and formed into different shapes for holidays and other special occasions. They freeze well or they can be stored in an airtight container until needed.

1 cup (2 sticks) margarine	3 drops yellow food coloring
1¼ cups powdered sugar	3 cups cake flour
¼ cup egg whites	1 teaspoon baking soda
1 teaspoon vanilla	1½ teaspoons cream of tartar
1 teaspoon butter flavoring	¼ teaspoon salt

Cream margarine and powdered sugar together until light and fluffy. Add egg whites, vanilla, butter flavoring, and food coloring to creamed mixture and beat 1 minute at medium speed.

Stir flour, soda, cream of tartar, and salt together to blend. Add to creamed mixture and mix at low speed for about 1 minute or until smooth.

Put dough into a pastry bag and form cookies on cookie sheets as desired. Let stand in a cool place or refrigerate 2 hours before baking.

Bake at 375° F. for 8 to 10 minutes or until lightly browned. Transfer to wire racks while still slightly warm.

Low sodium diets: This recipe is not suitable.

Yield: 5 dozen medium-sized cookies

MOCHA NUT BALLS (France)

1½ cups (3 sticks) softened
  margarine
¾ cup sugar
1 tablespoon vanilla
2½ cups all-purpose flour
1 tablespoon instant dry
  coffee

⅓ cup cocoa
½ teaspoon salt
2 cups chopped pecans or
  walnuts
Powdered sugar

Cream margarine, sugar, and vanilla together until light and fluffy.

Stir flour, instant dry coffee, cocoa, and salt together to blend. Add to creamed mixture. Mix at low speed about 2 minutes to blend well. Add nuts to dough and mix only to incorporate nuts into the dough.

Using a heaping tablespoonful of dough, form balls about the size of a walnut. Place balls on cookie sheets that have been lightly greased with margarine.

Bake at 325° F. for 20 minutes. Remove cookies from the pan while still warm. Cool cookies and shake in a bag containing powdered sugar. Keep cookies in an airtight tin until cookies are to be served.

Low sodium diets: Omit salt. Use salt-free margarine.

Yield: about 3½ dozen

PECAN DAINTIES (Southern United States)

Florence Jellings, who is an excellent cook, brought these to a tea one afternoon. She had made them with black walnuts instead of pecans and they were very good. I was happy to get the recipe because I loved them and I knew that Chuck would also like them.

1 egg white	1½ cups chopped pecans or
1 cup brown sugar	black walnuts

Beat the egg white at high speed in the small bowl of a mixer until stiff. Gradually add the brown sugar, continuing to beat at high speed. Carefully fold the nuts into the meringue by hand. Drop by heaping teaspoonfuls onto a cookie sheet that has been lined with aluminum foil.

Bake at 250° F. for about 30 minutes. Transfer from foil to a wire rack while still warm. Store cookies by themselves in an airtight container; if they are stored with other cookies, they will pick up moisture and will lose their crispness.

Note: Don't try to cut the amount of nuts in this recipe. I tried them that way and they aren't nearly as good. It's an expensive recipe but well worth the cost for a special occasion.

Low sodium diets: May be used as written.

Yield: about 2 dozen

PEPPERNUT COOKIES (Austria)

Rose Morris of Strawberry Point, Iowa, gave me the recipe for these spicy cookies from her native Austria.

⅔ cup (1⅓ sticks) margarine	1 teaspoon ground cloves
1½ cups sugar	¼ teaspoon coarsely ground
½ cup egg whites	black pepper
1 teaspoon rum flavoring	1 teaspoon baking powder
1 teaspoon ground cinnamon	3 cups all-purpose flour

Cream the margarine and sugar together at medium speed until light and fluffy. Add egg whites and rum flavoring and mix to blend.

Stir cinnamon, cloves, pepper, baking powder, and flour together to blend. Add to creamed mixture and beat 1 minute at low speed or until well blended.

Roll dough to about a ⅜-inch thickness on a lightly floured working surface. Cut with a lightly floured 3-inch round cutter. Place on cookie sheets that have been lightly greased with margarine.

Bake at 375° F. for about 15 minutes or until lightly browned. Transfer cookies from cookie sheet to a wire rack while cookies are still warm.

Low sodium diets: Use salt-free margarine and low sodium baking powder.

Yield: about 2½ dozen

PIONEER BARS (Midwestern United States)

The recipe for these spicy bars was given to me by Mabel Stafford, one of my mother's favorite cousins, for whom I was named. I'm sure that our grandmothers used lard instead of margarine, but this recipe uses the ingredients that were most plentiful when our grandmothers were baking. My grandmother used to say that she didn't know there were spices other than these, allspice, and pepper until she was in her middle sixties.

1½ cups raisins	3 cups all-purpose flour
1½ cups sugar	¾ teaspoon salt
1½ cups water	1½ teaspoons baking soda
¾ cup (1½ sticks) margarine	1 cup chopped dates
1 teaspoon ground cinnamon	1 cup chopped nuts
½ teaspoon ground cloves	Plain powdered sugar
½ teaspoon ground nutmeg	frosting (optional)

Place raisins, sugar, water, margarine, cinnamon, cloves, and nutmeg in a saucepan. Bring to a boil, stirring occasionally; remove from heat and cool to room temperature.

Place flour, salt, and soda in mixer bowl. Mix at low speed to blend. Add cooled mixture, dates, and nuts to flour and mix at low speed to blend well. Spread evenly in an 11″ × 15″ jelly roll pan that has been well greased with margarine.

Bake at 350° F. for 30 minutes or until the center springs back when touched. Cool on a wire rack to room temperature and then frost with plain powdered sugar frosting, if desired.

Low sodium diets: This recipe is not suitable.

Yield: 1 11″ × 15″ jelly roll pan

SHORTBREAD (Scotland)

1½ cups (3 sticks) margarine
1 cup sugar
3 cups all-purpose flour

Cream margarine and sugar together until light. Add flour to creamed mixture and mix until smooth.

Turn dough out onto a lightly floured working surface and knead about 10 times. Roll dough out ¼ to ½ inch thick and cut into about 2-inch squares.

Place cookies on ungreased cookie sheets and bake at 350° F. about 18 to 20 minutes or until lightly browned. Loosen cookies from pans while still warm and cool on racks.

Flavoring is not generally used in these cookies in Great Britain, but vanilla, almond, or other flavorings are frequently used in this country.

Note: If you would like to add a little fiber to these cookies, use 1½ cups of all-purpose flour and 1½ cups of graham flour instead of the 3 cups of all-purpose flour in the basic recipe.

Low sodium diets: Use salt-free margarine.

Yield: about 3 dozen

SUGAR COOKIES (United States)

These cookies are great favorites at the Lutheran nursing home where I work as a dietary consultant. I'd hate to have to count how many of these Erma Wiltse has made, but I'm sure it's an incredible amount. Cookies, especially the homemade kind, are always popular in the nursing home and I think they help to make the residents feel more at home.

1 cup sugar	4½ cups all-purpose flour
1 cup powdered sugar	1 teaspoon cream of tartar
1 cup (2 sticks) margarine	1 teaspoon baking soda
1 cup vegetable oil	1 teaspoon vanilla
2 egg whites	1 teaspoon lemon flavoring

Place sugars, margarine, oil, egg whites, flour, cream of tartar, soda, vanilla, and lemon flavoring in a mixer bowl. Mix at medium speed until well blended.

Form balls, using about 1½ tablespoons of dough. Place balls on cookie sheets that have been lightly greased with margarine. Flatten the cookies, using the bottom of a glass that has been dipped in water and then in sugar.

Bake at 350° F. for 10 to 12 minutes or until lightly browned. Transfer cookies from pan to a wire rack to cool while the cookies are still hot.

Low sodium diets: This recipe is not suitable.

Yield: 4 dozen

WEDDING COOKIES (Mexico)

1½ cups (3 sticks) margarine	1½ cups coarsely chopped
¾ cup powdered sugar	nuts
2 teaspoons vanilla	Powdered sugar
3 cups all-purpose flour	

Cream margarine, powdered sugar, and vanilla together at medium speed until light and fluffy. Add flour and mix at low speed about 1 to 2 minutes or until blended. Add nuts and mix lightly to combine.

Drop dough by the heaping tablespoonful onto cookie sheets that have been lightly greased with margarine. Bake at 350° F. for about 20 minutes or until cookies are lightly browned.

Shake cookies while they are still warm in a paper bag containing powdered sugar. Cool and keep in an airtight container until cookies are to be served.

Low sodium diets: Use salt-free margarine

Yield: about 3 dozen

FROSTINGS

COCOA FUDGE FROSTING (United States)

I've used this recipe in previous cookbooks, but it is so good that I don't want anyone to miss out on it. It tastes like fudge and is easy to make. It also freezes well and you can easily vary it by adding rum or peppermint or other flavoring. It is a good all-around frosting recipe that is handy to have on hand.

¼ cup white corn syrup   1 pound powdered sugar
2 tablespoons water   ½ cup cocoa
1 teaspoon vanilla   ¼ teaspoon salt
½ cup (1 stick) margarine

Combine syrup, water, vanilla, and margarine in a 2-quart saucepan; cook and stir over low heat until simmering, but do not allow to boil. Remove from heat. Stir powdered sugar, cocoa, and salt together to blend; stir into the hot syrup and mix until well blended. Frosting will be smooth and glossy and should be used as soon as possible since it will lose its gloss when it becomes cool. Frosting can be reheated in a double boiler over simmering water to restore the gloss if it is not all used the first time.

Low sodium diets: Omit salt. Use salt-free margarine.

Yield: frosting for 1 9″ cake

MARGARINE CREAM FROSTING (France)

This French frosting is richer than the butter cream frosting ordinarily used in this country and it is delicious. It freezes well, and it is handy to have several flavors stored in the freezer for use at a later date. If a butter flavor is considered necessary, a few drops of butter flavoring will do the trick.

¾ cup (1½ sticks) margarine   2 tablespoons skimmed milk
1 pound powdered sugar   2 teaspoons vanilla
¼ teaspoon salt

Cream margarine at medium speed until light and fluffy.

Add powdered sugar, salt, milk, and vanilla to creamed margarine. Beat at medium speed for about 2 minutes or until smooth and creamy.

Variations:
Chocolate Margarine Cream Frosting: Delete milk. Add ½ cup cocoa and ¼ cup boiling water.

Mocha Margarine Cream Frosting: Delete milk. Add 2 tablespoons cocoa and 3 tablespoons very strong coffee.

Chocolate Rum Margarine Cream Frosting: Delete milk. Add ½ cup cocoa and 3 tablespoons rum.

Peppermint Margarine Cream Frosting: Add 4 drops red food coloring and ¼ teaspoon peppermint flavoring.

Lemon Margarine Cream Frosting: Delete milk. Dissolve 1½ teaspoons dry lemonade mix in 2 tablespoons hot water. Cool to lukewarm and add.

Orange Margarine Cream Frosting: Delete milk and vanilla. Add 3 tablespoons orange juice and 1 tablespoon grated orange rind.

Low sodium diets: Omit salt. Use salt-free margarine.
Yield: 2½ cups

MERINGUE FROSTING (France)

You've undoubtedly heard the phrase "sinfully rich." To me, that describes this frosting, and you'll love it if you can afford the calories.

⅔ cup sugar
½ cup water
¼ teaspoon salt
1 tablespoon light corn syrup
3 egg whites

¼ teaspoon cream of tartar
⅓ cup sugar
1 cup (2 sticks) margarine
1 teaspoon vanilla or other
   flavoring or extract

Combine ⅔ cup sugar, water, salt, and corn syrup in a small saucepan. Stir over low heat until sugar is dissolved. Cook over moderate heat, without stirring, to 238° F. (soft ball stage).

While syrup is cooking, beat egg whites with cream of tartar until they form soft peaks. Gradually add ⅓ cup sugar, beating constantly, until whites and sugar are firm and will hold a stiff peak. Pour the boiling hot syrup over the whites while beating constantly. Use a wire whisk if you are beating the egg whites by hand. Beat mixture until it is cool.

Cream the margarine until it is light and fluffy. Beat the cooled meringue mixture into the creamed mixture, adding a couple of tablespoons of the meringue at a time to the margarine. Add flavoring to taste. A few drops of food coloring may be added and a variety of flavorings used. This frosting may be made ahead of time and refrigerated for a couple of days, but it does not freeze well.

Low sodium diets: Omit salt and cream of tartar. Use salt-free margarine.

Yield: 2½ cups

11
Pies

Unless your doctor has told you to cut down on calories and/or sugar, you can continue to make and serve pie as you always have, as long as you are careful to use a crust made with margarine or oil. Some pies are high in butter, eggs, and cream and, of course, they are taboo, but there is a multitude of good pie fillings waiting to be put inside your low cholesterol crusts. I may be coming on too strong about pies because we live in what I call "pie country." Church dinners and many large get-togethers around Wadena often feature pie. I remember when Chuck took my mother, Frances Nielsen, and me to a church dinner near our home when we first lived out here. The girl who was waiting on our table asked us what kind of pie we wanted. We asked her what kind she had and she told us she had any kind we wanted, so we each asked for our favorite. I couldn't believe it, but they really did have every kind we wanted. Chuck had strawberry, my mother had lemon meringue, Frances had groundcherry, and I had pecan. Of course, it was only about 11:30 and they had just started to serve, but I am still amazed when I remember it.

Poor Chuck didn't have any pie for the longest time after the doctor put him on a low cholesterol diet, and he does love pie. It took me a long time before I realized that there was no reason I couldn't make pie crusts with oil or margarine. Sometimes Chuck would just eat the filling and leave the crust, but that wasn't really satisfactory. I think what finally made me realize it could and should be done was when I found out that my friend Cracker Holton from Clearwater, Florida, made all her crusts with oil because she liked them that way and not because she had to. I decided that if she could do it that way, I probably could as well.

You shouldn't buy a pie from a bakery or store unless you know exactly what is in that crust because commercial pies are almost always made with hydrogenated fats, lard, or beef fat because they keep better. If the package says the crust was made with oil, be sure that it is not hydrogenated oil, which is as bad as shortening. It is best, if you want pie, to make your own so that you can control the fat in the crust and also in the filling. You can give the recipe for your low cholesterol crust to others in your family so they can prepare it when you are their guest, as Frances Nielsen does for Chuck, but don't eat any pie unless you know what is in the crust.

I'm happy to tell you that most instant puddings do not contain any cholesterol; therefore, you are free to use them in your own crusts for a variety of cream pies. Coconut is forbidden, but bananas, raisins, nuts, and fruits may be used with very good results. Just read the labels on the pudding packages and you'll know which ones to buy and prepare.

Any fruit pies that do not include eggs, cream, or butter may be used for a low cholesterol diet. There are countless numbers of fruit pies and I'm sure you have your own favorites. I haven't included them here, though I did put some of them into my first low cholesterol book. The prepared canned fruit fillings also may be used satisfactorily.

Pies are really not a great feature of the cuisines of most foreign countries, except for the meat pies of Great Britain. However, many immigrants to the United States accepted pies after they arrived here, and now many ethnic groups in this country feature them. Most regions have their own specialties, though some regional recipes are now prepared across the country. Pumpkin pie, which originated in New England, is a good example.

In many cases, it is the pie crust that determines whether or not the pie will be good. There are certain basic rules for making good pastry that should be followed for any recipe:

1. Read the recipe thoroughly and make sure you understand it before you start preparing it. Assemble all the ingredients and be sure they are at the temperature specified in the recipe. In this book, you can assume that all ingredients are at room temperature unless the recipe states otherwise.

2. Follow directions as written. Use even, accurate measurements and do not substitute one ingredient for another unless you are sure of the substitution ratio.

3. Refrigerate pie crust as directed but never less than ½ hour after it is mixed. It needs that time to rest before it is shaped.

4. Use half the amount of dough for a double crust, if preparing a single pie shell. Use a little more than half the crust for the bottom and a little less than half for the top crust when making a two-crust pie.

5. Roll the dough out on a lightly floured surface with a lightly floured rolling pin to avoid adding more flour to the dough. More flour will tend to make the dough tough. A pie cloth and a stockinette for the rolling pin are also useful, or the crust can be rolled out between two layers of wax paper or aluminum foil.

6. Roll the bottom crust into a circle about 2 inches larger than the pie tin. All recipes in this book are written for pie tins that are 1 to 1¼ inches deep. Pat the crust into the bottom of the pan to eliminate air holes under the crust. Fill the crust and brush the top edges of the crust with skimmed milk or water so the top edge will stick to the bottom crust.

7. Roll the top crust into a circle large enough to cover the filling, with about ½ inch extra on all sides. Fold the crust and make slits in it to allow the steam to escape.

8. Fit the top crust over the filling and trim the sides, if necessary, with a pair of kitchen scissors.

9. Seal the edges of the crust together and flute or crimp them.

10. If you want a shiny crust, brush the top lightly with a pastry brush dipped in skimmed milk before baking.

11. Bake the pie according to directions with the recipe for a double-crust pie. Bake a single shell to be filled later at 425° or 450° F. for 12 to 15 minutes or until lightly browned.

12. Prick the bottom of a pie crust to be filled later with a fork so it won't puff when it is baking, or put another pie tin of the same size inside the crust for the first ten minutes of baking time.

13. If you are making a cream pie, the filling should be put into the prebaked pie shell while the filling is still warm. However, a filling to be put into an unbaked pie crust should be allowed to cool before it is put into the crust.

Most pie crusts are made from flour, salt, fat, and water. Flakiness and tenderness are the most important characteristics of a good crust, and both of these depend on the proportion of ingredients used and the method of mixing. Therefore, it is important not to vary the proportions of the basic recipe unless you are deliberately trying to change the tenderness of the crust.

The flakiness of a crust depends on the method of mixing the fat into the flour. A mealy texture will result if the fat is mixed with the flour until the fat is in very small particles. If the fat is mixed with the flour until the fat particles are about the size of a pea, the crust will have a flaky texture.

Tenderness of the crust also depends to a large extent on proper handling of the dough. Since not all flours absorb the same amount of liquid, the proper amount of liquid needed will vary. Use only enough liquid to make a soft, pliable dough because excess liquid will cause the crust to become tough. Graham or whole wheat pie crust will seem soft at first if sufficient water is used, but it will become more firm after it stands for a while because the bran continues to absorb water after it is mixed. Margarine should be rather firm when it is added to the flour and the water should be very cold when added, about 40° F. or less.

Pie crusts may be mixed by hand or in the mixer. It is important not to overmix the dough because it will cause it to toughen and shrink while it is baking. Dough should be eased gently into the pan. It should never be stretched, because it will shrink while it is baking if it has been stretched.

Pie crust should not be allowed to stand in a warm room after it is mixed. It should be refrigerated almost until the time to use it, allowed to return to room temperature, and then used. Crusts that have been shaped and filled should be refrigerated if not baked immediately.

Meringue should touch all the inside edges of the crust to prevent it from pulling away from the sides of the crust while it is baked.

Baking temperatures for pies are very important. If the temperature is too low, the crust will be tough. If the temperature is too high, the crust will brown too quickly, leaving it browned on the outside with a layer of uncooked dough on the inside.

Dough trimmings should be rolled into a ball and used for a bottom crust, never a top crust.

Cream pies should be refrigerated if they are to be kept more than an hour or so before they are served because of danger of bacterial contamination. Therefore, it is a good idea to make them as close to serving times as possible since they don't taste as good after they have been refrigerated for a period of time.

Cleanliness of equipment and ingredients is very important in order to prevent bacterial contamination and maintain good flavor. Only good-quality ingredients should be used, since you always get out of the finished product exactly what you put into it. A margarine crust will taste much better if made from a well-flavored margarine than it will if made from a poor-quality margarine. Margarine for pie crusts should be of the stick type. Soft margarine doesn't make as good crusts as the firmer stick margarine, but when you are buying margarine for your crusts be sure to read the list of ingredients to be sure that it contains only unsaturated fats. At least be sure that the first ingredient in the list of ingredients is a liquid vegetable oil.

MARGARINE PIE CRUST (United States)

DOUBLE CRUST (8″ OR 9″ PIE)
1½ cups all-purpose flour
¾ teaspoon salt
¾ cup (1½ sticks) margarine
⅓ to ½ cup very cold water

SINGLE CRUST (8″ OR 9″ PIE)
1 cup all-purpose flour
½ teaspoon salt
½ cup (1 stick) margarine
¼ to ⅓ cup very cold water

Stir flour and salt together in mixer bowl to blend. Cut margarine into flour until the mixture resembles coarse meal. Add water and mix lightly with a fork. Round into a ball, cover with wax paper, and refrigerate at least 2 hours or overnight before crust is used.

Low sodium diets: Omit salt. Use salt-free margarine.

GRAHAM MARGARINE PIE CRUST (United States)

1 cup all-purpose flour
1 cup graham flour
¾ cup (1½ sticks) margarine

¼ teaspoon salt
About ½ cup very cold water

Stir flours in mixing bowl to blend. Cut margarine into flours until the mixture resembles coarse meal. Dissolve salt in water, add to flour mixture, and mix lightly with a fork. Round pastry into a ball, cover with wax paper, and refrigerate at least 2 hours or overnight before crust is used.

Low sodium diets: Omit salt. Use salt-free margarine.

Yield: crust for 1 9″ double-crust pie

OIL PIE CRUST (United States)

DOUBLE CRUST (8″ OR 9″ PIE)
1¾ cups all-purpose flour
1 teaspoon salt
½ cup vegetable oil
3 tablespoons cold water

SINGLE CRUST (8″ OR 9″ PIE)
1 cup plus 2 tablespoons all-purpose flour
½ teaspoon salt
⅓ cup vegetable oil
2 tablespoons cold water

Stir flour and salt together in mixing bowl to blend. Add oil and mix thoroughly with a fork. Sprinkle water on top of the dough and mix well. Press the dough firmly into a ball. If it is too dry to form a ball, add 1 to 2 tablespoons oil.

If you are making a double crust, use a little more than ½ the dough for the bottom crust and a little less than ½ for the top crust. Flatten the larger portion slightly and roll out between 2 aluminum foil circles. Peel off the top piece of foil. Put the pastry into a pie tin, foil side up. Peel off the top piece of foil, pat out any air bubbles, and fill. Roll out the top crust as you did the bottom crust. Put the top crust over the filling and cut slits to allow any steam to escape. Trim ½ inch beyond the edge of the pan. Seal the edges and flute them. Bake according to directions for the filling.

For a pie crust to be baked before it is filled, prick the dough in several places. Bake at 425° F. for 12 to 15 minutes or until lightly browned.

Low sodium diets: Omit salt.

GRAHAM CRACKER PIE CRUST (United States)

1½ cups graham cracker crumbs
3 tablespoons sugar

⅓ cup (⅔ stick) softened margarine

Combine cracker crumbs and sugar in a mixer bowl. Stir to blend. Add softened margarine and mix well. Press crumb mixture firmly against the bottom and sides of a 9″ pie tin. Bake at 350° F. for 10 minutes. Cool to room temperature before adding filling.

Low sodium diets: Use salt-free margarine.

Yield: 1 8″ or 9″ pie shell

CRUST FOR MEAT PIES (England)

The crust for meat pies is traditionally less rich than the crust used for dessert pies. This is a flaky, rather crisp crust that we like to use for pasties and meat pies or as a topping for chicken pot pies.

1½ cups all-purpose flour   **½ cup (1 stick) cold**
¾ teaspoon salt   **margarine**
                                          ⅓ to ½ cup very cold water

Stir flour and salt together in mixer bowl to blend. Cut margarine into flour until the mixture resembles coarse meal. Add water and mix lightly with a fork. Round into a ball, cover with wax paper, and refrigerate at least 2 hours or overnight before crust is used.

Low sodium diets: Omit salt. Use salt-free margarine.

Yield: crust for 1 9″ double-crust pie

MERINGUE FOR TOPPING PIES (France)

3 egg whites   **⅓ cup sugar**
¼ teaspoon cream of tartar   **½ teaspoon vanilla**

Place egg whites and cream of tartar in mixer bowl and beat at high speed, using a whip, until egg whites are foamy. Add sugar gradually, beating at high speed to form a meringue. Add vanilla near the end of the beating period.

Spread meringue on the pie filling, being careful to seal the meringue to the edges of the crust so that it will not shrink.

Bake at 325° F. for 15 to 20 minutes or until lightly browned.

Low sodium diets: May be used as written.

Yield: meringue for 1 9″ pie

CHOCOLATE PUDDING OR PIE FILLING
(United States)

This is one recipe that I gave to Anita Kane, rather than the other way around. She really is a chocoholic, and I knew she'd like this recipe because it is so rich and luscious. I especially like it in a graham cracker crust with a topping of Italian Meringue (see Index).

⅔ cup sugar	½ cup instant dry milk
3 tablespoons flour	2 cups water
1 tablespoon cornstarch	2 tablespoons margarine
⅛ teaspoon salt	1 teaspoon vanilla
¼ cup cocoa	

Combine sugar, flour, cornstarch, salt, cocoa, and dry milk in a bowl and stir until it is very smooth and well blended with no lumps. Bring water to a boil. Stir the dry mixture into the boiling water and continue to cook and stir over moderate heat, using a whip. (It is *essential* that you use a whip for this. A spoon simply won't work. If you don't have a whip, buy a small one. It is so much help in making this and other puddings and sauces that no kitchen should be without at least one whip, and preferably several of them in different sizes.) Continue to cook, stirring frequently, over low heat for 5 minutes. Remove from heat and add margarine and vanilla. Stir to mix and then pour into pudding dishes or cool before pouring into a prebaked pie crust. (Place the pudding pan in cold water to cool, stirring occasionally, to lukewarm.)

Low sodium diets: Omit salt. Use salt-free margarine and low sodium crust if used as a pie filling.

Yield: 4 servings of pudding or 1 8″ pie

JAM PIE (Wales)

I'd be the first to tell you that this pie isn't as rich as the original recipe made by my Welsh relatives with whole eggs and butter, but the flavor is just as good and we like it even better because it isn't as rich. It is traditionally made with damson plum preserves but they are often difficult to find, so I generally make it with strawberry or raspberry preserves and we like it that way.

¼ cup (½ stick) margarine
1 cup sugar
2 teaspoons vanilla
¼ cup cornmeal
1 cup skimmed milk

2 egg whites
1 cup damson plum
  preserves
1 unbaked 9″ pie shell

Cream margarine, sugar, and vanilla together until light and fluffy. Add cornmeal and milk and mix at low speed for ½ minute. Add egg whites and preserves and mix at low speed for 1 minute, scraping the bowl as necessary. Pour into an unbaked 9″ pie crust and bake at 400° F. for 10 minutes. Turn the oven down to 325° F. without opening the door and continue to bake for another 40 to 50 minutes or until a silver knife inserted in the center of the pie comes out clean. Place pie on a wire rack and cool to room temperature.

Low sodium diets: Use salt-free margarine and low sodium crust.

Yield: 1 9″ pie

JEFF DAVIS PIE (Southern United States)

¼ cup (½ stick) margarine
2 cups brown sugar
1 teaspoon vanilla
½ cup liquid egg substitute
¼ cup all-purpose flour
¼ teaspoon salt

¼ teaspoon ground nutmeg
1 cup evaporated skimmed
  milk
¼ cup chopped dates
¼ cup chopped nuts
¼ cup chopped raisins
1 unbaked 9″ pie crust

Cream margarine, brown sugar, and vanilla together until light and fluffy. Add egg substitute and beat at low speed until blended. Add flour, salt, nutmeg, milk, dates, nuts, and raisins and beat at low speed until blended. Pour into unbaked pie shell and bake at 425° F. for 10 minutes. Turn the oven down to 350° F. and bake for another 30 minutes without opening the oven door. Transfer pie to metal rack and cool to room temperature. (This is a very rich pie and is generally cut into 8 portions.)

Low sodium diets: Omit salt. Use salt-free margarine and low sodium crust.

Yield: 1 9″ pie

MOCHA CHIFFON PIE (United States)

This should probably be listed as a French recipe because it is based on a French cold soufflé, but I put it into a pastry shell because it also makes a beautiful pie.

1 envelope Knox gelatin
⅓ cup sugar
⅛ teaspoon salt
1 tablespoon instant or
  freeze-dried coffee
1½ cups water

2 tablespoons chocolate
  flavored liqueur
1 teaspoon chocolate
  flavoring
⅓ cup instant dry milk
1 prebaked 9″ low
  cholesterol pastry shell

Combine gelatin, sugar, salt, instant or freeze-dried coffee, and water in a small pan. Heat and stir over low heat until sugar and gelatin are dissolved. Add liqueur and flavoring and chill until the mixture is a little thicker than syrup. It should just be beginning to set but still not firm.

Add instant dry milk to gelatin and beat at high speed for about 5 minutes or until mixture is light colored and a little over double in volume. Pour filling into pastry shell and chill at least 1 hour before serving.

If you don't like to use liqueur in cooking, increase the water by 2 tablespoons and add 1 teaspoon chocolate flavoring.

Low sodium diets: Omit salt. Use low sodium crust.

Yield: 1 9″ pie

PECAN PIE (Southern United States)

This recipe is based on one that Mother Myers used to prepare for family dinner when we were all much younger and she was still with us. It gives us all a warm glow when we eat it, just thinking about Mother Myers and the many happy times we shared together.

¾ cup liquid egg substitute
½ cup sugar
1 cup dark corn syrup
1 teaspoon vanilla
¼ teaspoon salt

¼ cup (½ stick) melted margarine
1 cup coarsely chopped pecans
1 unbaked 8″ pie crust

Combine egg substitute, sugar, syrup, vanilla, salt, and margarine. Beat at low speed until smooth. Add pecans and pour into unbaked pie crust. Bake at 450° F. for 15 minutes. Reduce heat, without opening the oven, to 325° F. and bake for another 30 minutes or until a knife inserted in the center of the pie comes out clean.

Low sodium diets: Omit salt. Use unsalted margarine and low sodium crust.

Yield: 1 8″ pie

PUMPKIN PIE (United States)

1 1-pound can pumpkin	½ teaspoon ground nutmeg
¾ cup brown sugar	¼ teaspoon ground cloves
¾ cup liquid egg substitute	1⅔ cups (1 13-ounce can)
¼ teaspoon salt	evaporated skimmed milk
1 teaspoon ground cinnamon	1 unbaked pie shell

Place pumpkin, brown sugar, egg substitute, salt, cinnamon, nutmeg, cloves, and milk in mixer bowl. Mix at low speed until well blended. Pour filling into unbaked 9″ pie crust.

Bake at 400° F. about 50 minutes or until a silver knife inserted in the center of the pie comes out clean. Place on wire rack to cool and serve warm or at room temperature.

Low sodium diets: Omit salt. Use 2 cups pumpkin, which has been cooked without salt, and low sodium crust.

Yield: 1 9″ pie

RHUBARB-RAISIN PIE
(Midwestern United States)

This recipe was given to me by Eleen Woodmansee from Waukon, Iowa. Her husband is on a low cholesterol diet, so we exchange recipes and ideas for new recipes whenever we get together.

1 cup seedless raisins	½ teaspoon salt
3½ cups rhubarb, cut into 1-inch pieces	½ cup liquid egg substitute
	1 unbaked 9″ pie crust
¾ cup water	2 egg whites
1½ cups sugar	¼ cup sugar
5 tablespoons cornstarch	

Rinse and drain raisins. Add rhubarb and water to raisins and heat to a boil. Blend 1½ cups sugar, cornstarch, and salt together. Stir carefully into hot mixture to avoid breaking the rhubarb. Return to heat and bring to a boil, but do not allow to cook. Mix hot mixture into egg substitute and allow to cool slightly while preparing the pie crust. Turn cooled mixture into the pie crust and bake at 450° F. for 10 minutes. Reduce heat, without opening the oven door, to 350° F. and bake another 25 to 30 minutes.

Beat egg whites at high speed until foamy. Add ¼ cup sugar gradually, continuing to beat at high speed to form a meringue. Spread meringue over the top of the pie, being careful to seal the meringue to the pie by spreading it so that it touches the outer crust at all spots. Bake at 300° F. about 15 minutes or until meringue is lightly browned. Cool pie thoroughly before cutting it.

Low sodium diets: Omit salt. Use low sodium crust.

Yield: 1 9″ pie

SHOOFLY PIE (Pennsylvania Dutch)

1½ cups all-purpose flour	½ teaspoon baking soda
1 cup brown sugar	⅔ cup hot water
½ cup (1 stick) margarine	⅔ cup light molasses
¼ teaspoon salt	1 unbaked 9″ pie crust

Combine flour, brown sugar, margarine, and salt. Rub the mixture together with your fingertips to form crumbs and set aside.

Combine the soda, hot water, and molasses. Stir until blended and then pour into an unbaked 9″ pie crust. Sprinkle the crumbs evenly over the liquid, being careful not to pile the crumbs over the edge of the crust. The crust should be built up around the edge because the filling puffs up as it bakes. Bake at 350° F. for 35 to 40 minutes or until the filling is set. Cool on a wire rack to room temperature before serving.

Low sodium diets: This recipe is not suitable.

Yield: 1 9″ pie

STRAWBERRY-RHUBARB PIE
(Midwestern United States)

Mrs. Kennneth Ruroden brought this pie to one of the first senior citizen dinners I attended in Wadena. It was delicious, and I'd never seen that combination before, so I asked her for the recipe. I'm sure you will also enjoy it. It really gives you that first taste of spring when the rhubarb is ready around Memorial Day.

3 cups diced raw rhubarb
1 unbaked 9" pie crust
1 3-ounce package
  strawberry-flavored
  gelatin

½ cup all-purpose flour
1 cup sugar
½ teaspoon ground cinnamon
¼ cup (½ stick) melted
  margarine

Spread rhubarb evenly in pie crust. Combine gelatin, flour, sugar, and cinnamon and sprinkle evenly over the rhubarb. Pour the margarine evenly over the filling and bake at 350° F. for 50 minutes. Serve warm or at room temperature.

Low sodium diets: Use salt-free margarine and low sodium crust.

Yield: 1 9" pie

SWEET POTATO PIE (Louisiana)

This recipe is based on one from Pauline Lalande, a dietary consultant from Lafayette, Louisiana. She says she can't take credit for it because several people worked on it, including Lois Rivers and her food and nutrition class at the University of Southwestern Louisiana.

1½ cups brown sugar
1 teaspoon salt
1 teaspoon ground cinnamon
2 teaspoons maple flavoring
2 cups cooked and sieved
  sweet potatoes
¼ cup liquid egg substitute
1 cup evaporated skimmed
  milk

½ cup water
1 unbaked 10" pie crust
⅓ cup red currant jelly
3 egg whites
¼ teaspoon cream of tartar
⅓ cup sugar
½ teaspoon vanilla

Place brown sugar, salt, cinnamon, and maple flavoring in mixer bowl. Mix at low speed for ½ minute to blend well. Add sweet potatoes, egg substitute, milk, and water and mix 2 minutes at low speed or until very well blended.

Bake unfilled pie crust at 400° F. for 5 minutes. Pour filling into warm pie crust and bake at 325° F. for 50 to 60 minutes or until a silver knife inserted in the center of the pie comes out clean. Cool to room temperature.

Spread currant jelly in a thin layer over the pie filling. Avoid spreading jelly closer than ½ inch to the edge of the crust. Beat egg whites and cream of tartar at high speed until foamy. Add sugar a little at a time and beat at medium speed until meringue holds its shape. Stir in vanilla. Spread meringue over currant jelly, being careful to seal meringue to pie by spreading it so that it touches the outer crust at all spots. Bake at 350° F. for 15 minutes or until lightly browned. Serve at room temperature.

Low sodium diets: Omit salt. Cook potatoes without salt and use low sodium crust.

Yield: 1 10″ pie

12
Puddings and Sauces

It is discouraging to try to find a pudding recipe that doesn't include lots of eggs and whipped cream or whipped topping. I think that, originally, puddings probably were very simple desserts using fresh fruits and other equally available ingredients. However, they have grown more elaborate and complex until now some of them are truly too rich and elaborate for use on a low cholesterol diet. Sometimes it seems that most cooks think a pudding isn't a pudding unless it is topped with whipped cream or topping. I will admit that I like such treats as well as most people, but a pudding that is rich in eggs and cream is just not what I'm looking for these days. So, we have to find other puddings, just as attractive and often better, that concentrate on fruits and other ingredients that are allowed on our diet.

The problem of whipped cream or whipped topping can be solved by using Italian Meringue (see Index), which isn't an Italian topping but is a form of meringue used frequently in French recipes. It is very versatile since you can add different flavorings to it; it keeps well in the refrigerator for several weeks; it can be frozen if you are going to be gone or if you have made more than you think you'll need for 2 or 3 weeks. It is high in sugar and can't be used by anyone trying to cut down on sugar intake, but it is very useful when you feel a pudding simply must have a fluffy topping.

Egg whites can often be substituted for whole eggs, but I generally find that if the recipe includes more than 2 eggs, it is better to use liquid egg substitute than egg whites, using ¼ cup of the liquid egg substitute for each egg in the recipe. Of course, we do have those beautiful meringues that are made from egg whites. They are delicious and look very pretty when they are filled with pudding, fruit, or a mixture of both. They can also be made into melt-in-your-mouth cookies. However, even meringues are really not a perfect substitute for recipes such as custards and rice or bread puddings, which really need whole eggs. Before we had liquid egg substitute, we couldn't made custards that were quite as good as those we can now prepare.

We were happy to discover that we could use instant puddings because they are free of cholesterol but I was never really satisfied with them because the texture was different from that made with whole milk. However, I finally discovered that if I enriched the skimmed milk using ¼ cup instant dry milk for each cup of skimmed milk, I could produce a very acceptable pudding. This isn't necessary in the cooked puddings, but it is a great improvement in the instant puddings.

Many of the puddings use a great deal of fruit and, though this can become very expensive if you don't have your own fruit, they are very good desserts. They are tasty and pretty and add a lot of fiber to your diet. Research has indicated that a moderately high fiber diet will help keep the cholesterol count down, and fruit puddings and fresh fruits can both help a great deal in that way. I have a theory that years ago people enjoyed these fresh fruit puddings when the fruits were in season and then didn't see them again until the following year. Now that fresh, frozen, and canned fruits are so much more available to us, we are able to enjoy them during all seasons. Most regional and ethnic groups have their own favorite puddings, and they seem to be based on the foods, including fruits, that were in greatest supply in their own parts of the world.

Some puddings are glamorous, such as the English trifle, and some puddings are down to earth, such as the Indian pudding, but all of them are good. All the recipes in this chapter are suitable for your diet, so you can add a little variety to your diet with them and know that you are not eating prohibited foods.

The American Heart Association does say that you can enjoy ice milk, if you don't eat it too often, or sherbet, if it is made with juice or water and not whole milk. You can also have all the gelatin you want, as long as you don't add any saturated fats to it such as cream cheese or whipped cream. Fruit is always cholesterol-free and may be eaten as is or cooked and sugared or dried. Anyway you like it, it is always free of cholesterol unless you use a lot of saturated fat with it. Again, I suggest that if you want strawberry shortcake you use the baking powder biscuit dough recipe (see Index) instead of sponge cake, and Italian meringue instead of whipped cream. It is all just a question of learning to live with and enjoy the foods that are available to you as a whole new cuisine instead of worrying about what you can't have. Enjoy all the wonderful foods that you *can* have: think positive!

APPLE CRISP (Midwestern United States)

This is a crunchy topping that adds even more fiber and texture to the apples. The amount of sugar mixed with the cinnamon and cornstarch is right for a rather mild apple. If you are using a tart apple, you might want to increase the sugar to suit your taste.

1 cup rolled oats
½ cup brown sugar
⅓ cup all-purpose flour
½ teaspoon salt
¼ cup (½ stick) margarine
½ cup chopped nuts

8 cups cored and chopped apples
½ cup sugar
1 teaspoon ground cinnamon
1 tablespoon cornstarch
Italian Meringue (see recipe) or milk

Combine oatmeal, brown sugar, flour, salt, and margarine and mix together to form a coarse crumb. Add nuts, mix lightly, and set aside for later use.

Spread apples evenly in an 8"-square pan. Combine sugar, cinnamon, and cornstarch. Mix well and sprinkle over the apples. Mix lightly with a fork and cover evenly with the oatmeal mixture.

Bake at 350° F. for 45 minutes. Serve warm or at room temperature topped with Italian Meringue (see Index) or milk.

Low sodium diets: Omit salt. Use salt-free margarine and low sodium Italian Meringue (see Index).

Yield: 6 to 8 servings

APPLESAUCE PUDDING (Denmark)

2 cups finely crushed zwieback crumbs (about 6 ounces)

⅓ cup (⅔ stick) melted margarine

2 cups unsweetened applesauce

1 cup raspberry jam

Italian Meringue (see recipe)

Toss zwieback crumbs with margarine. Spread ½ cup crumbs in the bottom of a 2-quart glass serving dish. Spread 1 cup applesauce evenly over the crumbs. Add a layer of ½ cup crumbs and then a layer of the jam. Top with ½ cup crumbs and then the remaining applesauce topped with the remaining crumbs. Refrigerate until serving time. Serve chilled with a topping of swirls of Italian Meringue (see Index).

If you want the crumbs to remain crisp, prepare the pudding just before it is served. If you want the crumbs to meld into the fruit, prepare the pudding 4 to 12 hours before it is served.

Low sodium diets: Use salt-free margarine.

Yield: 4 to 6 servings

BAKED FRUIT DESSERT
(Southern United States)

3½ cups (1 29-ounce can)   ½ cup brown sugar
  sliced peaches   ⅓ cup (⅔ stick) margarine
3½ cups (1 29-ounce can)   1 teaspoon ground cinnamon
  apricot halves   ¼ teaspoon ground ginger
3½ cups (1 29-ounce can)   ¼ teaspoon ground cloves
  pear halves   Italian Meringue (see recipe)
3½ cups (1 29-ounce can)
  pineapple chunks

Drain fruit well. Place fruit juice in saucepan and reserve fruit
for later. Cook juice over moderate heat until it is reduced by
about ½. Add brown sugar, margarine, cinnamon, ginger, and
cloves to juice and simmer another 2 minutes. Add the reserved
fruit and simmer for another 2 minutes. Pour fruit and juice into
a shallow casserole and bake at 325° F. for from 30 minutes to 1
hour or until the juice is absorbed and the fruit is lightly
browned. Serve hot with cookies or chilled with Italian Meringue
(see Index) and cookies.

Low sodium diets: Use fresh fruits and simmer in a mixture of 1
  cup water and 1 cup sugar plus the brown sugar, margarine,
  and spices. Use salt-free margarine.
Yield: 12 to 16 servings

BAKED INDIAN PUDDING (New England)

1 quart hot water   1 cup raisins
1⅓ cups instant dry milk   1 teaspoon ground cinnamon
⅓ cup cornmeal   ½ teaspoon ground nutmeg
½ cup light molasses   ½ teaspoon salt
½ cup brown sugar   1 cup cold skimmed milk
½ cup liquid egg substitute Cold skimmed milk
2 tablespoons (¼ stick)
  margarine

Combine hot water and dry milk in top of a double boiler. Stir to dissolve milk. Add cornmeal and cook over simmering water, stirring occasionally, for 15 minutes. Remove from heat and cool to lukewarm. Add molasses, brown sugar, egg substitute, margarine, raisins, cinnamon, nutmeg, and salt to cornmeal mixture. Mix well and pour into an 8"-square pan that has been well greased with margarine. Pour 1 cup cold skimmed milk carefully over batter. *Do not stir milk into batter.*

Bake at 350° F. for 1 hour. Serve warm or refrigerated with cold skimmed milk.

Low sodium diets: Omit salt. Use salt-free margarine.

Yield: 6 to 9 servings

BLUEBERRY BUCKLE (New England)

2 cups (1 15-ounce can)
  canned blueberries
⅓ cup sugar
½ cup all-purpose flour
1 teaspoon ground cinnamon
¼ cup (½ stick) margarine
½ cup (1 stick) margarine
⅓ cup sugar
2 egg whites

2 cups all-purpose flour
¼ teaspoon salt
2 teaspoons baking powder
½ cup skimmed milk
1 tablespoon lemon juice
2 tablespoons sugar
1 tablespoon cornstarch
Water

Drain blueberries well, reserving both berries and juice. Combine ⅓ cup sugar, ½ cup flour, cinnamon, and ¼ cup margarine. Mix to form a coarse crumb and set aside for later use. Cream ½ cup margarine and ⅓ cup sugar together until light and fluffy. Add egg whites and mix at low speed to blend. Stir 2 cups flour, salt, and baking powder together to blend and add with the milk to the creamed mixture. Mix at medium speed only to blend well. Spread batter evenly in a 9" × 13" cake pan that has been well greased with margarine. Pour the lemon juice over the blueberries and then sprinkle the blueberries evenly over the batter.

Spread the cinnamon mixture evenly over the blueberries and bake at 350° F. for about 40 minutes or until a cake tester inserted in the center comes out clean.

While the buckle is baking, combine the reserved blueberry juice, 2 tablespoons sugar, cornstarch, and enough water, if necessary, to make 1 cup. Cook and stir over low heat until smooth and thickened. Pour hot over the hot buckle as it comes out of the oven. Cut into squares and serve hot.

Low sodium diets: Omit salt. Use fresh or frozen blueberries. Use salt-free margarine and low sodium baking powder.

Yield: 1 9″ × 13″ pan of pudding

BREAD PUDDING (Midwestern United States)

Vera Wilson not only makes a great custard pie, she also makes a really good bread pudding that we like very much. This was one of my mother's favorites, and I used to make it often for her.

1 cup brown sugar	1 teaspoon vanilla
4 slices bread	¾ cup liquid egg substitute
Margarine	¼ cup raisins
2¼ cups skimmed milk	¼ teaspoon ground cinnamon

Spread the brown sugar evenly in the top part of a double boiler. Spread margarine evenly on both sides of the bread. Cut bread into 1-inch cubes and layer over brown sugar. Beat milk, vanilla, and egg substitute together and pour over the bread. Sprinkle raisins into custard mixture and then sprinkle with cinnamon. Place over simmering water. Cover and cook for 1 hour and 10 minutes. Remove from heat, remove lid and cool, away from drafts, to room temperature.

Low sodium diets: Use salt-free margarine.

Yield: 4 servings

BOILED-BAKED APPLES (Shaker)

Chuck likes these with about 2 tablespoons of those hot cinnamon candies sprinkled over the apples along with the sugar. It
isn't traditional, but it does add a taste of cinnamon and a pretty
red color.

6 baking apples
Cold water
¾ cup sugar

Wash apples well, core them, and place them in a saucepan that
is large enough to hold all the apples in a single layer. Add water
carefully until it is about ½ inch deep. Sprinkle the sugar over the
apples. Cover and simmer gently, turning the apples several
times, about 20 minutes or until the apples are tender. Serve
warm or chilled with the syrup.

Low sodium diets: May be used as written.

Yield: 6 servings

CINNAMON APPLESAUCE PUDDING
(Minnesota)

1 cup all-purpose flour
½ teaspoon baking soda
1 teaspoon baking powder
½ teaspoon salt
1 teaspoon ground cinnamon
¼ teaspoon ground cloves
1 cup brown sugar

½ cup (1 stick) softened
  margarine
2 egg whites
1½ cups sweetened
  applesauce
1¼ cups rolled oats
½ cup raisins or chopped
  dates

Place flour, soda, baking powder, salt, cinnamon, cloves, and
brown sugar in mixer bowl and mix at low speed about 1 minute
to blend well. Add margarine, egg whites, and applesauce. Beat
at medium speed for 1 to 2 minutes or until thoroughly blended.

Add oatmeal and raisins or dates and mix at low speed just to blend well. Spread the batter evenly in an 8"-square baking dish that has been well greased with margarine.

Bake at 350° F. for 35 to 40 minutes or until a cake tester inserted in the center comes out clean. Cut into 9 equal portions and serve hot with Lemon Sauce (see Index), Hard Sauce (see Index), or skimmed milk.

Low sodium diets: Omit salt. Delete baking soda and increase the baking powder to 2 teaspoons, using a low sodium baking powder. Use salt-free margarine.

Yield: 9 servings

FRUIT AND NOODLE KUGEL (Jewish)

8 ounces wide noodles	1 orange
2 large tart apples	¼ cup sugar
1 cup drained canned crushed pineapple	1 teaspoon cinnamon
	1 teaspoon vanilla
½ cup washed and drained raisins	2 tablespoons (¼ stick) melted margarine
¾ cup liquid egg substitute	½ cup dry bread crumbs

Cook noodles according to package directions until tender. Drain well. Rinse with cold water and set aside until needed. Peel and core apple. Grate into a bowl. Add pineapple, raisins, egg substitute, juice and grated rind of orange, sugar, cinnamon, and vanilla. Mix lightly but thoroughly. Add the noodles and mix well. Spread evenly in a 9" × 13" cake pan that has been well greased with margarine. Sprinkle evenly with bread crumbs.

Bake at 425° F. for 15 minutes. Reduce heat and bake at 350° F. for about 20 minutes or until a knife inserted in the center comes out clean. Cut into 3" × 4" pieces and serve hot.

Low sodium diets: Use salt-free margarine. Cook noodles without salt and use low sodium canned pineapple.

Yield: 9 servings

OZARK PUDDING (Missouri)

½ cup liquid egg substitute
¾ cup sugar
2 teaspoons vanilla
¾ cup all-purpose flour
1 tablespoon baking powder
½ teaspoon salt

3 cups cored and diced tart
  apples
½ cup chopped black or
  English walnuts
Lemon Sauce or Custard
  Sauce (see recipes), or
  skimmed milk

Combine egg substitute, sugar, and vanilla. Beat at medium speed for 1 minute. Stir flour, baking powder, and salt together to blend. Add to egg mixture and beat at medium speed just until smooth and blended. Do not overbeat. Remove beater from mixer and stir apples and nuts into pudding by hand. Pour pudding into an 8″-square baking pan that has been well greased with margarine. Bake at 350° F. for 35 to 40 minutes or until the center springs back when touched. Serve warm, if possible, with Lemon Sauce (see Index), Custard Sauce (see Index), or skimmed milk.

Low sodium diets: Omit salt. Use low sodium baking powder and sauces.

Yield: 4 to 6 servings

RED BERRY PUDDING (Norway)

1 10-ounce package frozen
  strawberries
1 10-ounce package frozen
  raspberries
Water

⅓ cup cornstarch
⅓ cup sugar
½ cup water
Sugar
Italian Meringue (see recipe)

Defrost the berries. Measure them and add an equal amount of water. Place berries and water in a saucepan and simmer for 5 minutes. Strain through a sieve. You should have 4½ cups liquid. If you have less than that, add enough water to yield 4½ cups. Stir the cornstarch and sugar into ½ cup water to make a thin paste. Slowly pour the paste into the liquid, cooking and stirring over moderate heat. Cook and stir for 2 minutes after the cornstarch mixture has been added. Cool slightly and pour carefully into a pretty glass bowl or individual glass serving dishes. Sprinkle lightly with sugar to prevent the formation of a film on top. The pudding should be prepared several hours or a day before it is to be served, chilled with swirls of Italian Meringue (see Index).

Note: Different combinations of fruits may be used. Strawberries and rhubarb are good, and combinations of blueberries, blackberries, and currants may also be used.

Low sodium diets: The pudding may be served as written. Use low sodium Italian Meringue (see Index).

Yield: about 6 servings

RICE PUDDING (United States)

2 egg whites
1½ cups skimmed milk
2 drops yellow food coloring
⅓ cup sugar
¼ teaspoon salt

1 teaspoon vanilla
½ cup raisins
¼ teaspoon cinnamon
1½ cups cooked rice

Combine egg whites, milk, food coloring, sugar, salt, vanilla, raisins, and cinnamon. Mix to blend well. Add rice and pour into a shallow 1-quart casserole.

Bake at 325° F. for about 45 minutes or until a knife inserted in the center comes out clean. Remove from oven and serve warm or chilled with additional milk or Custard Sauce (see Index).

Low sodium diets: Omit salt.

Yield: 4 to 6 servings

SWEET POTATO PUDDING
(Southern United States)

2 cups grated sweet potatoes
or yams (about 1 large or 2
medium)
1½ cups skimmed milk
½ cup liquid egg substitute

⅓ cup (⅔ stick) melted
margarine
1 teaspoon vanilla
1 cup brown sugar
¼ teaspoon salt
Ground cinnamon

Add the grated sweet potatoes or yams to the milk. Mix lightly.
Add the egg substitute, margarine, vanilla, brown sugar, and salt
to the mixture and mix lightly. Pour into a 1½-quart casserole
that has been well greased with margarine. Sprinkle with cinnamon and bake at 350° F. for about 1 hour or until golden
brown. Serve chilled or at room temperature.

Variation: Squash Pudding (Midwestern United States): Substitute 2 cups cooked sieved winter squash for the sweet potatoes or
yams and add 1 teaspoon pumpkin pie spice mixed with the
pudding. Delete the cinnamon. Use 1 cup skimmed milk instead
of 1½ cups.

Low sodium diets: Omit salt. Use salt-free margarine and cook
the squash without added salt.

Yield: 4 to 6 servings

STRAWBERRY MERINGUES (France)

Remember the old saying, "If you can't lick them, join them"?
This is how I feel about meringues. If we are forced to give up
egg yolks and concentrate on egg whites, let's make the most of it
and do something really pretty and glamorous with those egg
whites

Cornstarch

½ cup (about 4) egg whites

⅛ teaspoon cream of tartar

⅛ teaspoon salt

¼ cup strawberry-flavored gelatin

¾ cup sugar

3 cups strawberries and juice

Prepare a large cookie sheet by lining it with aluminum foil with the shiny side down. Draw 6 4-inch circles on the foil. I do it by tracing around a 4-inch soup cup with the handle of a knife, being careful not to cut the foil. Sift cornstarch lightly over the aluminum circles of foil and set aside.

Beat egg whites, which have been allowed to come to room temperature, at high speed until foamy. Gradually add cream of tartar and salt. Blend gelatin and sugar together and add 1 tablespoon at a time to the meringue, continuing to beat at high speed. Continue beating until the meringue will stand in soft peaks.

Drop equal amounts of the meringue, using a serving spoon, onto each of the circles on the foil. Spread the meringue with the back of the spoon, making an indentation in the center and building up the sides. This may also be done with a pastry bag, if desired.

Bake at 225° F. for 1 hour. Turn off the oven without opening the door and let the meringues stay in the oven for another hour. Store in an airtight can in the freezer for up to 2 or 3 months if not to be used immediately.

Fill each meringue shell with ½ cup strawberries and juice. Italian Meringue (see Index) may be used as a topping, but it is not necessary.

Note: Other flavors of gelatin may be used, such as raspberry gelatin with raspberries or lemon gelatin with lemon sherbet or chocolate pudding.

Variation: Strawberry Meringue Kisses: Drop meringue by the tablespoonful onto a foil-lined pan that has been dusted with cornstarch and bake as directed for meringue shells. One cup chopped nuts, candied fruit, dates, or raisins may be added, if desired.

Low sodium diets: Omit salt. Use low sodium Italian Meringue (optional, see Index).

Yield: 6 shells

CHOCOLATE MERINGUE (France)

Cornstarch	1 cup sugar
½ cup (about 4) egg whites	¼ cup cocoa
⅛ teaspoon cream of tartar	1 teaspoon vanilla
⅛ teaspoon salt	

Prepare a large cookie sheet by lining it with aluminum foil with the shiny side down. Draw 6 4-inch circles on the foil. I do it by tracing around a 4-inch soup cup with the handle of a knife, being careful not to cut the foil. Sift cornstarch lightly over the circles on the foil and set aside for later.

Beat the egg whites, which have been allowed to come to room temperature, at high speed until foamy. Gradually add cream of tartar and salt. Blend sugar and cocoa together and add 1 tablespoonful at a time to the meringue, continuing to beat at high speed. Continue to beat until the meringue is stiff and stands in stiff peaks. Beat vanilla into meringue at high speed.

Using a serving spoon, drop equal amounts of the meringue onto each of the circles in the foil. Spread the meringue with the back of the spoon, making an indentation in the center and building up the sides. This may be done with a pastry bag, if desired.

Bake at 225° F. for 1 hour. Turn off the oven without opening the door and let the meringue stay in the oven for another hour. Store in an airtight can in the freezer for up to 2 to 3 months, if not used immediately.

Fill each meringue shell with chocolate or lemon pudding or other filling. Top with Italian Meringue (see Index), if desired.

Variations: Hard Meringue: Delete cocoa.

Meringue Kisses: Drop meringue onto foil-lined pans that have been dusted with cornstarch, using a heaping tablespoon of meringue for each kiss. Either Chocolate Meringue or Hard Meringue may be used. One cup chopped nuts, candied fruit, dates, or raisins may be added, if desired. Bake as directed for meringue shells.

Low sodium diets: Omit salt. Use low sodium fillings and Italian Meringue (optional, see Index).

Yield: 6 large shells

ITALIAN MERINGUE (France)

I like to keep some of this on hand because it is so versatile. I generally use it as a topping for puddings or pies or it can be used as a quick frosting for cakes. It can also be turned into a good cream frosting by beating ½ cup softened margarine into it.

1 cup sugar	**⅛ teaspoon salt**
½ cup water	**¼ teaspoon cream of tartar**
½ cup (about 4) egg whites at room temperature	**1 teaspoon vanilla**

Combine the sugar and water in a heavy saucepan and stir to dissolve the sugar. Cook over moderate heat for about 10 minutes or until the syrup registers 238° F. on a candy thermometer (soft ball stage).

While the sugar is cooking, combine the egg whites, salt, and cream of tartar and beat at high speed until it forms soft peaks. Pour the hot syrup slowly into the egg whites, beating at high speed. Add the vanilla and beat at moderate speed for 5 minutes or until the topping is cool. Put the topping into a clean container, cover tightly, and refrigerate until needed.

Low sodium diets: Omit salt.

Yield: about 2 quarts

CRANBERRY WHIP (New England)

1½ cups boiling hot
  cranberry juice cocktail
1 3-ounce package lemon-
  flavored gelatin

½ cup instant dry milk
2 to 3 tablespoons cranberry
  sauce

Combine hot cranberry juice cocktail and gelatin and stir until gelatin is dissolved. Refrigerate until it just begins to firm. Place in a mixer with dry milk and beat at high speed until light and fluffy and about doubled in volume. Pour into a glass bowl or individual serving dishes. Garnish with cranberry sauce to serve.

Note: This recipe may be varied by using other fruit juices and flavors of gelatin.

Low sodium diets: May be used as written.

Yield: 4 to 6 servings

GELATIN TRIFLE (England)

This is a very popular dish at our house. A friend of ours, Bud Gunsallus, had a ball last year when he was in Great Britain, trying to find out just how many different combinations of fruit and gelatins he could find. It lends itself well to serving in a plain glass bowl or in individual servings in goblets, sherbet dishes, or parfait glasses. It is especially pretty in a regular trifle dish with several different layers of fruit, gelatin, and pudding.

1 3-ounce package
  strawberry-flavored
  gelatin
1¼ cups boiling hot water
1 10-ounce package frozen
  strawberries

2 cups skimmed milk
½ cup instant dry milk
1 3¾-ounce package instant
  vanilla pudding
2 medium-sized bananas
¼ cup thinly sliced nuts

Add gelatin to boiling water and stir until gelatin is completely dissolved. (Use 1 cup hot water and 1 cup cold water if the fruit is not frozen in sugar to form liquid). Add the frozen strawberries to the gelatin and stir gently to defrost the fruit. Pour the gelatin into a square 8″ glass baking dish. Refrigerate until the gelatin is firm.

Combine the skimmed milk and the dry milk and beat until the dry milk is dissolved. Add the pudding mix and continue to beat until the pudding mix is also dissolved. Slice the bananas over the gelatin and pour the pudding over the bananas. Sprinkle the top with chopped nuts and refrigerate until thoroughly chilled. Cut into squares and serve.

Note: Any variety of gelatins and fruits may be used, such as raspberry gelatin with frozen raspberries, orange gelatin with mandarin oranges, or lemon gelatin with peaches for the bottom layer.

Low sodium diets: Use low sodium pudding mix and fruit prepared without salt.

Yield: 6 to 8 servings

STRAWBERRY CHEESE MOLD (Iowa)

People here in Iowa can hardly believe that in other parts of the country a fruit or vegetable gelatin mold is not just automatically included in any company dinner. I've gone to small potluck dinners since I've been out here where there would only be thirty-five or forty people and there would be at least five or six beautiful shimmering gelatin molds of various kinds.

1 3-ounce package strawberry-flavored gelatin
1½ cups boiling water

1 10-ounce package frozen strawberries
1 cup creamless cheese (see recipe)

Dissolve the gelatin in the boiling water. Add the frozen strawberries and stir until the strawberries are thawed. Strain off 1 cup liquid and set aside at room temperature. Pour the gelatin and fruit into a 1-quart glass bowl and refrigerate until firm. When the mixture is firm, combine the reserved liquid gelatin and the Creamless Cheese (see Index) and pour over the firm gelatin. Refrigerate until firm and served chilled.

Low sodium diets: Use low sodium Creamless Cheese (see Index).

Yield: 4 to 6 servings

INSTANT VANILLA PUDDING (United States)

½ cup instant dry milk   1 3¾-ounce package instant
2 cups skimmed milk   dry vanilla pudding

Stir the dry milk into the skimmed milk until smooth. Add the vanilla pudding mix and beat until smooth. Pour into bowl or serving dishes and chill.

Note: Instant pudding made with skimmed milk is a different texture and color than that made with whole milk, but the addition of the instant dry milk to the skimmed milk will give you approximately the same taste and texture as you would get with the whole milk.

Low sodium diets: Use low sodium pudding mix.

Yield: 4 servings

CUSTARD SAUCE (United States)

2 cups skimmed milk   ⅓ cup instant vanilla pudding
⅓ cup instant dry milk   powder
½ teaspoon vanilla

Combine skimmed milk, dry milk, and vanilla and beat until smooth. Add instant pudding powder and beat until smooth. Refrigerate until used as a topping for sauce or plain cake.

Notes: Other flavorings such as rum may be added to the sauce to vary the flavor. The texture of this sauce, with or without the addition of the instant dry milk, is very different. You might try it both ways to see which texture you prefer.

Low sodium diets: Use low sodium instant pudding.

Yield: about 2 cups

HARD SAUCE (England)

⅓ cup (⅔ stick) margarine   1 teaspoon vanilla or rum
1 cup sifted powdered sugar   flavoring
                                    ⅛ teaspoon salt

Cream the margarine until light colored and smooth. Add the powdered sugar and beat until light and fluffy. Add the vanilla or rum flavoring and salt and mix well. Serve well chilled.

Low sodium diets: Omit salt. Use salt-free margarine.

Yield: about ¾ cup

LEMON SAUCE (California)

½ cup sugar   2 tablespoons lemon juice
1 tablespoon cornstarch   1 tablespoon grated lemon
⅛ teaspoon salt   rind (optional)
1 cup boiling water   1 tablespoon margarine

Place sugar, cornstarch, and salt in small saucepan. Stir to mix well. Gradually add boiling water. Bring to a boil and cook and stir over low heat until thickened and clear. Stir lemon juice, rind, and margarine into the hot sauce. Mix well and serve hot.

Variation: California Sauce: Use 1 cup boiling hot orange juice instead of 1 cup water and increase the cornstarch to 1½ table-spoons.

Low sodium diets: Omit salt. Use salt-free margarine.

Yield: about 1¼ cups

PIONEER PUDDING SAUCE (Iowa)

This is the sauce my grandmother made and used on apple dumplings, puddings, and plain cakes. Occasionally she would add a little cinnamon and nutmeg to it, but she always said that this was the way her mother prepared it when they were still living in a log cabin.

2 tablespoons all-purpose   1 cup sugar
   flour   1 tablespoon white vinegar
1 tablespoon margarine   2 cups water

Mix flour and margarine together with your fingers to form a coarse crumb. Combine the sugar, vinegar, and water together in a small saucepan and bring to a boil. Add the margarine mixture to the boiling sauce and cook and stir over moderate heat until the starchy taste is gone. Serve hot over puddings or dumplings.

Low sodium diets: Use salt-free margarine.

Yield: about 2 cups

13
Pancakes

Some foods give you a nice warm feeling when you see them or smell them cooking, and pancakes do that for me. I have such happy memories of my grandmother baking those big pancakes in a 10″ iron skillet, of my father frying pancakes on a cold frosty morning before he went to work and we went to school, and of the many times Chuck and I have celebrated some special occasion by going to the pancake house in Chicago before we moved out here. We often order pancakes on trips and I have many happy memories of these occasions, but especially of one time when we had them at a pancake house in Marblehead, Massachusetts. The oldest son of my cousin, Virginia Ballantine, was getting married that day and all the Iowa relatives who were there to attend the wedding gathered that morning at a pancake house for breakfast before the wedding. We all talked at once and had such an assortment of pancakes that we still talk about them today when we get together.

I would have hated to give up pancakes because of Chuck's low cholesterol diet. He does have to figure that the pancakes use up most of his allowance of eggs for the week when we go out, but I can prepare them at home without worrying about them. Now that we have liquid egg substitute to use, along with the egg whites and vegetable oil or melted margarine, we can make any of a great variety of pancakes.

Pancakes are very easy to make at home and some very good mixes are available if you don't want to make them from scratch. Beware of the ones that say they are complete mixes. That means they may contain dehydrated egg yolks and some saturated fat. It is much better to buy the mixes that instruct you to add eggs, milk, and melted fat. You can always add egg whites, liquid egg substitute, skimmed milk, and melted margarine or vegetable oil. However, they are so easy to make from scratch that I'm hoping you will try some of the recipes in this chapter.

You can even make good crepes using the liquid egg substitute. Some of the pancake recipes are good with egg whites, but many of the recipes need liquid egg substitute. Chuck has always loved crepes and can eat them just about as fast as I can make them. In fact, I have a hard time making any to put in the freezer because he seems to sense that I'm preparing them and appears in the kitchen when I start baking them for his snack. I have included several crepe recipes in this book, but I didn't include a recipe for Swedish pancakes because it would be the same as the basic or dessert crepe recipes. You can use that batter and fry it in the special pans used to make those delightful small Swedish pancakes.

There are certain basic rules that apply to most recipes that you should remember when you are making pancakes.

1. It is a good idea to use an electric grill because you can control the amount of heat better. Most pancakes cook best at 375° F. If the heat is too high, the pancakes will be too brown on the outside and raw in the center. If the grill is too low, the pancakes won't brown well and will be tough and have a poor color.

2. Most pancake batter can be kept covered in the refrigerator for several hours. Most restaurants make a big batch of it at a time and just keep using it all morning until it is gone. It can be kept overnight and, if it is too thick, the next morning you can add a little water or skimmed milk to thin it.

3. It is handy to put the batter into a pitcher so that you can pour it out onto the grill. I even use a pitcher for crepe batter. After a while, you will be able to judge how much to use so well that you no longer need to measure it.

4. The pancakes shouldn't be turned over until there are bubbles on them and they are dry around the edges. It generally takes about 3 minutes on one side and 2 minutes on the other side to bake pancakes. They are baked when they have stopped steaming.

5. A no-stick grill is best because it needs very little or no fat and, if you must use some fat, vegetable oil is better than margarine because it doesn't burn as easily.

6. Extra pancakes can be frozen with wax paper between them in moisture-resistant paper, aluminum foil, or plastic freezer wrap and reheated in the microwave oven or toaster.

7. If you make crepes often, it is a good idea to have a 6″ or 8″ crepe pan reserved exclusively for the crepes. Keep it conditioned by rubbing it with vegetable oil if you have to wash it out. Generally speaking, it will only have to be wiped out with a paper towel after each use. I have one with a no-stick lining that I think is excellent.

BUCKWHEAT PANCAKES (Germany)

This recipe was given to me by Susan Weger of Strawberry Point, Iowa. She told me that the recipe came from her grandmother, Mrs. Hulda Weger.

1½ teaspoons active dry yeast
1 teaspoon sugar
1 cup warm (85° to 87° F.) water
⅓ cup all-purpose flour

⅔ cup buckwheat flour
¼ teaspoon baking soda
1 tablespoon hot water
2 tablespoons milk

Stir yeast and sugar into the warm water. Add all-purpose and buckwheat flours and beat until smooth. Cover and let stand at room temperature overnight.

The next morning, dissolve the soda in the hot water and add with the milk to the batter. The texture of the batter should be like that of regular pancake batter. Add a little more milk, if necessary, for the right thickness. Fry pancakes on a 375° F. griddle and serve hot with margarine and syrup, jam, jelly, or honey.

Low sodium diets: This recipe is not suitable.

Yield: 2 or 3 servings

BUTTERMILK PANCAKES (United States)

Frances Nielsen sometimes makes these for us as a special treat on cold frosty mornings or when we are leaving on a trip.

2 cups all-purpose flour	**½ teaspoon vanilla**
1 teaspoon baking powder	**½ cup liquid egg substitute**
1 teaspoon baking soda	**2 cups low-fat buttermilk**
1 tablespoon sugar	**2 tablespoons vegetable oil**
½ teaspoon salt	

Stir flour, baking powder, soda, sugar, and salt together to blend. Beat vanilla, egg substitute, buttermilk, and oil together with a rotary beater or whip. Add to flour mixture and beat with a rotary beater or whip until smooth.

Pour about ⅓ cup batter onto a lightly greased griddle that has been preheated to 375° F. Cook about 3 minutes on one side or until bubbles begin to form on the surface and the edges of the pancakes are dry. Turn and cook about 2 minutes on the other side or until nicely browned. Repeat with remaining batter and serve hot with margarine and jam, jelly, honey, syrup, or molasses.

Variation: Graham Buttermilk Pancakes: Substitute 1 cup graham flour for 1 cup of the all-purpose flour.

Low sodium diets: This recipe is not suitable.

Yield: 12 6″ pancakes

CORNMEAL BUTTERMILK PANCAKES
(Midwestern United States)

I do believe this is my favorite pancake. I love the color and the texture. It doesn't taste much like cornmeal, but it is very good.

1 cup cornmeal	1 teaspoon baking soda
1 cup all-purpose flour	2 cups low-fat buttermilk
¼ cup sugar	2 large egg whites
2 teaspoons baking powder	2 tablespoons vegetable oil

Stir the cornmeal, flour, sugar, baking powder, and soda together to blend. Beat the buttermilk, egg whites, and oil together with a rotary beater. Add to the flour mixture and beat with a rotary beater only until smooth.

Pour about ⅓ cup batter onto a lightly greased griddle preheated to 375° F. Cook about 3 minutes or until bubbles begin to form on the surface and the edges of the pancake are dry. Turn and cook about 2 minutes on the other side or until nicely browned. Repeat with remaining batter. Serve hot.

Low sodium diets: This recipe is not suitable.

Yield: 12 6″ pancakes

GRIDDLE CAKES (New England)

These are the pancakes I knew as a child and I still like them. They must have been served only in the winter because I don't remember eating them in the summer—only on cold mornings before we left for school. They were served with margarine and brown sugar, peanut butter, and homemade brown sugar syrup.

2 cups all-purpose flour
4 teaspoons baking powder
½ teaspoon salt
¼ cup sugar

½ cup liquid egg substitute
2 cups skimmed milk
⅓ cup vegetable oil

Stir flour, baking powder, salt, and sugar together to blend. Beat the egg substitute, milk, and oil together and add to the flour mixture. Beat with a whip or rotary beater only until smooth.

Pour ¼ to ⅓ cup batter onto a lightly greased griddle that has been preheated to 375° F. Cook about 3 minutes on one side or until bubbles begin to form on the surface and the edges of the pancake are dry. Turn and cook about 2 minutes on the other side or until nicely browned. Repeat with the remaining batter and serve hot with margarine, jam, jelly, honey, brown sugar, syrup, or molasses.

Variation: Graham Griddlecakes: Substitute 1 cup graham flour for 1 cup of all-purpose flour.

Low sodium diets: Omit salt. Use low sodium baking powder.

Yield: 12 to 16 pancakes

OVEN-BAKED PANCAKES (Germany)

⅔ cup all-purpose flour
3 tablespoons sugar
¼ teaspoon salt
⅛ teaspoon ground nutmeg
¾ cup evaporated skimmed milk

1 cup liquid egg substitute
1 teaspoon vanilla
2 tablespoons (¼ stick) margarine
Lemon juice
Powdered sugar

Stir flour, sugar, salt, and nutmeg together to blend well. Combine milk, egg substitute, and vanilla. Beat well with a hand beater until smooth. Add to flour mixture and beat with a hand beater until smooth.

Melt margarine in the bottom of a 10″ iron frying pan with an ovenproof handle. Pour batter into the pan and bake at 400° F. for 25 minutes. Serve hot with lemon juice and powdered sugar.

Note: Do not try to put more batter into the 10″ pan. If more pancakes are desired, use additional 10″ frying pans.

Low sodium diets: Omit salt. Use salt-free margarine.

Yield: 2 servings

PANCAKES (Denmark)

These pancakes are light and delicate—a lot like crepes except that you need to fry them as soon as the batter is mixed.

1¼ cups all-purpose flour
¼ cup sugar
1 teaspoon salt
½ teaspoon ground
  cardamom
¼ cup liquid egg substitute
1⅔ cups skimmed milk

⅓ cup vegetable oil
½ cup (about 4) egg whites
Lingonberries or whole-
  cranberry sauce
Melted margarine or
  vegetable oil

Stir flour, sugar, salt, and cardamom together to blend. Mix egg substitute, milk, and oil together with a fork and add to flour mixture. Blend until smooth, using a rotary beater or a whip. Whip egg whites until stiff and fold into the pancake batter.

Fry the pancakes in a 6″ crepe pan, using 3 to 4 tablespoons of batter per pancake. Pour the batter into a hot pan that has been brushed with melted margarine or oil, rotating the pan as you pour to spread the batter over the entire bottom of the pan. Stir the batter lightly occasionally as you fry the pancakes. Fry on both sides until browned and serve hot, folded into quarters, with lingonberries or whole cranberry sauce. The pancakes can be kept warm in a preheated 250° F. oven, if desired.

Low sodium diets: Omit salt. Use salt-free margarine.
Yield: 12 to 16 pancakes

BLINTZES (Jewish)

Anita Kane gave me this recipe, which is based on one her mother made. Anita serves the blintzes with applesauce or other fruit. We like them that way or with apricot or strawberry jelly or jam and we like them for any meal, including breakfast and late night snacks.

1-pound carton dry cheese (hoop cheese, baker's cheese, or well-drained cottage cheese)
¼ cup liquid egg substitute
2 teaspoons sugar
Salt to taste

Pepper to taste (optional)
¾ cup liquid egg substitute
1 cup water
½ teaspoon salt
¾ cup all-purpose flour
2 tablespoons vegetable oil
Margarine

Combine cheese, ¼ cup liquid egg substitute, sugar, and salt and pepper to taste. Mix well and refrigerate until needed.

Beat ¾ cup liquid egg substitute, water, ½ teaspoon salt, flour, and vegetable oil together until smooth.

Heat a little margarine or oil in a 6″ frying pan. (The shallow kind used for making crepes is excellent. Anita says that she generally uses wax paper or the margarine wrapper brushed against a stick of margarine, which she rubs lightly over the inside of the teflon pan she uses.) Pour about 2 tablespoons batter into the frying pan, tilting the pan so that the batter coats as much of the pan surface as possible. It should make a very thin pancake. Let the bottom of the pancake brown lightly. The sides will curl up and the pancake will lose its shine. Carefully turn the pancake out onto a clean white dish towel. You can stack the pancakes, if you like, as you would solitaire cards. The pancakes won't stick together.

When all the pancakes are cooked, spread about a tablespoon of the filling in the center of each pancake. Fold in both sides and then the ends so that you have a little package of pancake holding the filling.

When you are ready to serve the blintzes, brown them on both sides in margarine over moderate heat and serve hot.

These freeze very well. I freeze them individually on a cookie sheet and then put them in a freezer bag until I need them. I partially thaw them before I brown them when I'm ready to serve them.

Low sodium diets: Omit salt. Use salt-free margarine.

Yield: 18 blintzes

CREPES (France)

Chuck loves crepes. He can eat them as fast as I can make them. He likes them best plain without any filling, just served hot with margarine and a little syrup, but I like them with various fillings and I especially like them filled with a mixture of applesauce and chunky peanut butter mixed together or with jelly and Creamless Cheese (see Index).

INGREDIENTS	ALL-PURPOSE	DESSERT	CHOCOLATE
All-purpose flour	1 cup	—	—
Cake flour	—	1 cup	1 cup
Cocoa	—	—	¼ cup
Sugar	1 tablespoon	¼ cup	2 tablespoons
Salt	⅛ teaspoon	—	—
Baking soda	⅛ teaspoon	⅛ teaspoon	⅛ teaspoon
Skimmed milk	1 cup	1 cup	1¼ cups
Liquid egg substitute	½ cup	½ cup	½ cup
Vegetable oil	2 tablespoons	2 tablespoons	3 tablespoons
Rum	—	2 tablespoons	—
Vanilla	—	—	1 teaspoon
Melted margarine	As necessary	As necessary	As necessary

Stir dry ingredients together to blend. Mix liquid ingredients together with a fork to blend. Add liquid ingredients to dry ingredients and beat until smooth with a whip or rotary beater. Cover and refrigerate for from 4 hours to overnight.

It is best to use a regular pan meant for crepes. The best ones are either 6" or 8" in diameter and I like mine with a no-stick lining very much. They should be tempered before they are used and I like to use mine only for crepes.

Preheat the pan until a drop of water sizzles in the pan. Brush the pan with melted margarine. Pour 2 tablespoons batter into a 6" pan or 3 tablespoons batter into an 8" pan. Rotate the pan as soon as you pour in the batter so that the batter will cover the bottom of the pan. Allow the crepe to cook on one side for about 1 minute, then turn it over and cook it on the other side for about ½ minute, cooking the crepe over medium heat. (You will eventually establish the exact heat on your stove that does it the most efficiently.) Turn out onto a plate or a cloth. Stack crepes on an ovenproof plate or baking dish and keep warm in the oven.

Crepes may easily be prepared ahead of time and frozen with a piece of wax paper between them. They will stay fresh in the freezer for from 4 to 6 weeks. They must be thawed at room temperature in their wrappings. If the filling is to be put into warm crepes, reheat the crepes in a 350° F. oven for 8 to 10 minutes, fill, and serve.

Low sodium diets: Omit salt and baking soda. Use salt-free margarine.

Yield: 12 to 16 crepes

CREPES SUZETTE (France)

1 recipe Dessert Crepes
½ cup (1 stick) margarine
3 tablespoons sugar
½ cup orange juice

1 teaspoon grated orange
  rind
2 tablespoons Grand Marnier

Prepare Dessert Crepes (see Index) in advance. Cool the crepes and keep them covered so they will not dry out. They can be prepared earlier in the day and kept covered or several days earlier and frozen. If frozen, they must be removed from the freezer and allowed to come to room temperature naturally.

When you are ready to serve them, melt the margarine with the sugar, orange juice, and rind in a chafing dish before your guests or in a frying pan in the kitchen. Stir the sauce to dissolve the sugar and add the Grand Marnier. Turn the crepes over in the hot sauce, using a fork. Fold them into quarters and place them on warmed dessert plates, 4 to a portion. Serve hot with some of the sauce.

Low sodium diets: Prepare low sodium Dessert Crepes (see Index) and use salt-free margarine.

Yield: 3 or 4 servings

BLACK FOREST CREPES (France)

1 recipe Chocolate Crepes	2 tablespoons sugar
2 cups (1 20-ounce can)	Powdered sugar
canned cherry pie filling	Italian Meringue (see recipe)
2 tablespoons (¼ stick)	
softened margarine	

Prepare Chocolate Crepes (see Index) in advance. Cool the crepes and keep covered so they won't dry out. They can be prepared earlier in the day and kept covered or several days earlier and frozen. If frozen, they must be allowed to come back to room temperature naturally.

When you are ready to serve the crepes, place 1 to 2 tablespoons of the pie filling in the center of each crepe. Roll the crepe around the filling and place them, seam side down, in a shallow pan that has been well greased with margarine. (I use a shallow 2-quart glass pan.) Spread the softened margarine over the tops of the crepes, using a pastry brush. Sprinkle them with sugar and bake at 375° F. for about 10 to 12 minutes or until the edges are crisp.

Serve hot, 3 to a portion, sprinkled with powdered sugar. Italian Meringue (see Index) and the remaining pie filling, which has been heated, may be served with the crepes, if desired.

Low sodium diets: Prepare low sodium Chocolate Crepes (see Index). Use salt-free margarine.

Yield: 4 or 5 servings

STRAWBERRY CREAM CREPES (France)

1 recipe Dessert Crepes
1 pint fresh strawberries
½ cup sugar

1 cup creamless cheese (see recipe)
¼ cup sugar

Prepare Dessert Crepes (see Index) in advance. Cool the crepes and keep them covered so they will not dry out. They can be prepared the day you plan to serve them and kept covered or prepared earlier and frozen. If frozen, they must be allowed to come back to room temperature naturally.

Clean and wash the strawberries and divide them into 2 equal portions. Slice the first portion, combine with ½ cup sugar, and refrigerate until needed. Combine the Creamless Cheese (see Index) with ¼ cup sugar and the remaining strawberries. Spread about 1 tablespoon filling on each crepe. Roll the crepes and place them, 3 to a serving, on a dessert dish and top them with the refrigerated strawberries.

Low sodium diets: Use low sodium Creamless Cheese (see Index).

Yield: 4 or 5 servings

WAFFLES (United States)

1½ cups all-purpose flour
2 teaspoons baking powder
½ teaspoon salt
3 tablespoons sugar

1⅓ cups skimmed milk
½ cup vegetable oil
½ cup liquid egg substitute

Place flour, baking powder, salt, and sugar in mixer bowl and mix at low speed to blend. Combine milk, oil, and egg substitute. Mix until smooth. Add to flour mixture and mix at low speed until free of lumps. Bake according to manufacturer's directions for your waffle iron. Serve hot with margarine, syrup, or other low cholesterol toppings.

Low sodium diets: Omit salt. Use low sodium baking powder.

Yield: 4 to 6 waffles

CRISP CORNMEAL WAFFLES
(Southern United States)

¾ cup white cornmeal
2 tablespoons all-purpose
  flour
¼ teaspoon salt
¼ teaspoon baking soda

½ teaspoon baking powder
1 tablespoon sugar
2 egg whites
1 cup low-fat buttermilk
¼ cup vegetable oil

Place cornmeal, flour, salt, soda, baking powder, and sugar in mixer bowl. Mix at low speed to blend well. Combine egg whites, buttermilk, and oil and add to flour mixture. Beat at low speed until smooth. Bake according to manufacturer's directions for your waffle iron. Serve hot with margarine, syrup, or other low cholesterol toppings.

Low sodium diets: This recipe is not suitable.

Yield: 4 waffles

FRENCH TOAST (United States)

These thicker slices of bread make really outstanding toast. The mixture may also be used with regular bread, but I think you'll appreciate how good it is with the thicker slices. It also works well with "Texas Toast" bread or thick slices of homemade bread. Use of the almond flavoring is Frances's idea. You can also use vanilla, but try it with the almond flavoring. I think you'll like it that way.

1 cup skimmed milk
1 cup liquid egg substitute
½ teaspoon salt
½ teaspoon almond flavoring

2 tablespoons sugar
8 1-inch-thick slices of Italian
   or French bread

Combine milk, egg substitute, salt, flavoring, and sugar in a bowl and beat until well blended with a whip or rotary beater. Soak the bread slices in the mixture and fry in a small amount of margarine or oil over moderate heat until browned on both sides. Serve hot with margarine and syrup, honey, brown sugar, cinnamon sugar, or powdered sugar.

Low sodium diets: Omit salt. Use salt-free margarine for frying the toast.

Yield: 4 servings

Index

A

Almond cookies, 208
American Heart Association, xviii
Andalusian rice, 184–85
Apples
  boiled-baked, 246
  crisp, 241–42
  Ozark pudding, 248
  fruit and noodle kugel, 247
  and raisin stuffing, 81–82
  salad, 155–56
Applesauce
  cinnamon pudding, 246–47
  cookies, 208–9
  pudding, 242
Apricot barbecued chicken, 65

B

Bagels, 125–26
Baked beans (Sweden), 166

Baked bean sandwich, 166–67
Baked bean soup, 16
Baked brown bread, 131–32
Baked chicken and noodles, 66
Baked fruit dessert, 243
Baked Indian pudding, 243–44
Baked lamb stew, 54–55
Baking powder, 109
Baking powder biscuits, 135
Baking soda, 109
Barbecue sauce, 56–57
Barm brack, 110–11
Basic french dressing, 158–59
Beans
  baked (Sweden), 166
  baked bean sandwich, 166–67
  baked bean soup, 16
  red bean soup, 28
  three-bean bake, 168
Beef
  and bean stew, 38–39
  bourguignon, 36–37